IMAGES
of America

ALTAMONTE SPRINGS

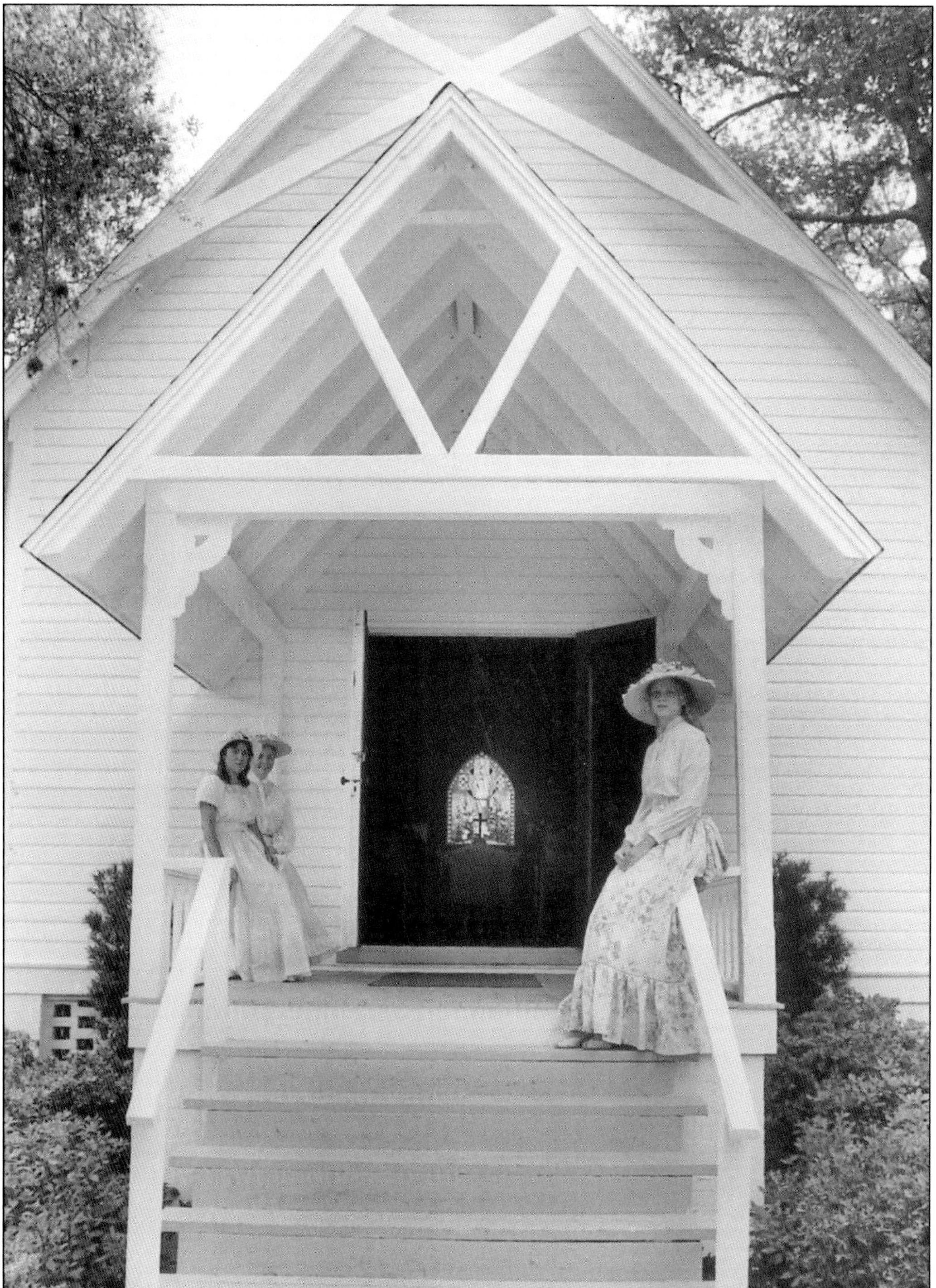

This 1985 photo was taken during the Altamonte Chapel's centennial celebration. Kate Adams (far right), Lisa Tournour (left front), and Cheryl Cornelius (back left) wear period dresses for the festival.

IMAGES
of America

ALTAMONTE SPRINGS

Jim Robison

ARCADIA
PUBLISHING

ISBN 978-0-7385-1397-3

Published by Arcadia Publishing
Charleston, South Carolina

Printed in the United States of America

Library of Congress Catalog Card Number: 2001097629

For all general information contact Arcadia Publishing at:
Telephone 843-853-2070
Fax 843-853-0044
E-Mail sales@arcadiapublishing.com
For customer service and orders:
Toll-Free 1-888-313-2665

Visit us on the Internet at www.arcadiapublishing.com

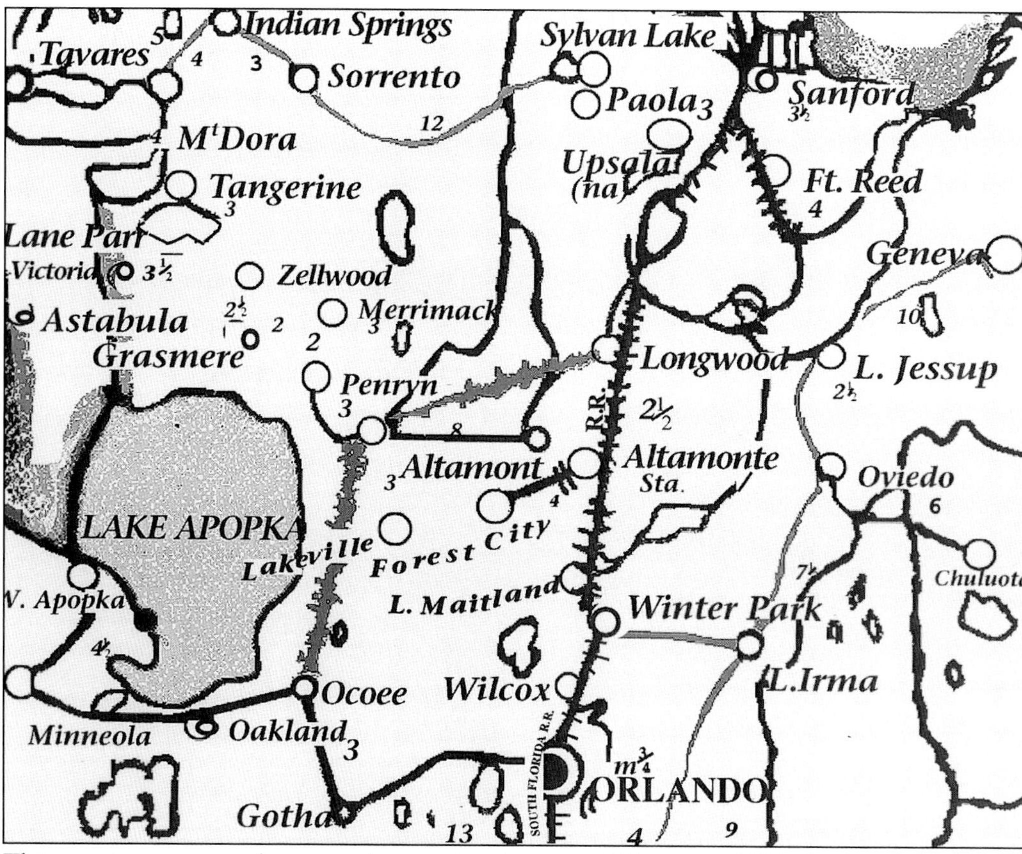

This map is an excerpt from postal routes for the state of Florida in 1884. At that time, the old Altamont and the newer Altamonte Station were separate communities.

Contents

ACKNOWLEDGMENTS

This book was made possible because of the efforts of Richard Miller, director of the Altamonte Springs City Library, who has preserved an extensive photographic history of the city and its people. He cheerfully donated his time, office space, and trusted counsel in the selection of each of these photographs. A special thanks also is due to Bill Goddard for his careful attention to detail in researching the materials used to write the text for this book. Also, many thanks go to Lee Fiedler for the never-ending donation of her skills to rescue and restore photographs. The author also thanks Robyn Robison for donating her time, energy, and dining room table to design and organize the photographs. Future generations of Altamonte Springs residents will owe thanks to the families who donated their photo collections to the library's archives. The majority of the photographs used for this book came from the Fuller, Haines, and Bates families. Additional contributions came from the region's historical museums and societies, including the Museum of Seminole County History as well as the Florida State Archives collection. Sales of this book will help the Altamonte Springs Historical Society continue to buy scale models of some of the city's landmark houses and other architectural treasures.

INTRODUCTION

During Florida's railroad era, the center of community life in Altamonte Springs stretched from the few stores near the railroad depot at Longwood and Altamonte Avenues and west about a half-mile to the winter resort hotel at Maitland Avenue. The little village of Altamonte Springs blossomed into Seminole County's leading retail center with the opening of the Altamonte Mall in the early 1970s just as Walt Disney was turning what had been Central Florida's wilderness, pastureland, and groves into theme parks that drew tourists from throughout the world.

A century earlier, the town's commercial center was Fuller's Store near the railroad depot. Few people lived here year-round. Fuller's Store, which included the post office, was among the few businesses open all year. People gathered at the railroad depot, Fuller's Store, the resort hotel, and the brown, two-story Community House across from the hotel on Maitland Avenue where they held covered-dish dinners and Christmas parties. Surrounding the hotel, wealthy families lived in fine winter homes among the tall pines and mossy oaks and along the spring-fed lakes. About a half-mile east of the hotel, the trolley met guests arriving at the Atlantic Coast Line Railroad's station. Altamonte Springs was reborn every November when the first winter residents arrived, opening up their houses or checking into the resort. Northerners with wealth came to soak up the sun and bathe in Florida's springs. The Altamonte Hotel, which was on the rise between Lakes Adelaide and Orienta, attracted those seeking treatment for consumption, later determined to be tuberculosis. Florida offered something doctors called "rest cures." Nearby springs had become known for "medicinal qualities and the beautiful tropical scenery," writes Nathan H. Fogg, who managed citrus groves owned by the winter residents, sold real estate, and promoted the community in newspapers. In one of those promotions, he writes, "This beautiful little village is now in possession of tourists and winter residents." The hotel's orchestra entertained with classical and popular music at Saturday dances and Sunday concerts. The hotel hosted theatric shows, masquerade balls, Christmas parties, and New Year's Eve celebrations. On Monday nights, it showed movies. The grounds included a golf course where the hotel organized tournaments. Many pines covered the links, called the "Damned Trees Course" by some guests. The hotel added tennis courts at the southeast corner of Altamonte and Maitland Avenues.

Soon, the automobile was making its entrance into Altamonte Springs. B.A. Galloway's Winter Park Telephone Co. (now part of Sprint) reached 10 phone subscribers in Altamonte Springs a few years later. Commerce near the depot and Fuller's Store picked up in the 1920s when the area was becoming the world's leading fern grower. The Altamonte Garage opened in 1921. G.A. Bryant opened another store. Lumber was cut and shipped from B.D. McIntosh's Fargo Lumber Co. near the railroad depot. In the mid-1920s, the ACL replaced the depot, spending about $100,000. A pharmacy, a barbershop, and a grocery store and meat market opened in the block of businesses built by investor Ray Trovillion of Winter Park. Other businesses included an antiques store, a teashop, a canteen, and a barber.

Besides the hotel, year-round and winter visitors were treated to entertaining nights at the Jasmine Theater, built for social gatherings by Charles D. Haines when he owned a winter retreat on Lake Orienta. After a cruise on the lake and a barbecue, his guests were treated to shows at the Jasmine. Each winter, Haines set aside one week to entertain guests from nearby towns at the theater and enjoy a tour of the lake aboard his party boat. The theater at 447 Orange Drive off Boston Avenue was later remodeled as a residence. Haines was among the many winter residents whose hobbies started in Florida to fill up their free time providing jobs and industries for the young town. With help from his son, B.F. Haines, he established south Seminole County as the home of the world's largest ferneries. The other leading gathering area was the Community House, which sat on the site that now includes the city library. The Community House became the city hall as well as a meeting place for the chamber of commerce and civic and religious groups.

Emma Lyman and her husband, Howard, both New York entertainers, first came to Altamonte Springs as guests and performers at the Jasmine. And both would take leading roles in the town's social and political life. Both voted to create the town at referendum that passed on November 11, 1920, by 38-7. Howard Lyman won election to the county school board. The Lyman School, which opened in 1924, was named in honor of Howard Lyman who died that year. The original Lyman, now the campus of Milwee Middle School, became a gathering place for community and athletic events, dramatic performances, and public meetings. As chairman of the town's board of aldermen in 1925, Emma Lyman often served as mayor when B.L. Maltbie was out of town on business. To keep civic organizations active during the lean years of the Great Depression, she put on community picnics and political rallies. She also formed a civic association that took over maintenance of the center when the town was having trouble keeping up with the bills. Many of her organized activities took place at the Community House.

The town's first streetlights were at the Community House across Maitland Avenue from the hotel. As cities across Florida paved old dirt trails with bricks to lure tourists and new residents, boom-time boosterism sparked newspaper and chamber of commerce demands to re-create the bright lights of Broadway. In the mid-1920s, the town council sanctioned its "White Way." The route was south along Longwood Avenue (County Road 427), then west on Altamonte Avenue to Maitland Avenue, where it turned south again. Today, the downtown spotlight is focused a few miles to the west along the interstate and at the lakefront Cranes Roost Park.

One

Early Settlers

The rolling pineland along spring-fed lakes drew the first settlers to what became Altamonte Springs in the years just after the Second Seminole War opened up Florida's interior along the St. Johns River valley. By the early 1870s, the Altamont settlement between what today is Interstate 4 and the Rolling Hills neighborhoods north of the Altamonte Mall included some of the area's first orange groves. The community's post office opened in 1874 about where State Road 434 crosses the Little Wekiva River. Houses were built west to Lake Brantley and east to Palm Springs. Year-round residents found investments or employment in lumbering, citrus, and turpentine businesses. Sanford and Longwood's railroad builders opened the South Florida Railroad and the Orange Belt Railroad in the 1880s, bringing winter visitors. The Snow Station (Altamonte Springs) flag stop appears on the first printed schedule for the South Florida Railroad in 1882. The settlement of Snowville had only a few year-round families, but its population grew to more than 300 during the winters.

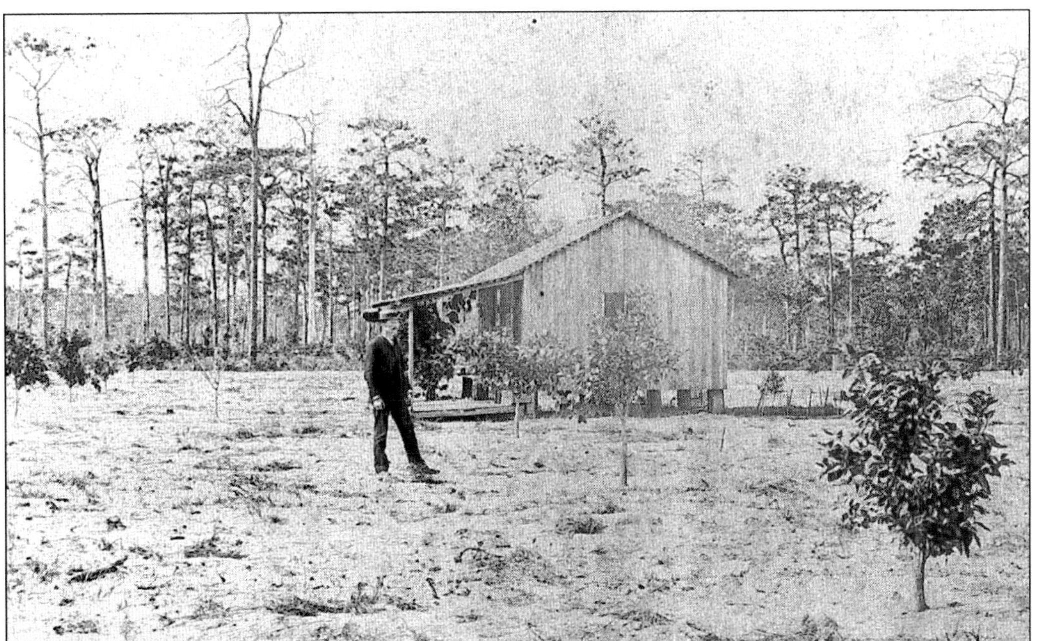

Roswell S. Fuller lived at this simple house at the old Altamont community when he first came to the area. He called it his "bachelor's quarters."

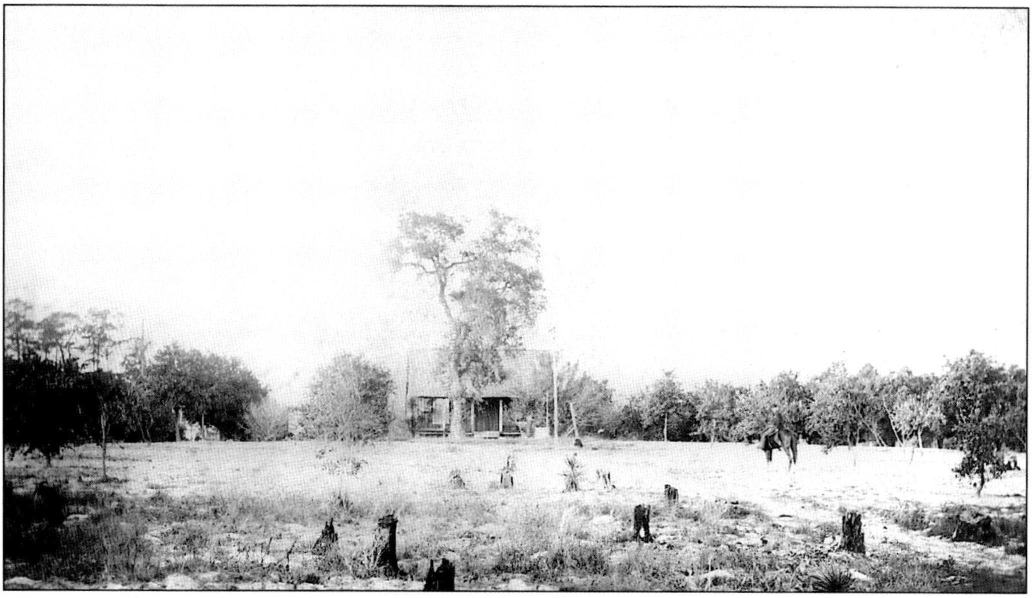

This scene shows Roswell S. Fuller's bachelor's quarters at the old Altamonte community just after the land was cleared for one of the early orange groves. The cracker-style house survived into the late 1800s. Fuller owned the community store nearby at Palm Springs. In the early 1900s he moved the store to Altamonte Springs as postmaster.

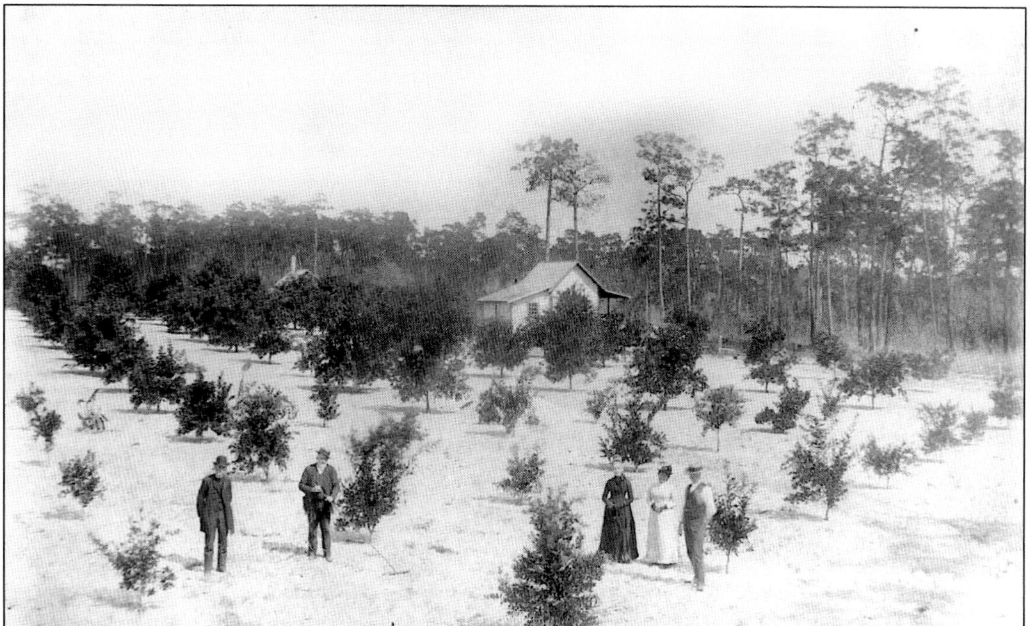

Early residents at the old Altamont community stand among the young citrus trees at the Fuller grove. Fuller's bachelor's quarters is in the background. This photo was taken after an addition in the late 1890s.

These early Altamonte Springs residents pose after a hunting trip into the giant cypress forests only miles from their village. Much of Central Florida still had its first-growth forests in the late 1800s.

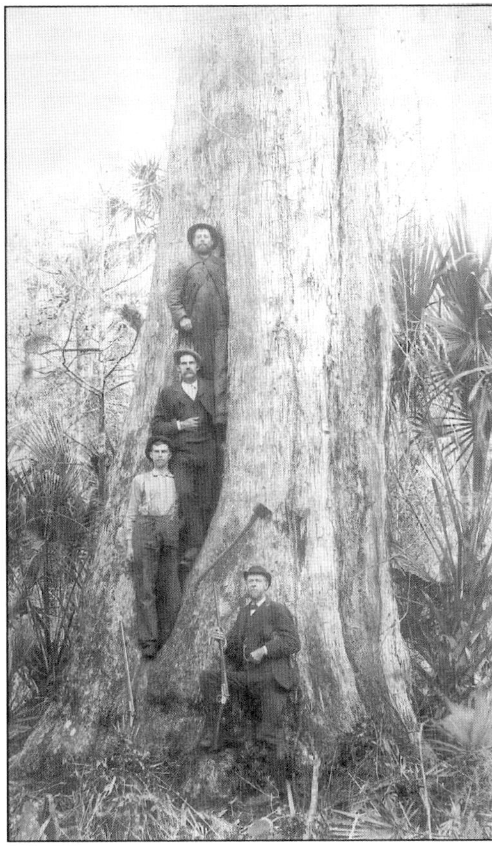

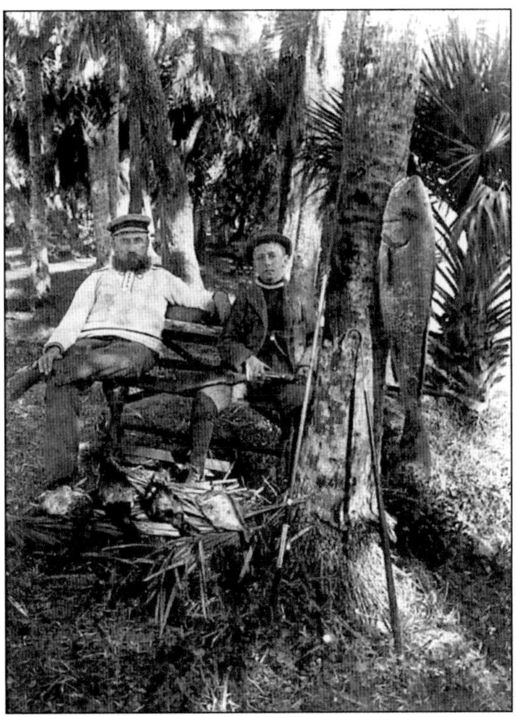

Everette and Chester Bates are shown after a hunting and fishing trip.

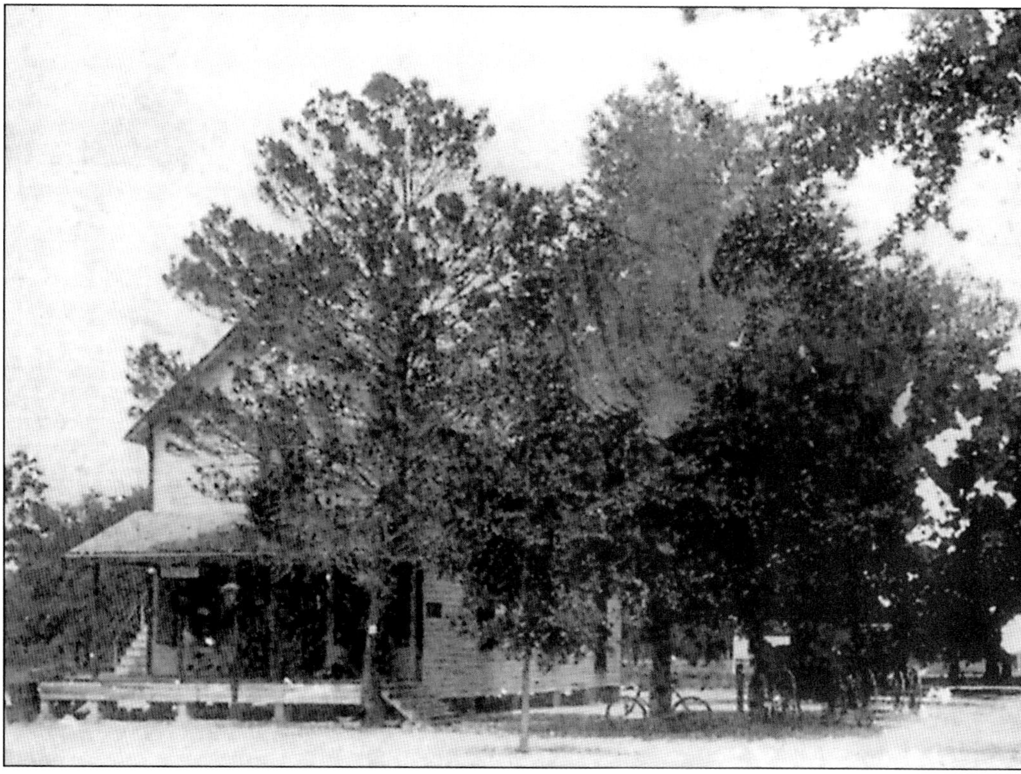

The Fuller store was run by Roswell S. Fuller at what would become Longwood and Altamonte Avenues. Fuller was also the postmaster. His son, Arthur, would later build a new store on the same site.

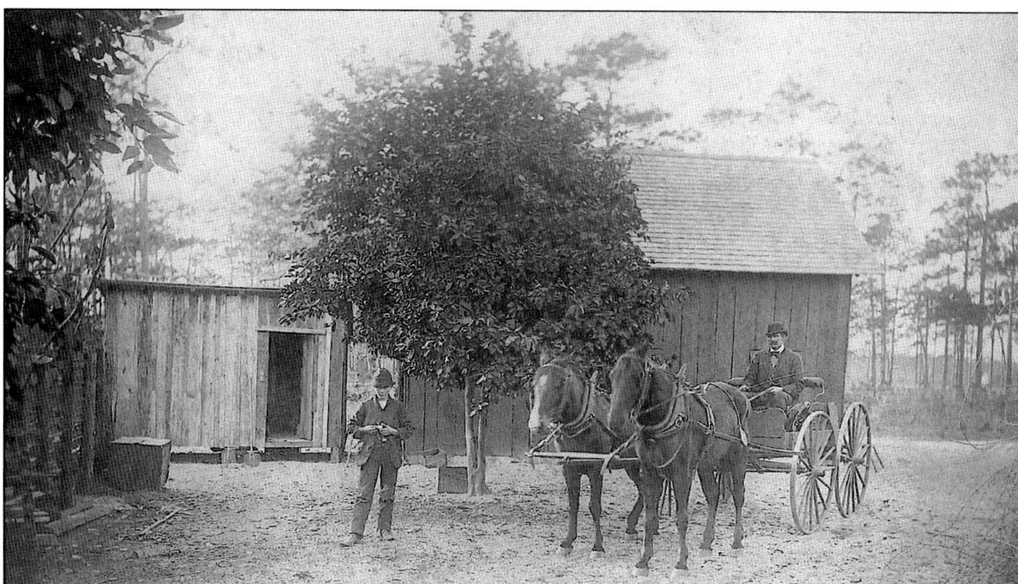

Arthur Fuller, who succeeded his father as postmaster and storekeeper, is shown here at the reins of a wagon at the family's barn. The Fullers used the wagon to deliver dry goods, hardware, and other items from their store to customers.

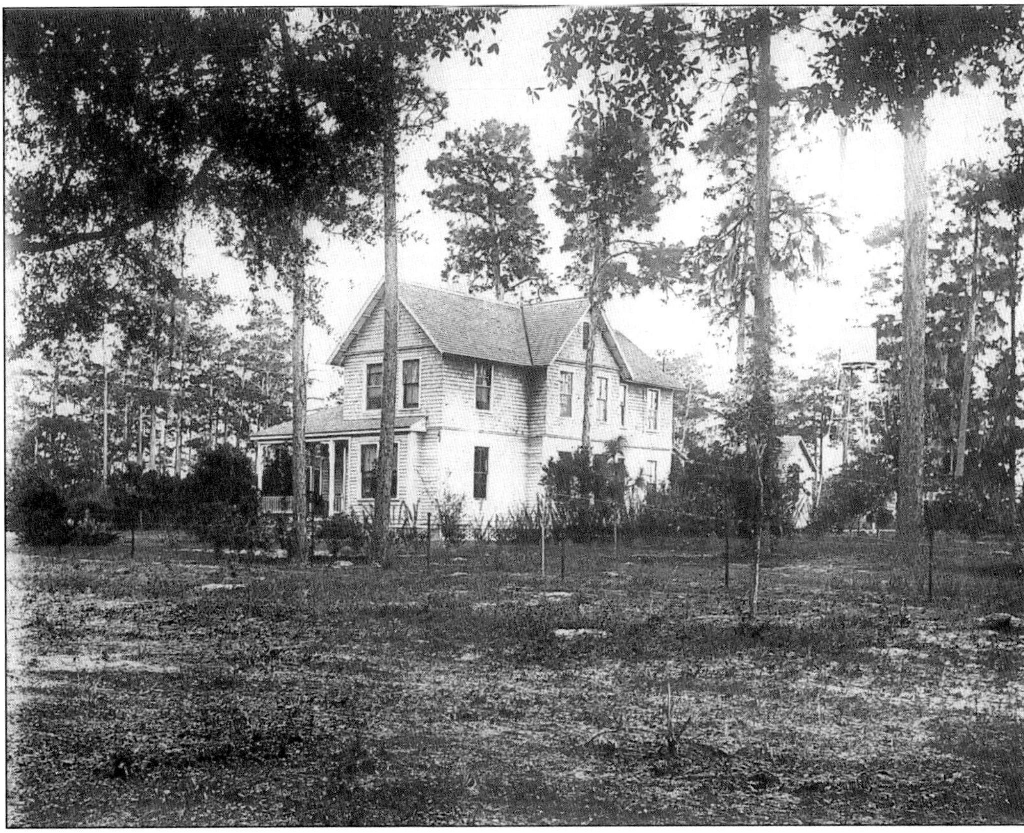

The west side of the Fuller residence is shown on Altamonte Avenue. Houses were scattered along both sides of Altamonte Avenue.

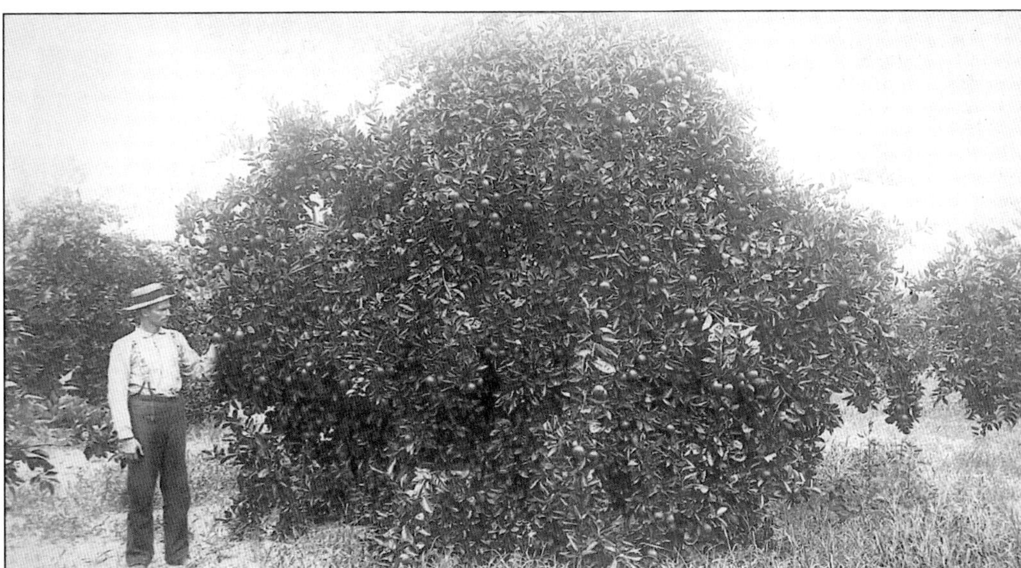

This is one of Fuller's groves. The Fullers owned their own groves and managed other groves owned by winter visitors.

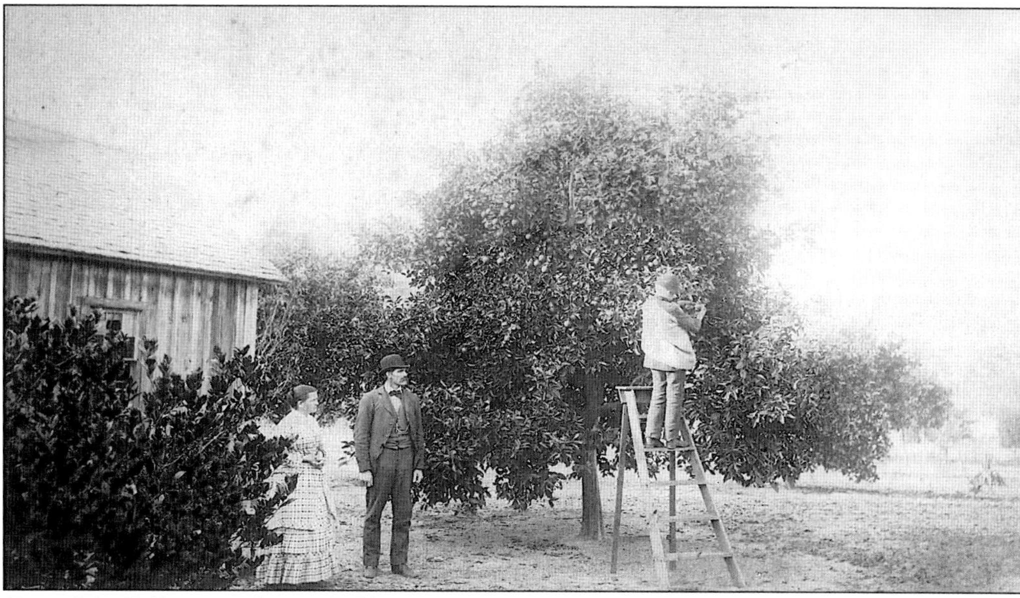

One of the Fullers stands on a ladder to pick fruit at the grove northeast of the family home.

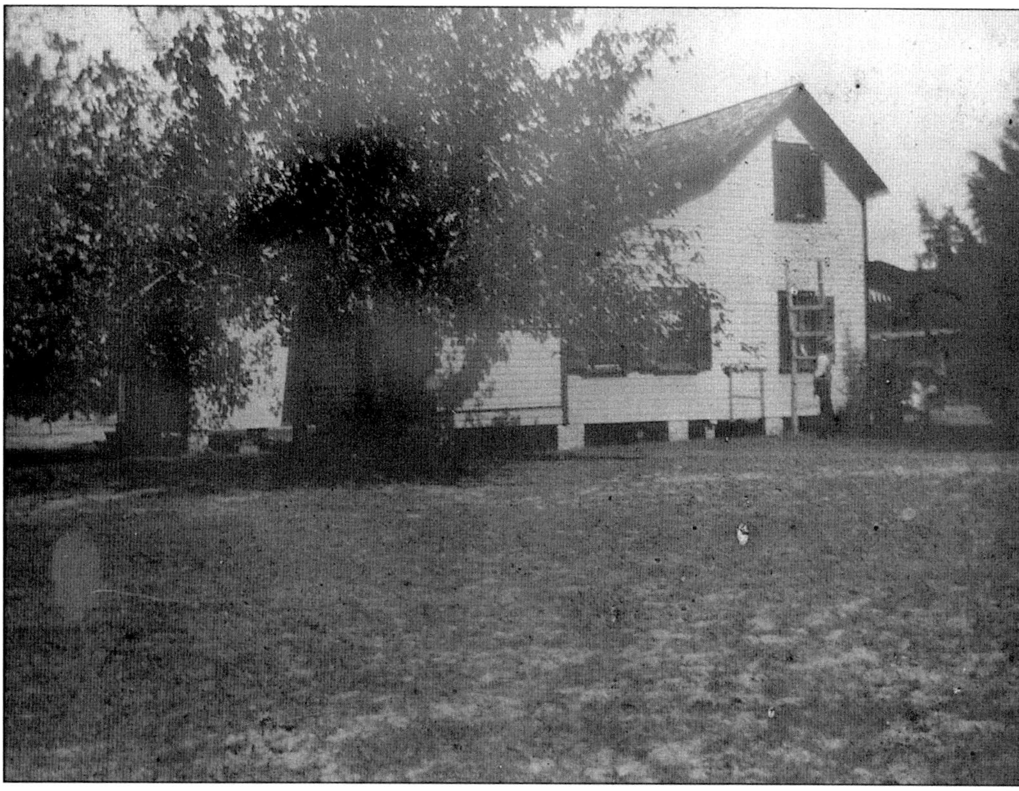

Herbert E. Fuller was born in this family house at Spring Lake, shown around 1890. Fuller was among the original 28 residents who voted in favor of incorporating Altamonte Springs on November 11, 1920. He became the first town marshal, serving until 1922. He also ran the family store, and he served as an alderman.

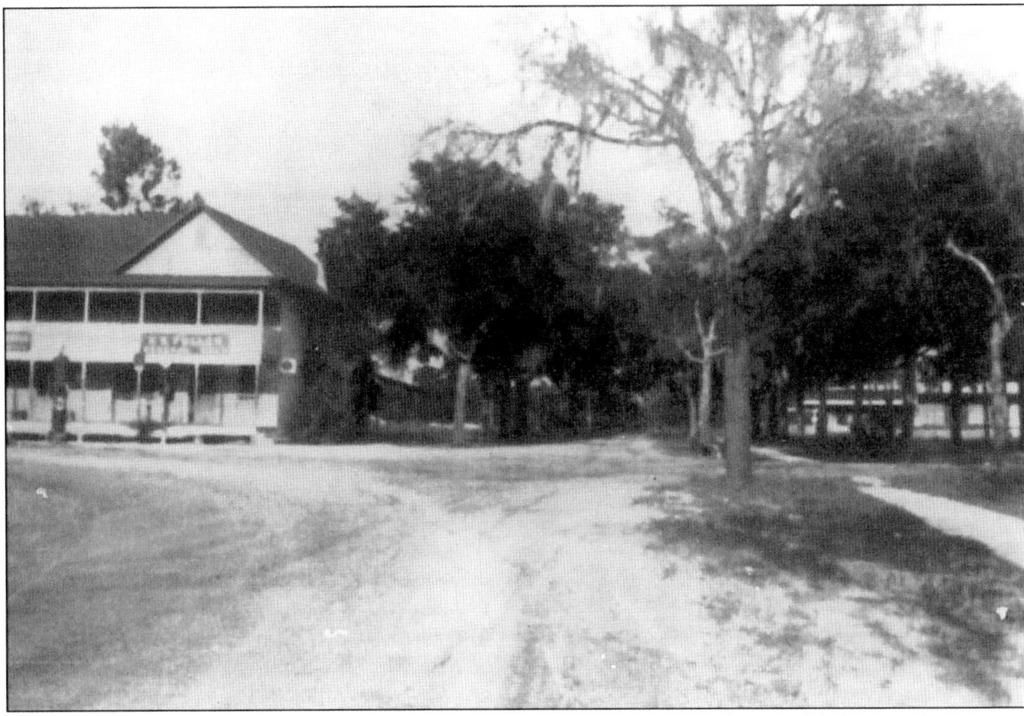

Fuller's store in Altamonte Springs, which included the post office, sold dry goods, general merchandise, medicines, and hardware. Roswell S. Fuller had owned a store nearby at Palm Springs.

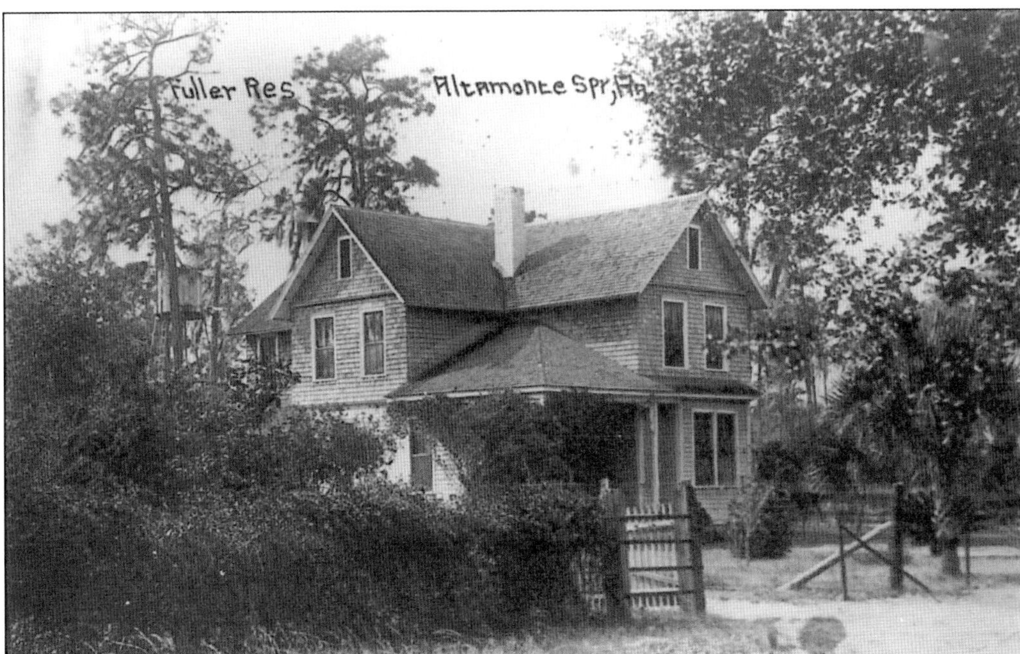

This is the residence of Arthur Fuller on Altamonte Avenue. The family store was to the east.

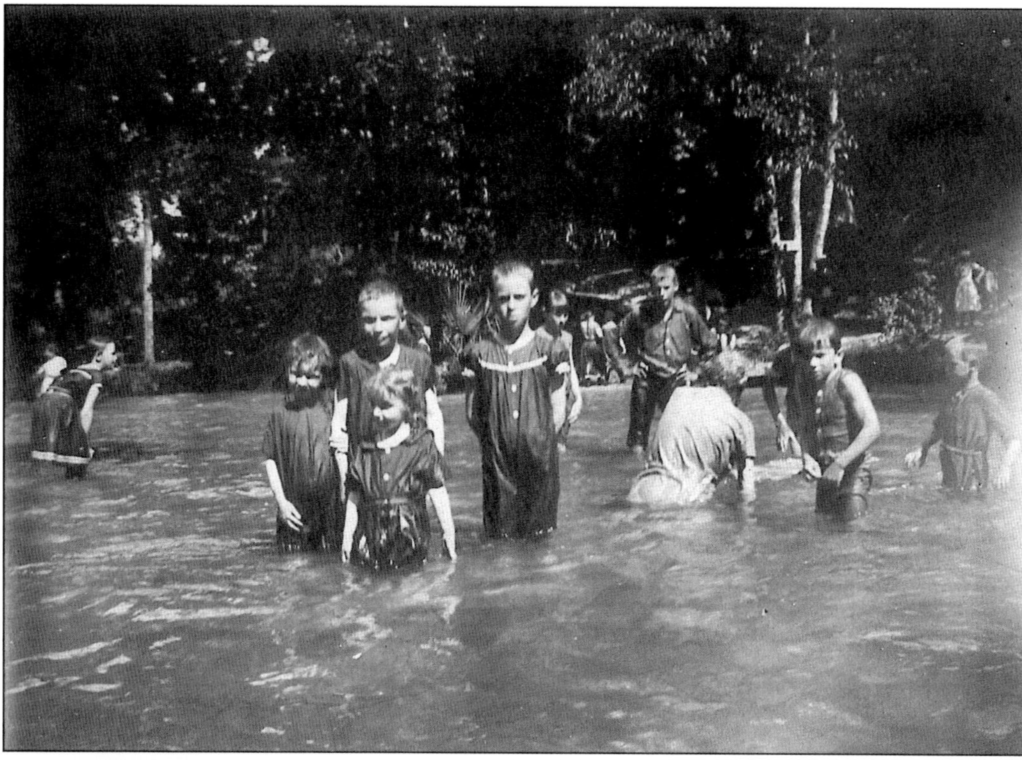

The Fullers and other children play at one of the many springs, which in years to come would draw tourists for mid-winter bathing.

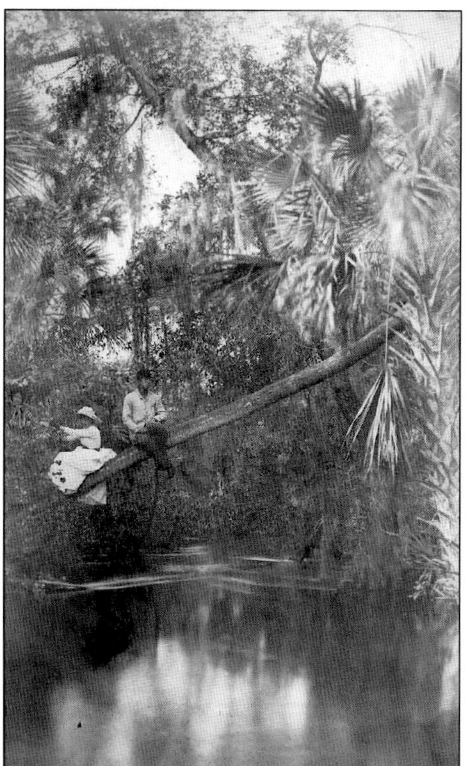

A Mr. Biggs sits with Annie Farnham on a palm bent over a creek at the springs. Spring boils dotted many areas along the Wekiva and Little Wekiva Rivers.

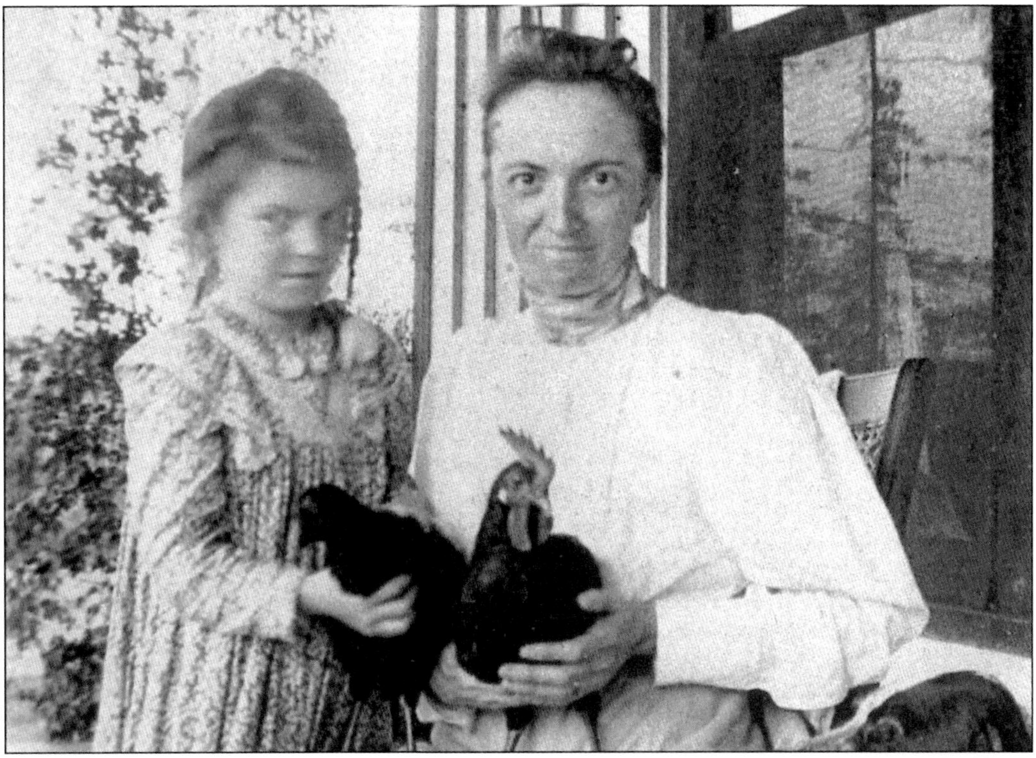

Mary Ann Fuller, shown sitting on the porch of the Fuller's Spring Lake farm in 1900, holds a Minorca chicken. With her is daughter Irene.

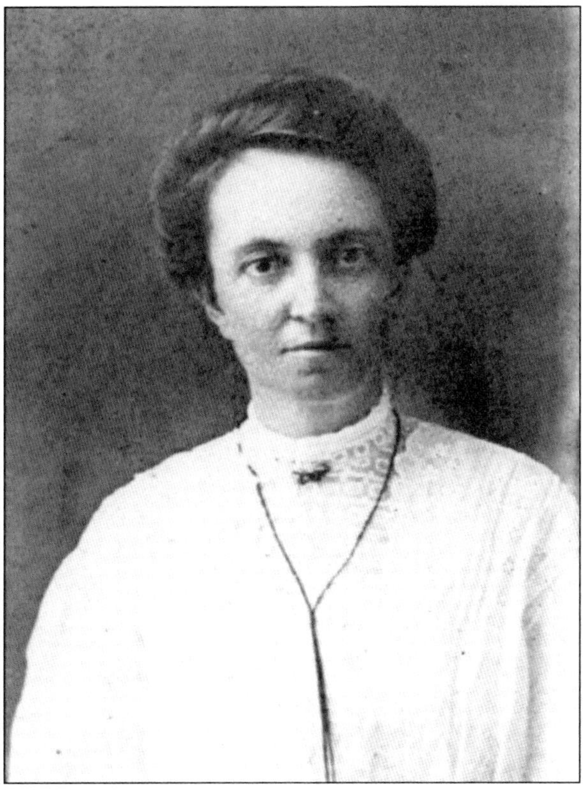

Mary Ann "Mamie" Fuller, one of the 10 women among the 28 qualified voters, cast one of her most important votes in 1920 and helped form the new town of Altamonte Springs; it was born during the boom times. Just a few years after Seminole County broke away from Orange County in 1913, 28 Altamonte voters called for a town referendum. The vote passed on November 11, 1920, by a count of 38 to 7.

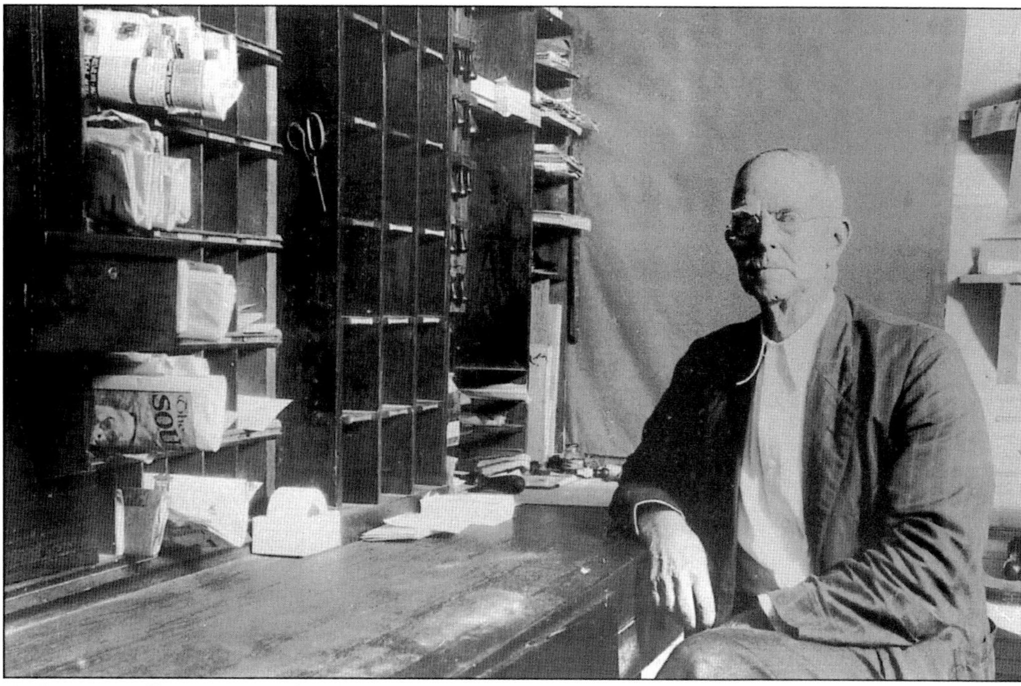

Arthur H. Fuller is seen at his desk at the post office.

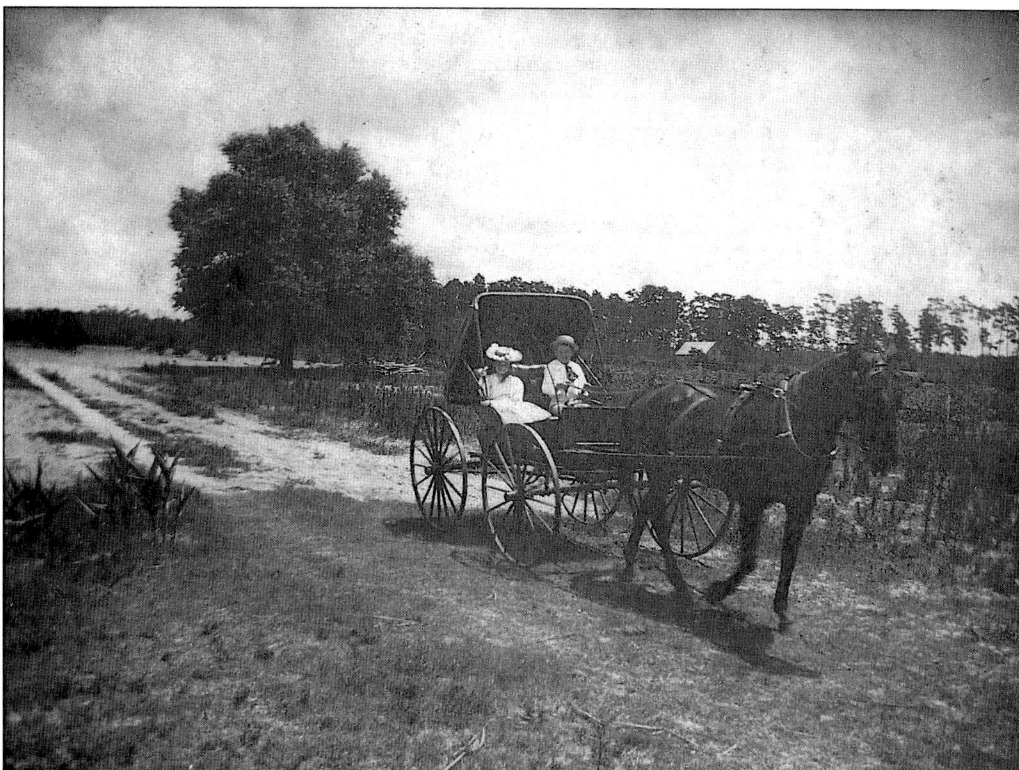

The Fullers' carriage is shown while out for a ride in the late 1800s.

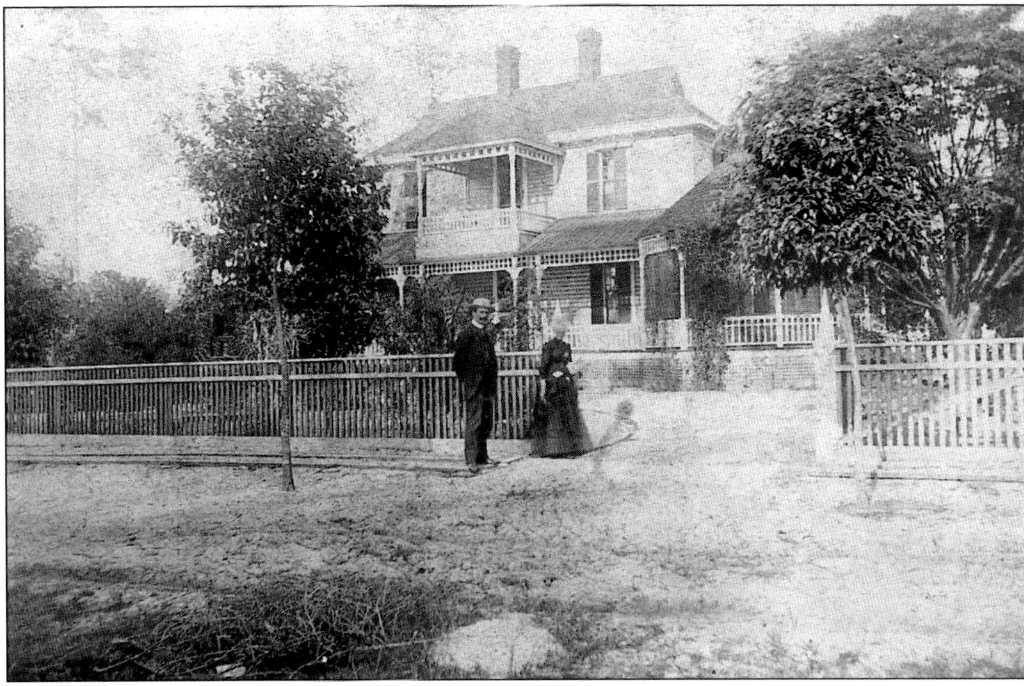

Known as the Julia Day House on Park Avenue, this residence was also the home of the Briggs family.

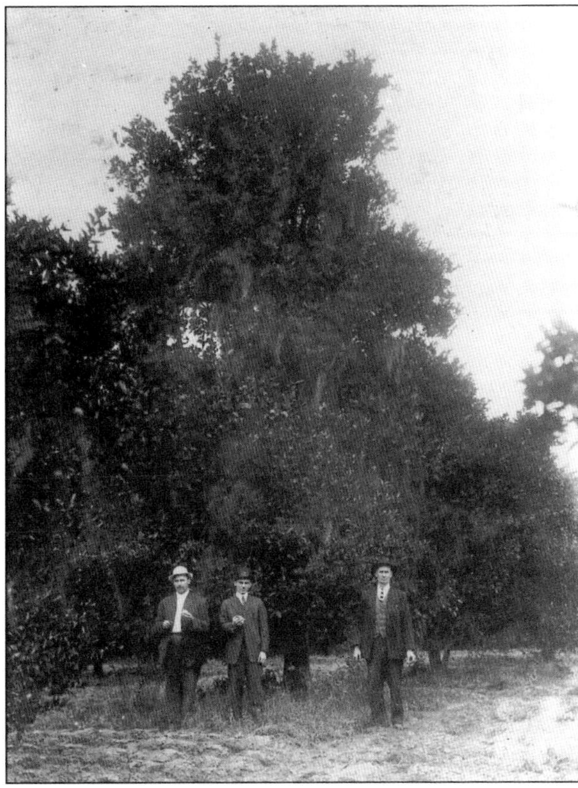

The Phillips family is shown at their grove that include massive citrus trees. Altamonte, Spanish for "high hill," offered rolling sand hills with good drainage for groves. Citrus profits pushed out other crops. The young trees required year-round care. Winter residents left their groves in the care of year-round residents, who were paid a share of the crop.

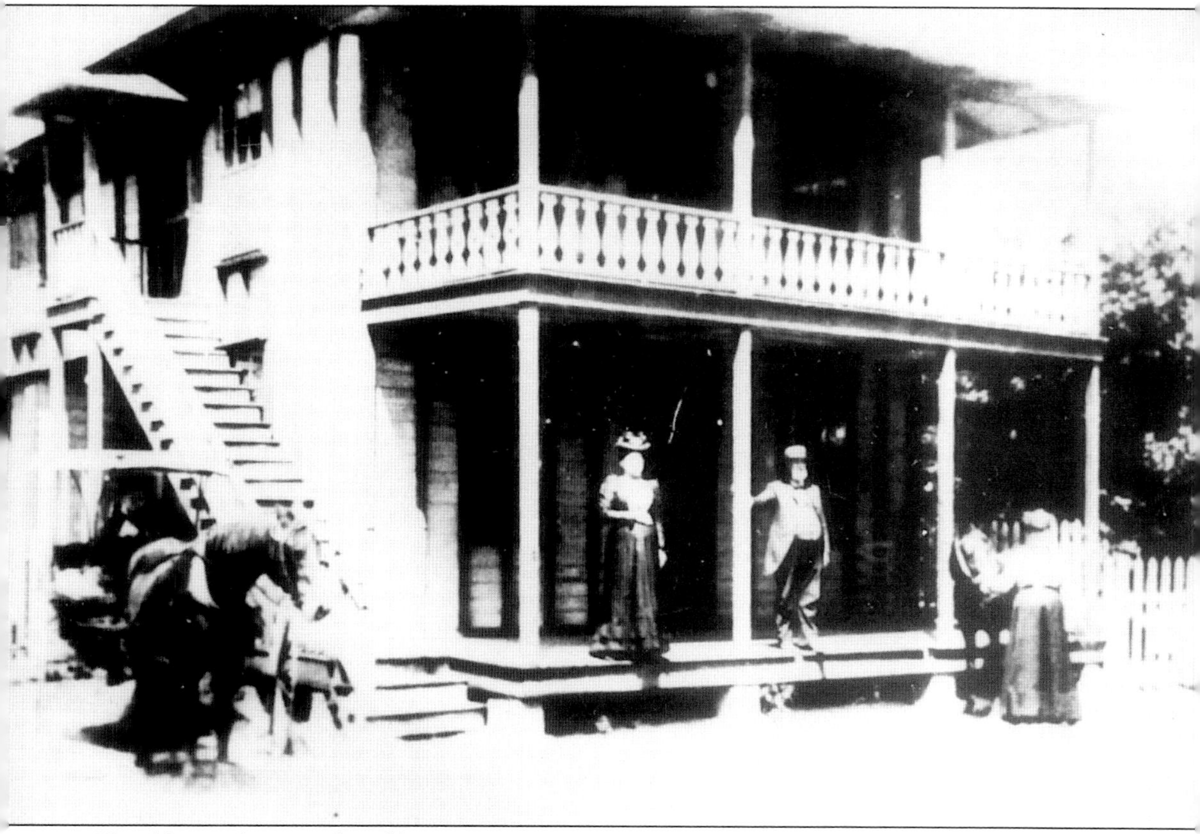

This blurry photo is the oldest surviving view of the Inside-Outside House when it was on Boston Avenue in Altamonte Springs. The man on the porch could be the sea captain, known only as W. Pierce. Built for Pierce in Boston, the house was disassembled and shipped by steamer to Sanford and by mule team to Altamonte Springs in 1883. The house takes its odd name from its unusual exposed stud framing on the outside. It was once part of a cluster of winter cottages at Snow Station in the 1880s. The captain did not move into the house right away. Soldiers used it for a way station when the federal government occupied Florida after the Civil War. The captain moved into the house about 1878. The coming of the railroad would soon turn the little village into a winter resort town. The two-story house was moved in the 1970s to Longwood's historic district, claiming its spot on the National Register of Historic Places as one of the first examples of prefabricated housing. By day, the Inside-Outside House is a gift shop, but by nightfall, the captain and his black cat, Brutus, return.

Two

A Winter Retreat

Five investors from Boston purchased 1,200 acres along the railroad at Snow Station. They formed a land company and built a grand hotel between Lakes Adelaide and Orienta and laid out a village of winter houses for wealthy Northerners. Two landmarks—the Bradlee-McIntyre House, a Queen Anne–style winter home built in 1885, and the Inside-Outside House, built in Boston, taken apart, and shipped by steamer and mule team for reassembling in Altamonte Springs in 1883—date to this period. Chartered in 1882, the Altamonte Land, Hotel and Navigation Co. promoted land sales for groves and farms and homesites for winter visitors. The centerpiece Altamonte Hotel, built with yellow pine cut nearby, would provide "ample facilities, for boating, fishing, gunning, mid-winter open-air bathing and commanding an outlook for miles over picturesque scenery," boasted the company's literature.

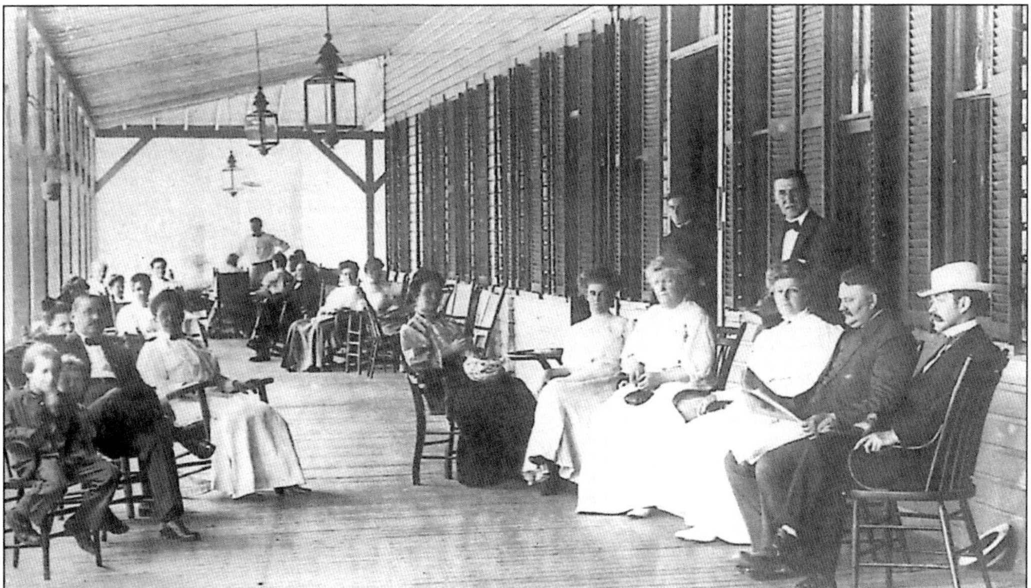

Winter guests at the Altamonte Hotel gather on its wrap-around porch in the 1890s.

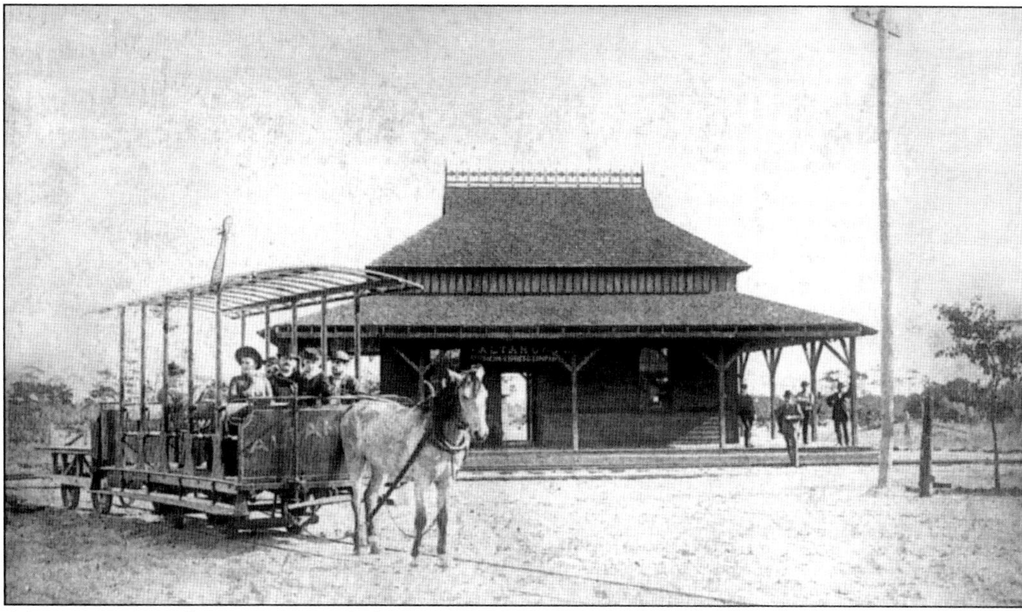

Altamonte Hotel's tram, named the "Dixie Flyer," prepares to leave the depot at Altamonte Springs for the hotel in 1887.

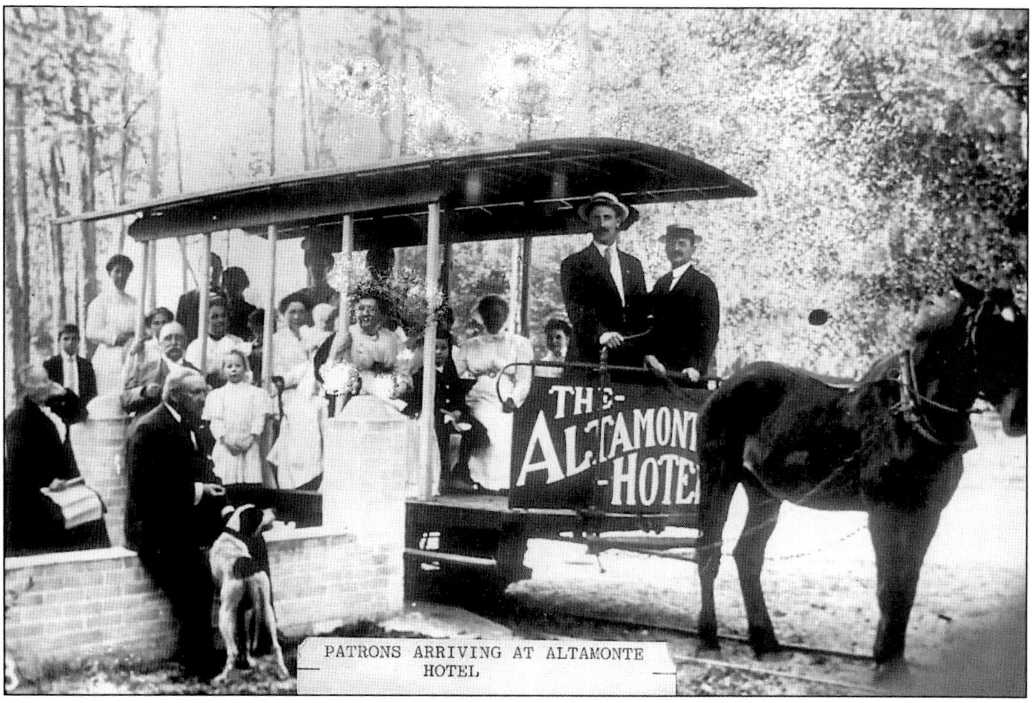

The Altamonte Hotel's tram arrives at the hotel in 1887. The tramway ran from the railroad depot to the grand hotel on the rise between Lakes Adelaide and Orienta, which attracted those seeking treatment for consumption. Florida offered something doctors called "rest cures."

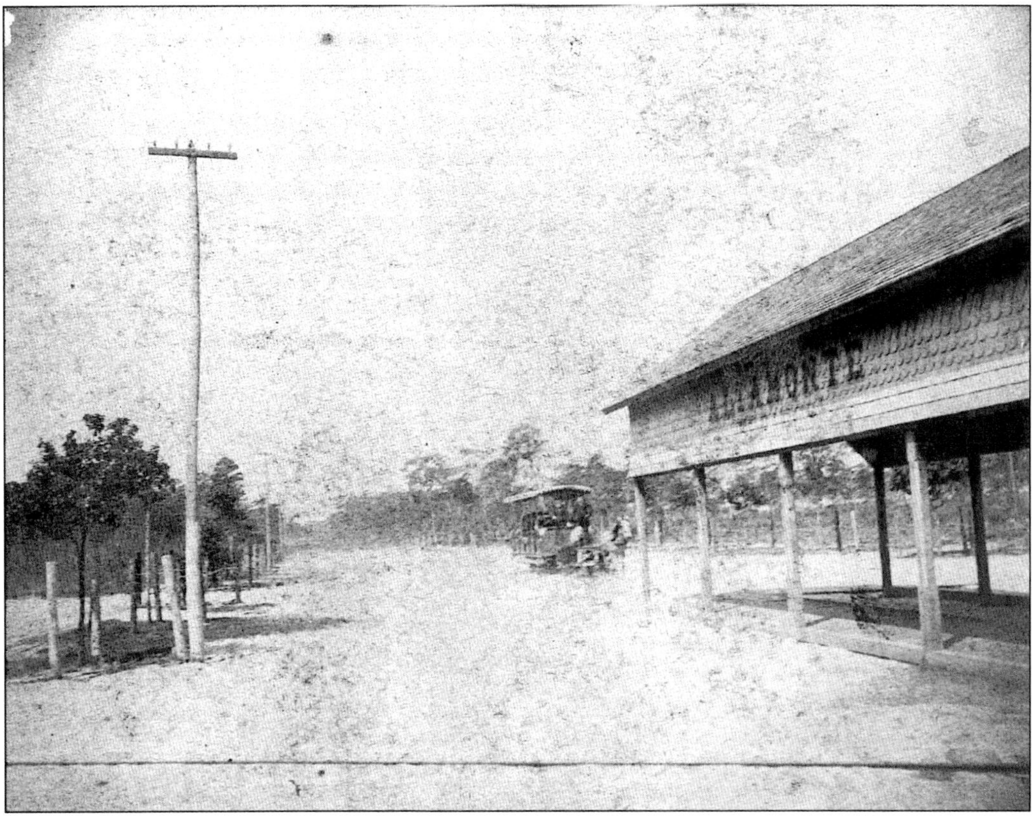

The Altamonte Hotel's Dixie Flier arrives at the depot. The tram's horse was named Dixie and was brought to Altamonte Springs by railroad.

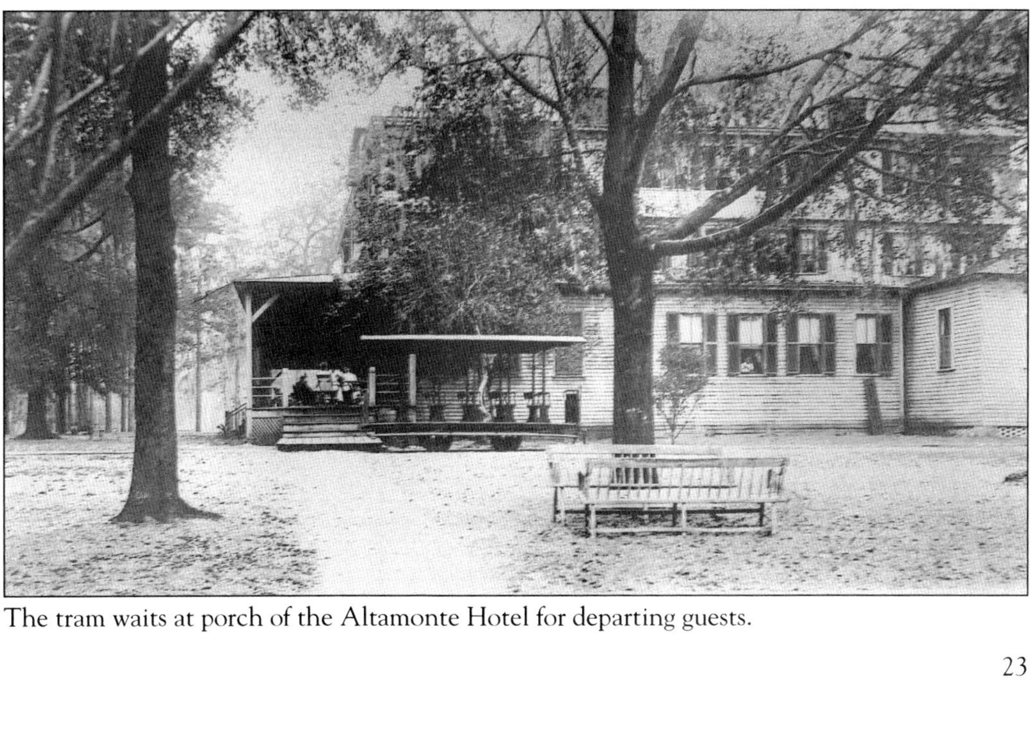

The tram waits at porch of the Altamonte Hotel for departing guests.

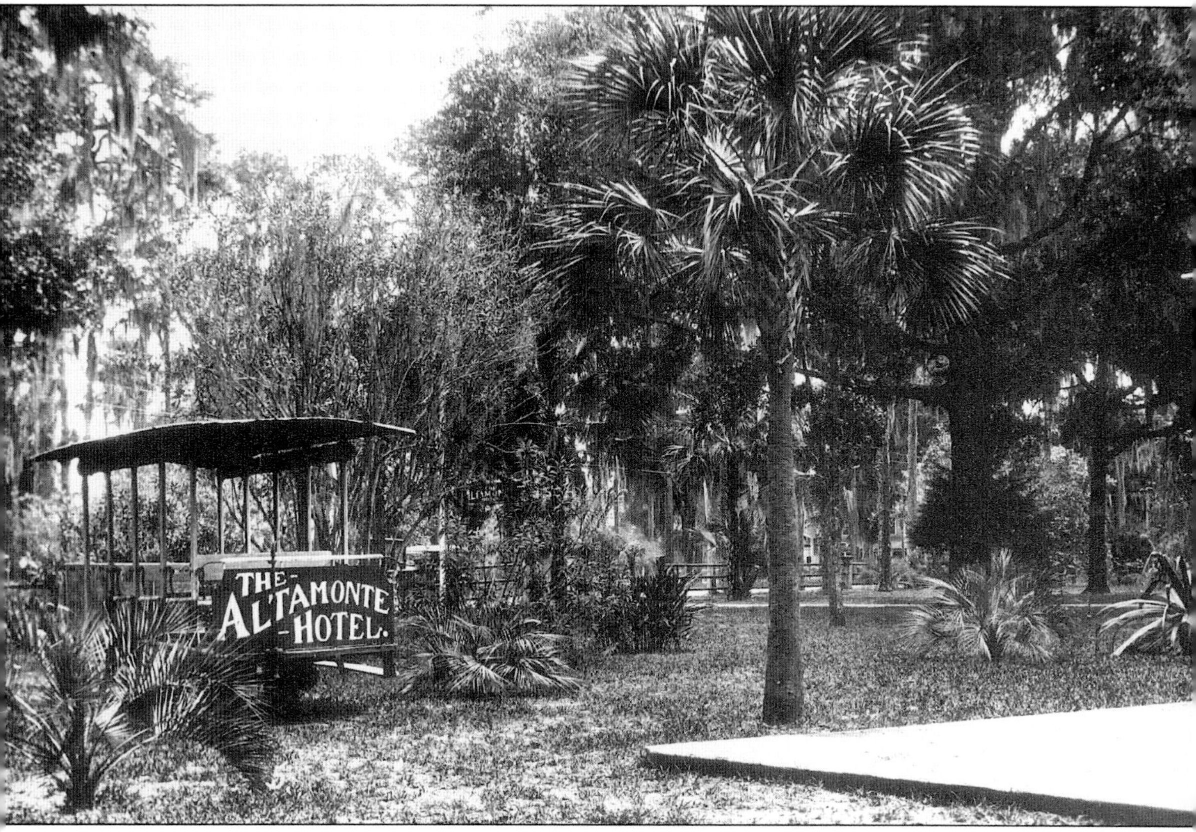

The Altamonte Hotel's tram is parked to the side of the hotel. The tramway, added after the hotel opened, became the most popular way to get to the hotel from the South Florida railroad depot. Railroads replaced steamboats as the leading transportation to Florida and towns along the tracks prospered.

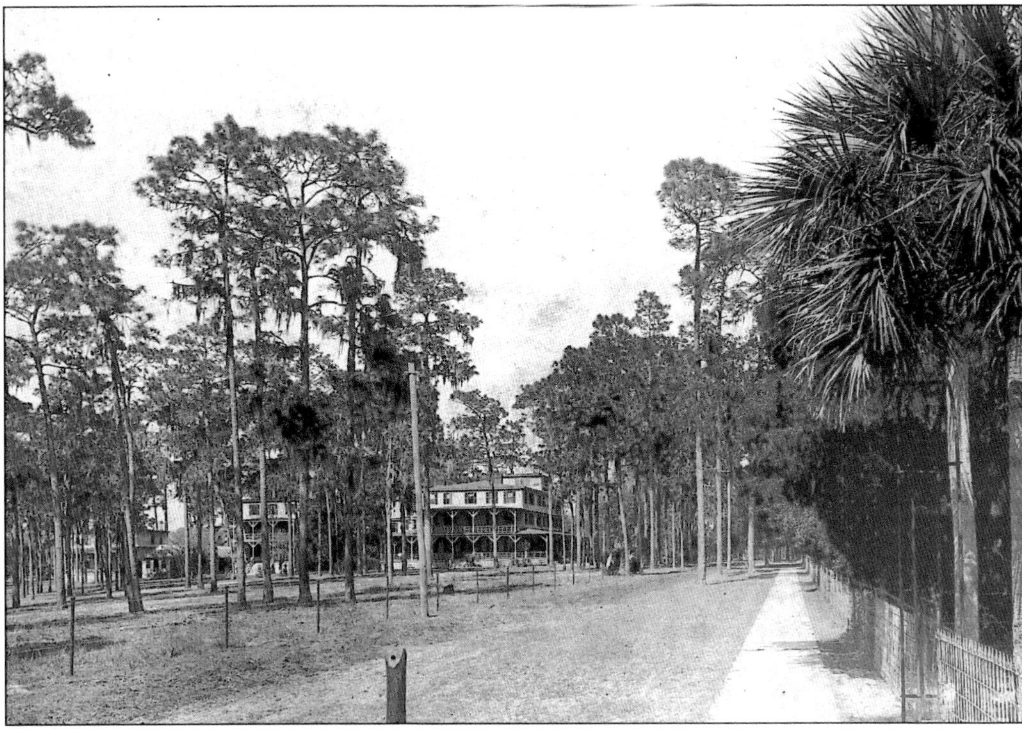

Looking north on Maitland Avenue toward Lake Adelaide, the Altamonte Hotel is shown on Lake Orienta. The site is now condominiums.

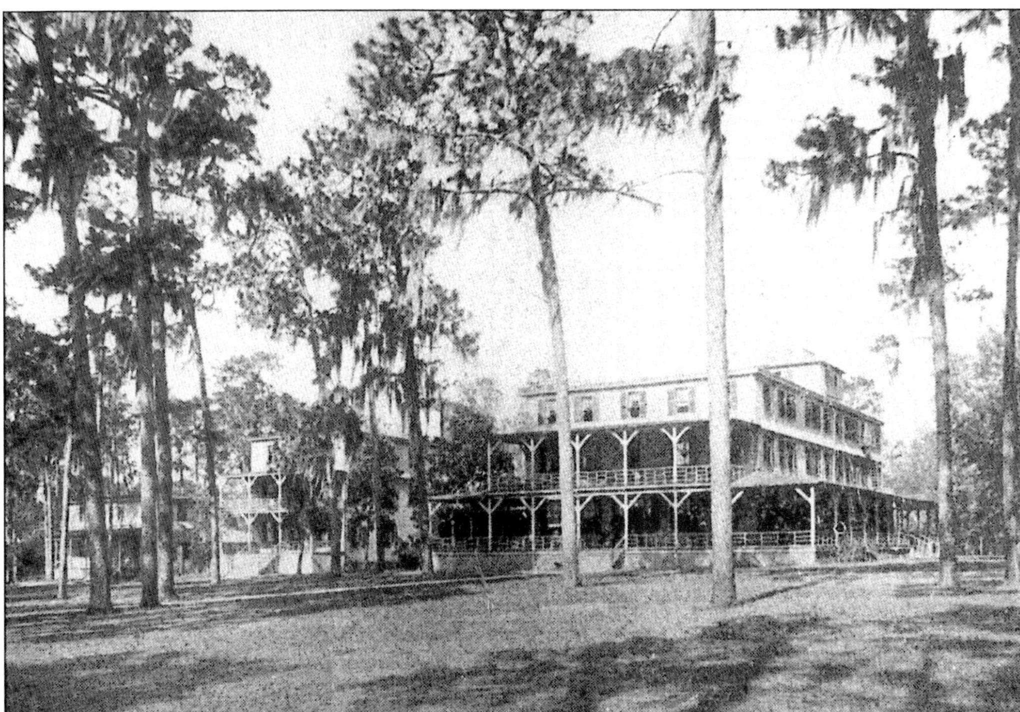

The Altamonte hotel is shown through the pines along the lakefront.

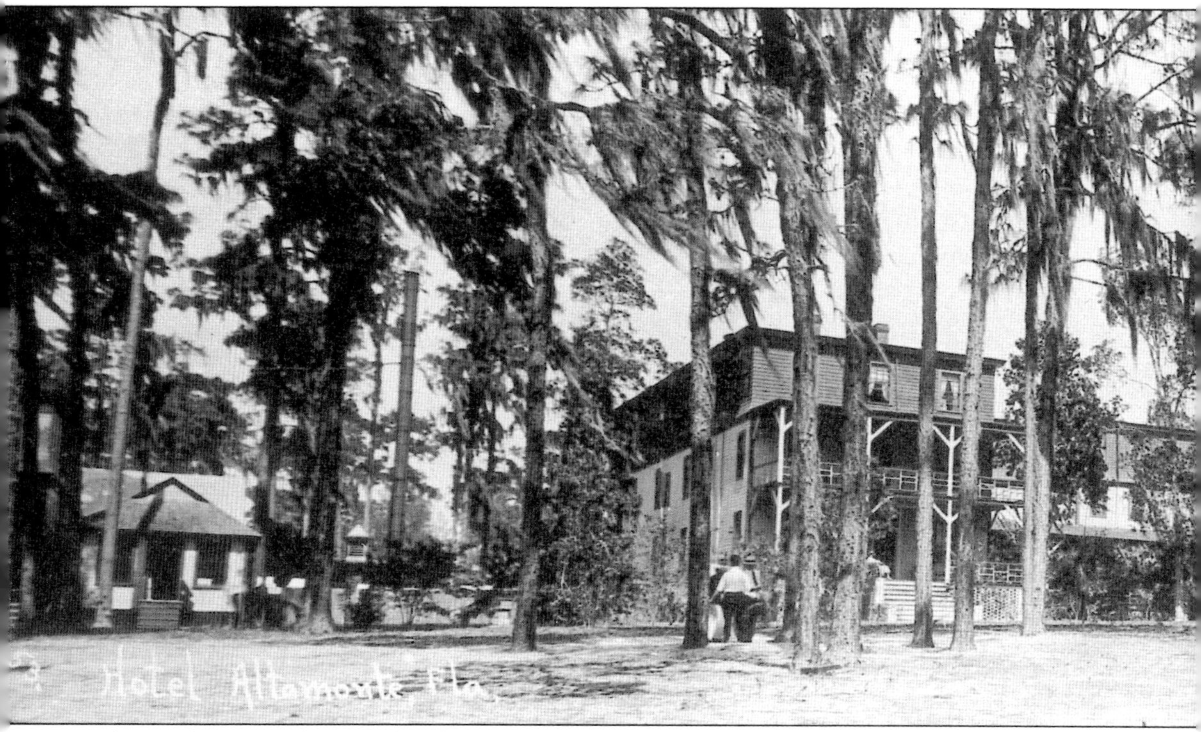

This early 1890s photograph of the Altamonte Hotel was taken from the shoreline of Lake Orienta. The first guests registered in early 1883. The winter guests at the hotel and others who

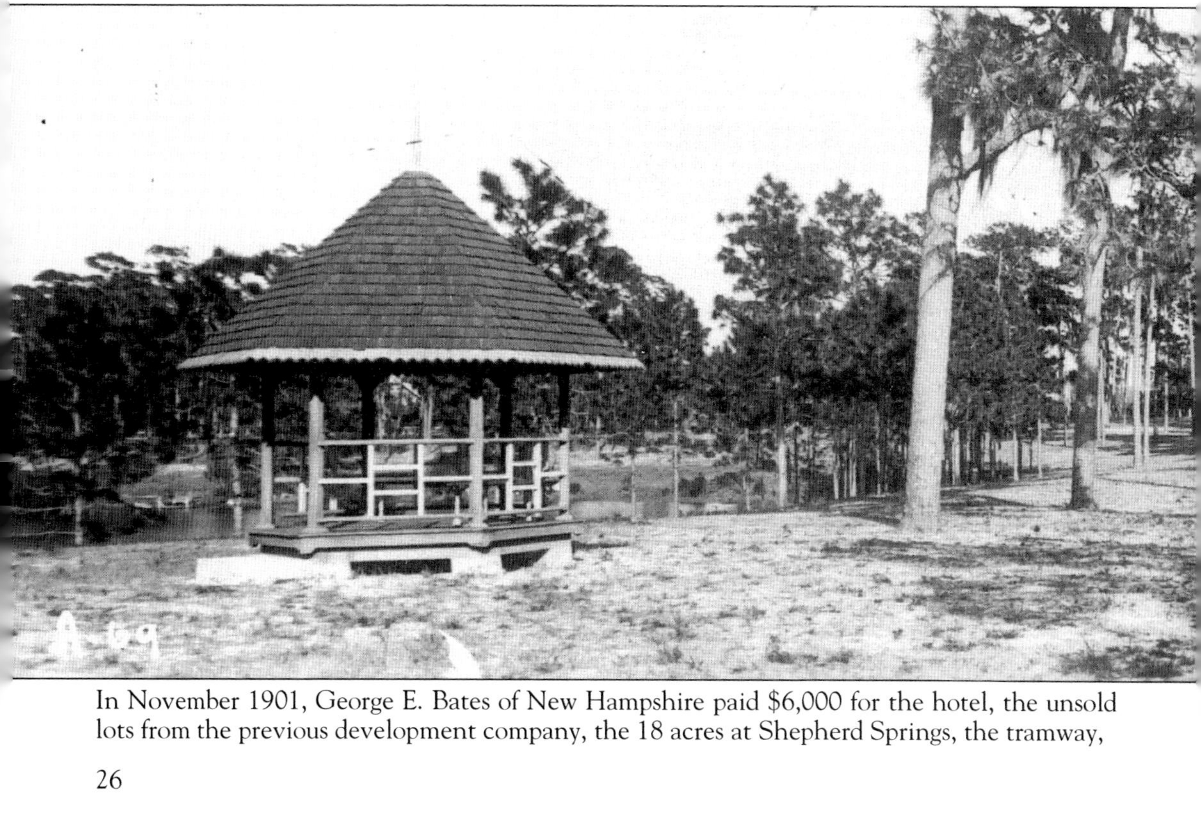

In November 1901, George E. Bates of New Hampshire paid $6,000 for the hotel, the unsold lots from the previous development company, the 18 acres at Shepherd Springs, the tramway,

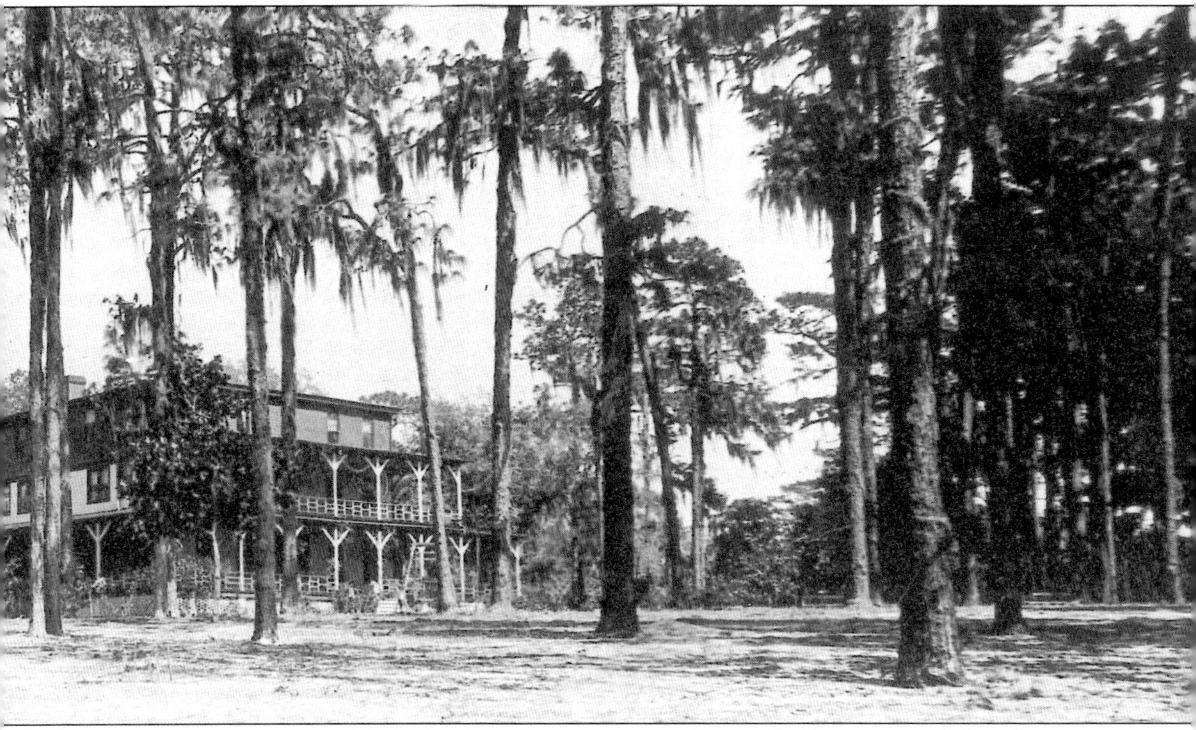

built winter homes established Altamonte Springs when old Altamont faded. Altamonte Springs had schools, public services, and better transportation.

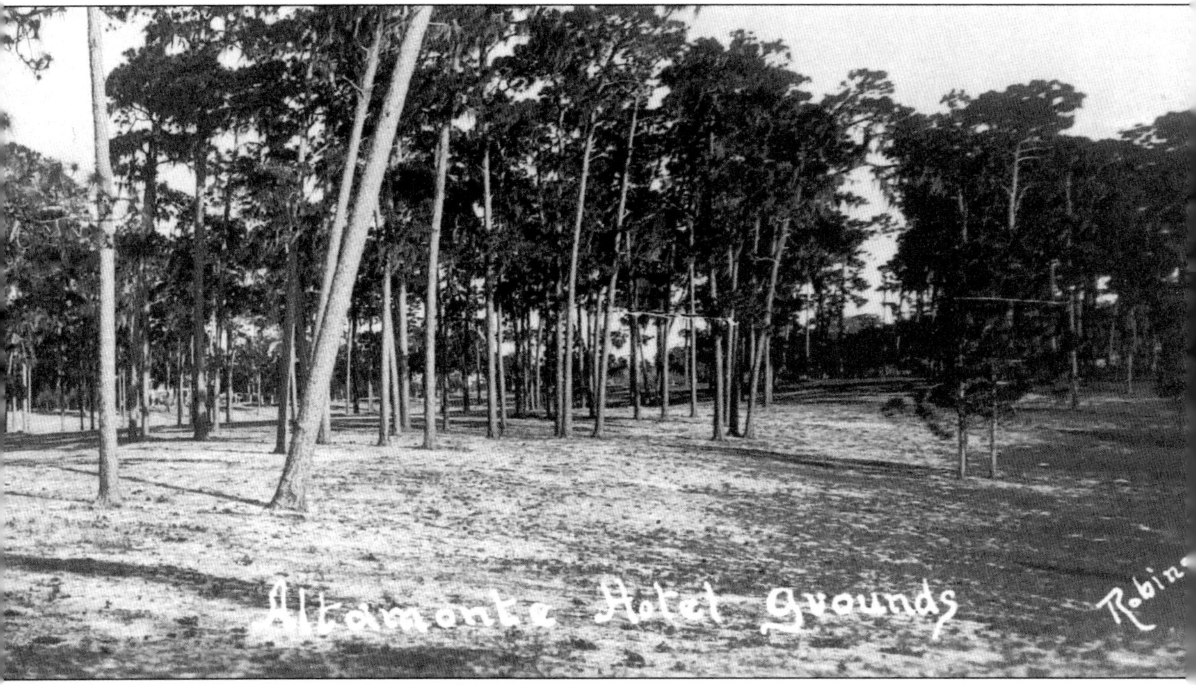

and the hotel's grounds, which included gardens and a gazebo.

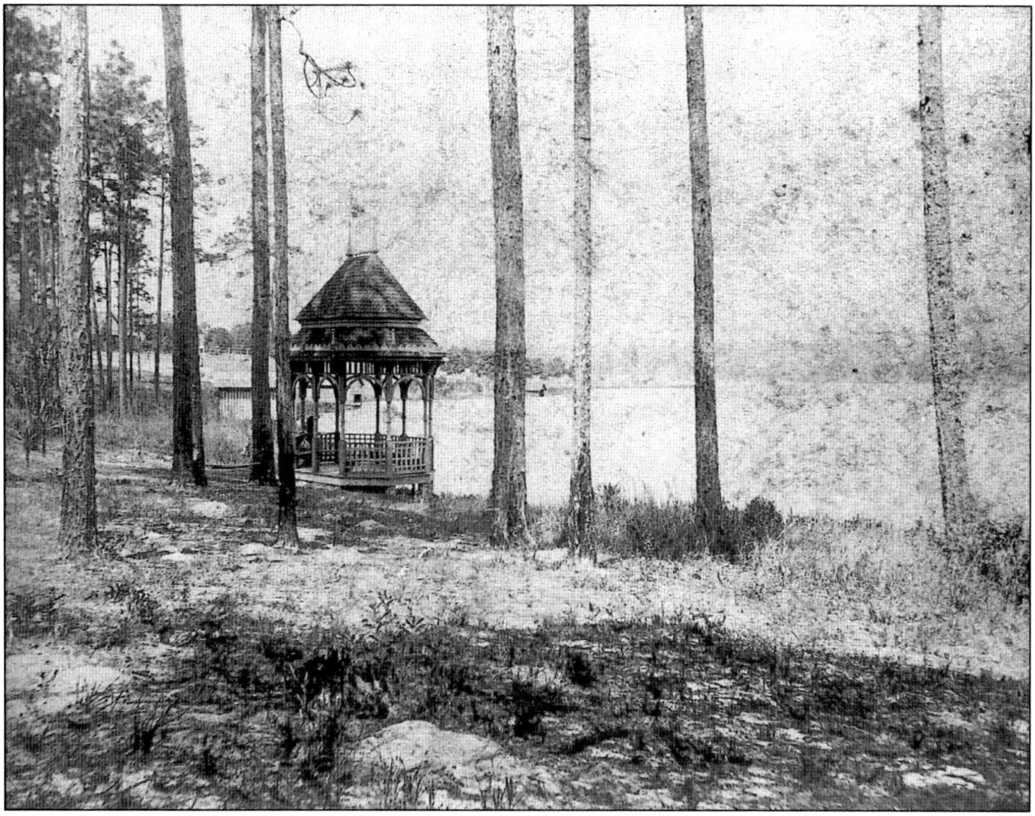

This 1888 scene is one of the oldest views of the Altamonte Hotel's springhouse on Lake Adelaide. Bathing in and drinking springwater was part of the hotels "rest cures." The hotel was a haven for the ill.

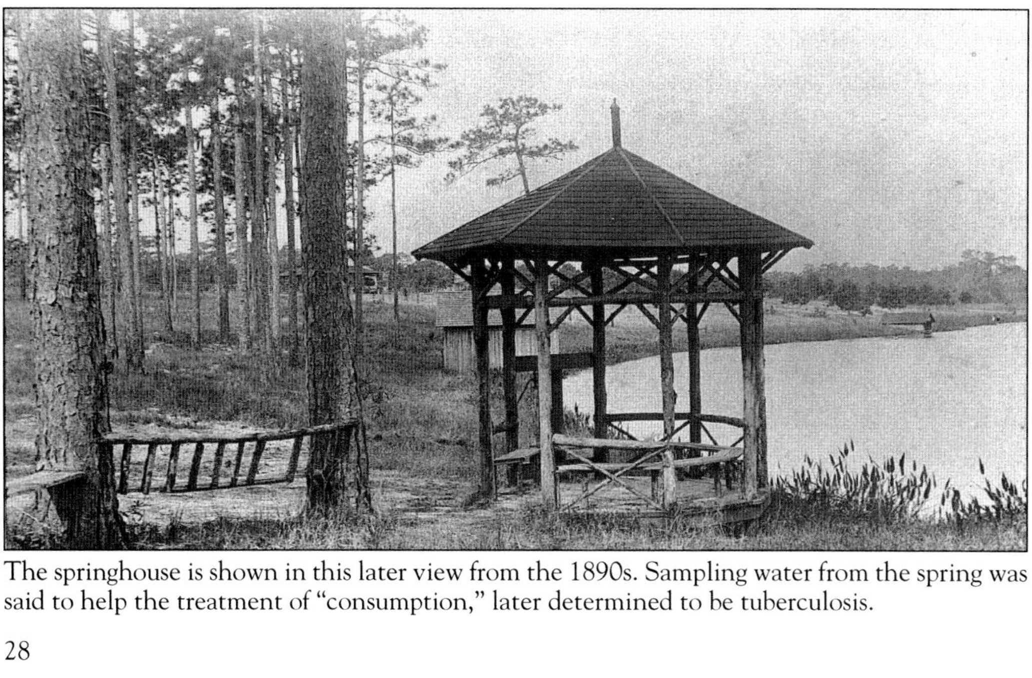

The springhouse is shown in this later view from the 1890s. Sampling water from the spring was said to help the treatment of "consumption," later determined to be tuberculosis.

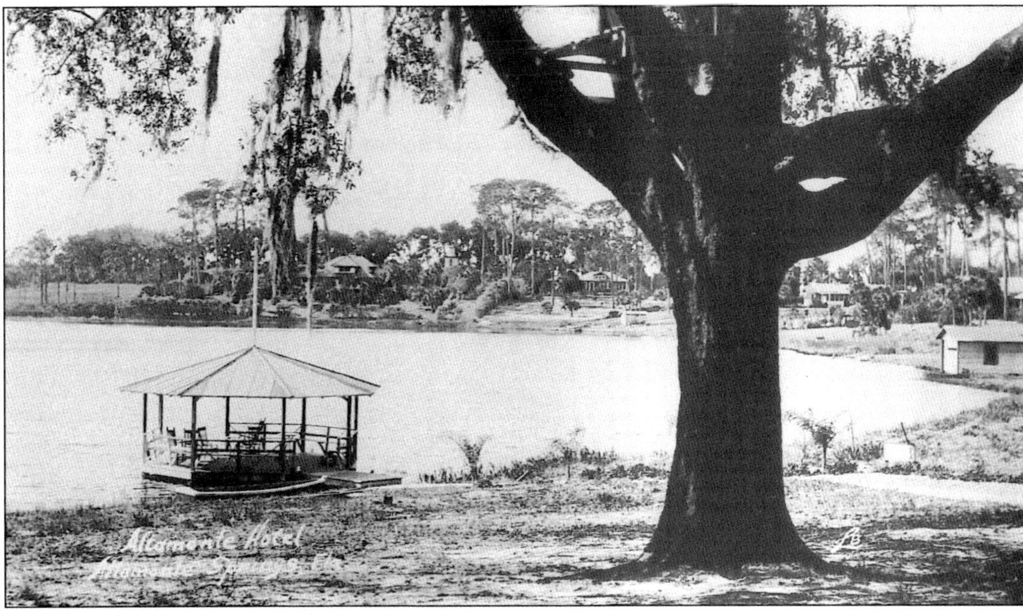

The Altamonte Hotel's dock on Lake Orienta included a gazebo, shown here. Looking southwest across the lake is the Briggs-Hoffman House and Fuller House in background.

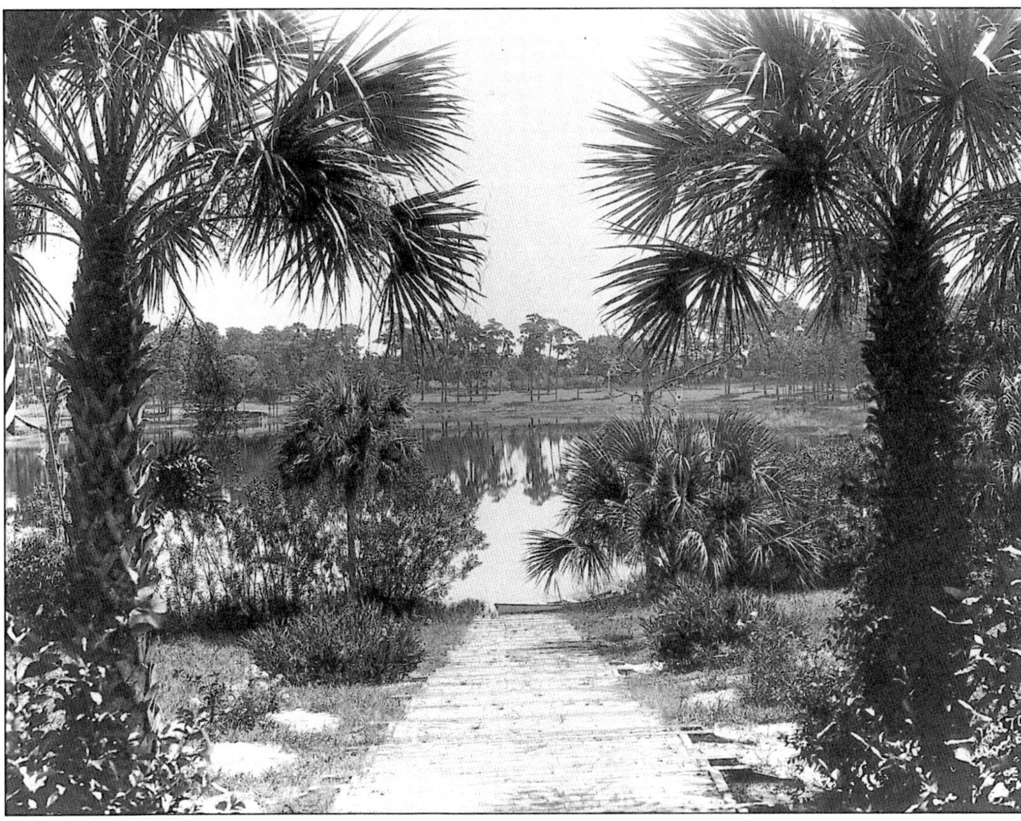

In this view, the walkway from the Altamonte Hotel leads through the eighth and ninth holes of the golf course to the dock at Lake Orienta.

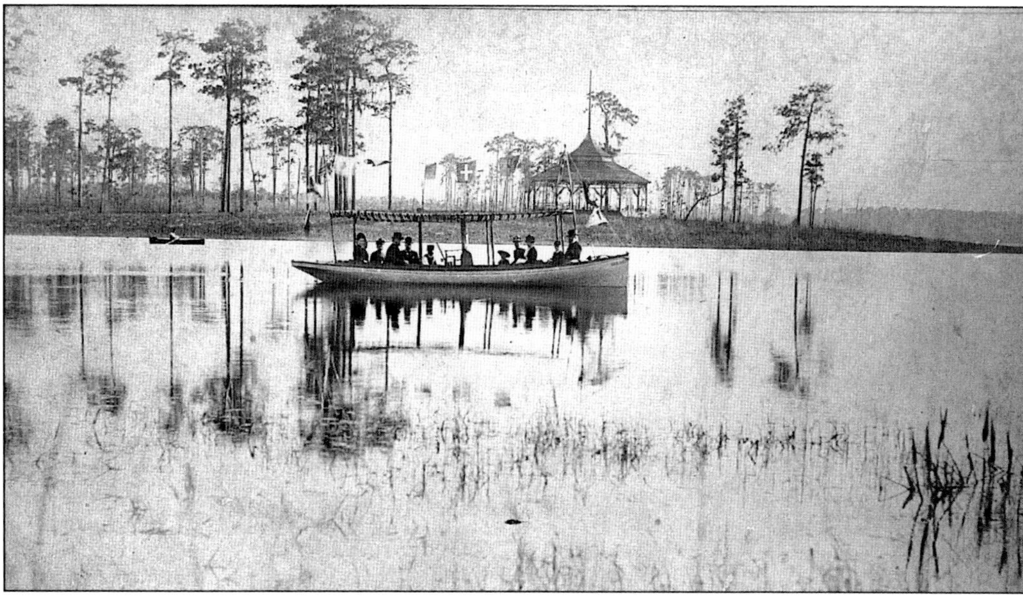

Altamonte Hotel guests cruise Lake Orienta on the hotel's boat in this c. 1887 photograph. The lake and the beautiful hotel grounds made the Altamonte Hotel the region's leading destination. It was booked to capacity for its December-April season throughout the early 1900s.

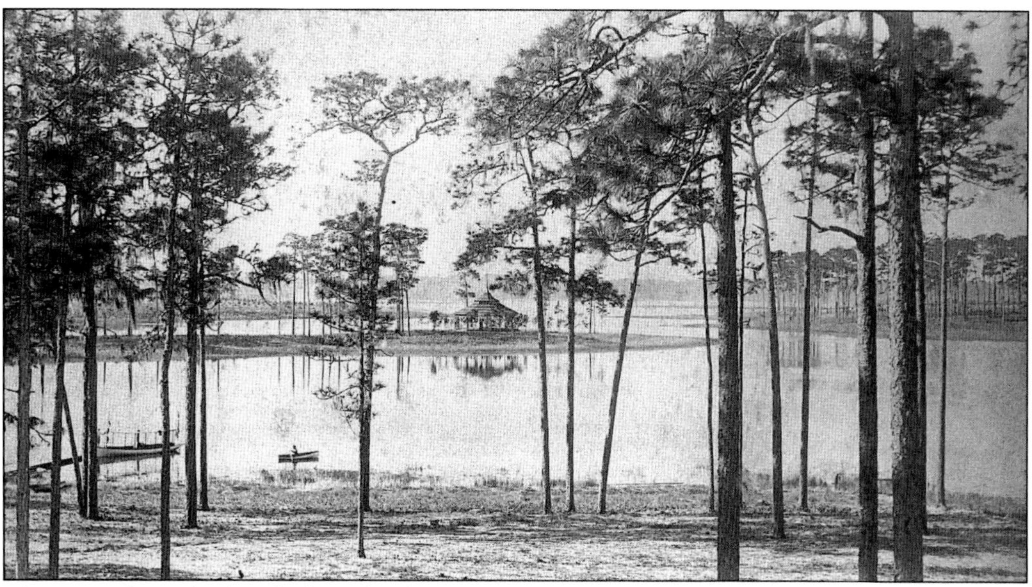

This view from the hotel's boat landing across to the point on Lake Orienta shows another gazebo built for guests.

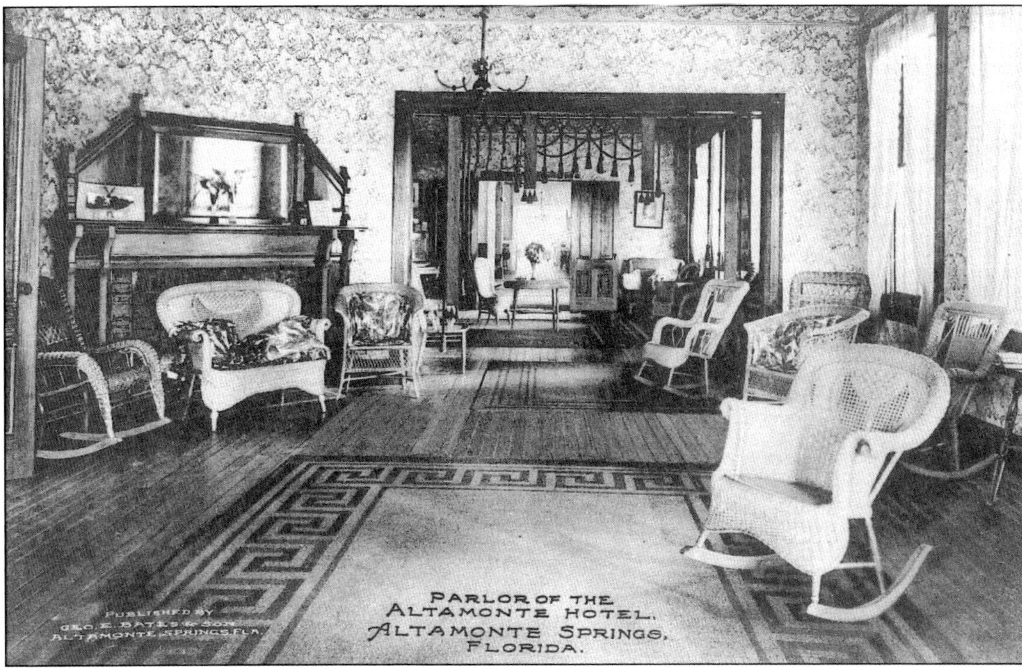

The parlor of the Altamonte Hotel is shown as it appeared in the early 1900s when it was owned and managed by the Bates family.

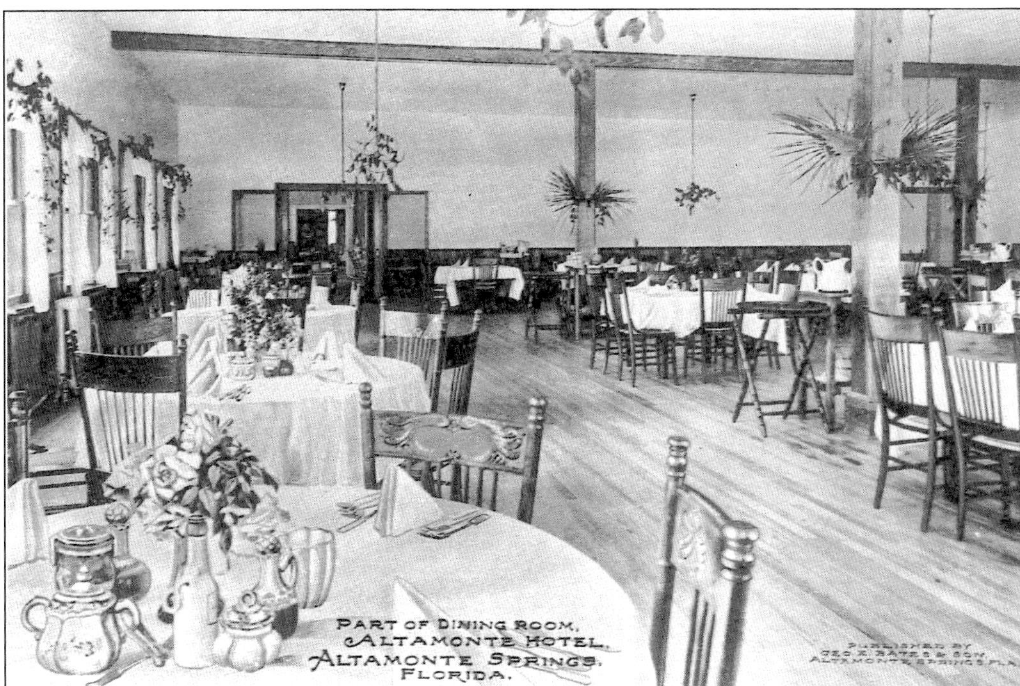

The hotel's dining room, shown here in the early 1900s, served some of the best meals in Central Florida. Most of the cottages in Altamonte were built without kitchens, so many of the winter visitors ate their meals at the hotel.

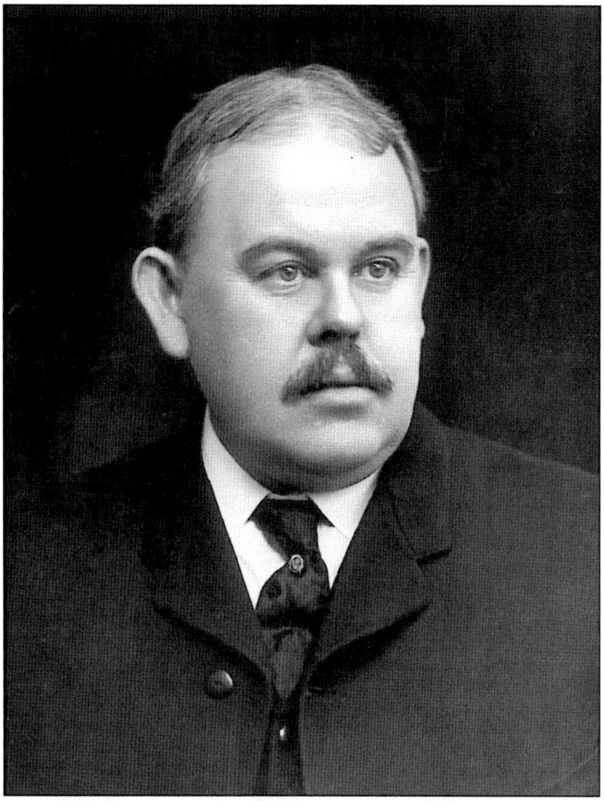

Henry Westinghouse, the younger brother of the investor, spent many winters in Altamonte Springs and built at least six houses using the same designs. The best known is the Bradlee-McIntyre, which was rescued and moved to the downtown Longwood historic district.

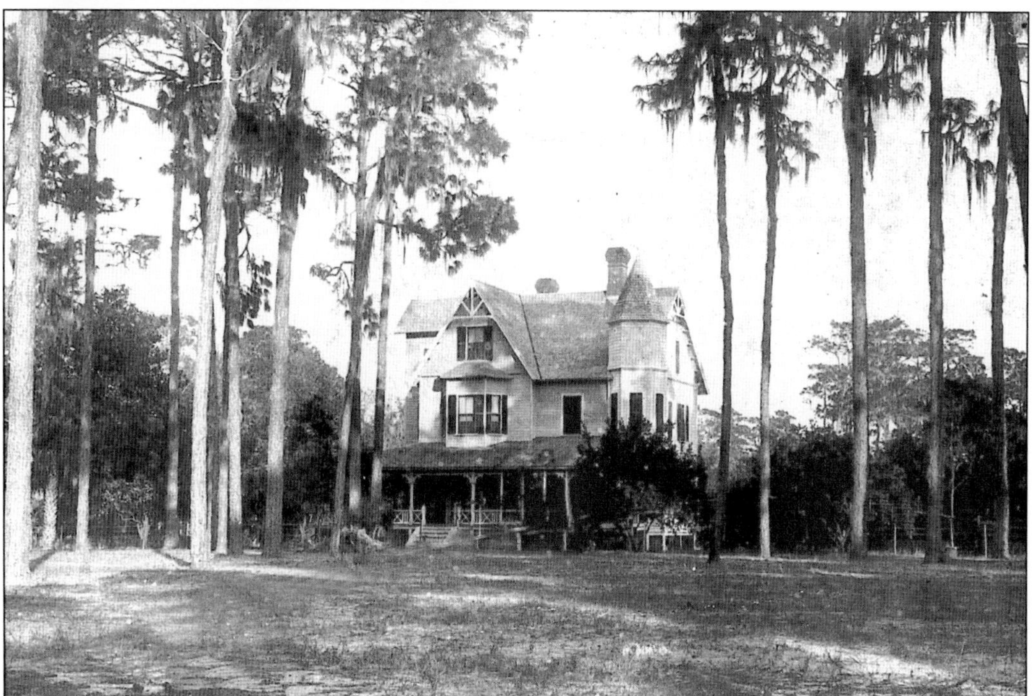

The winter home of August Richardson was one of the houses built by Henry Westinghouse.

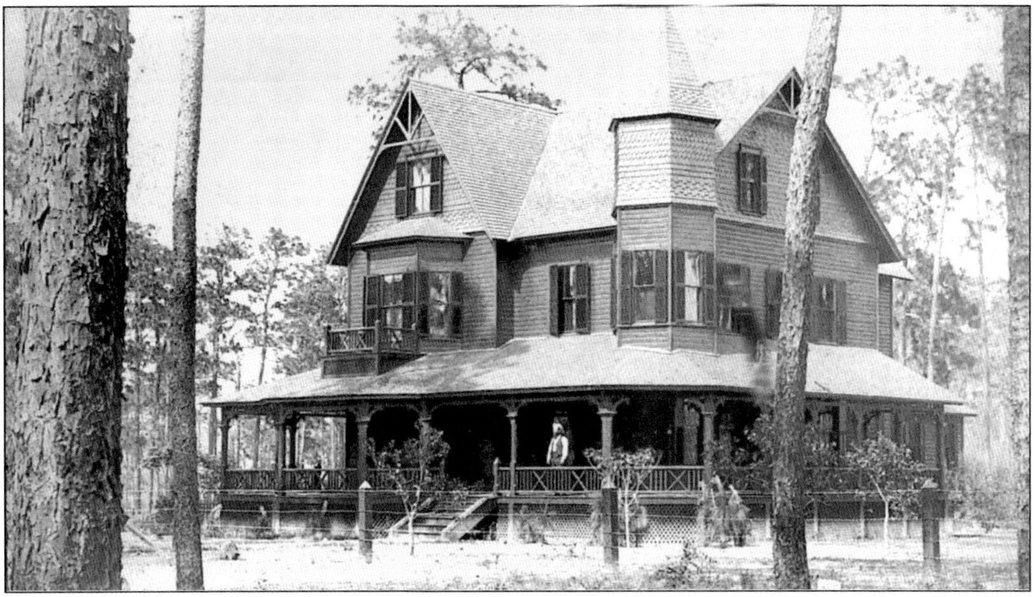

August Richardson of Boston stands on the porch of his winter residence, *c.* 1887. The house is a mirror image of the Bradlee-McIntyre House, both of which were exactly alike except with reversed facades. They were among at least six Altamonte Springs houses with similar designs built by Henry Westinghouse.

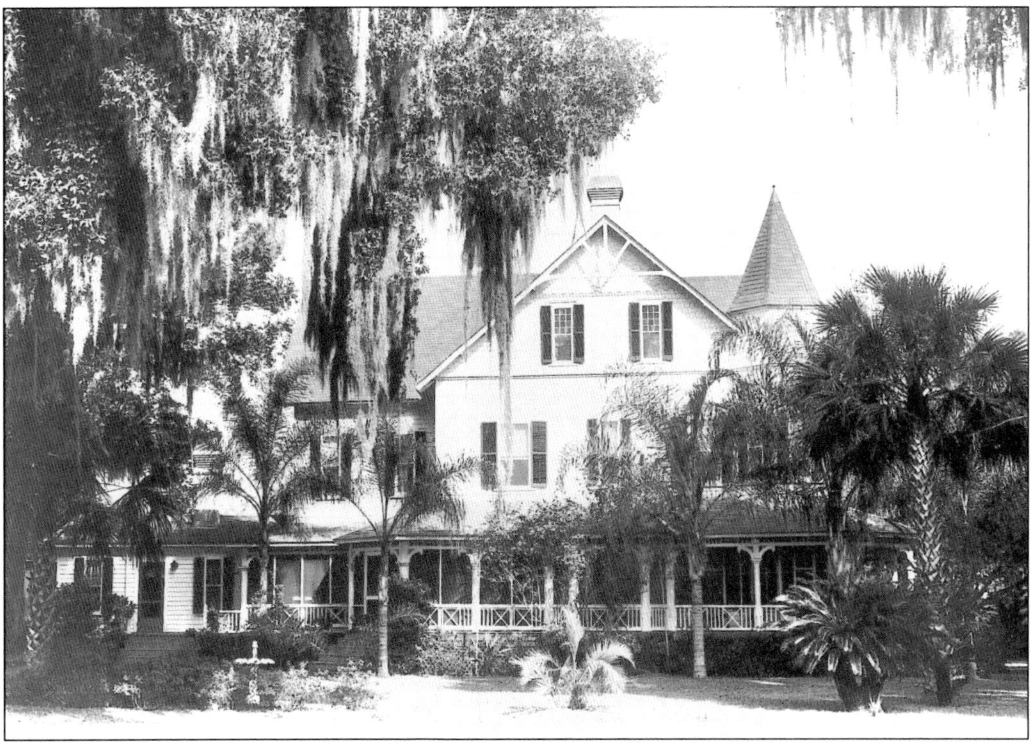

This is the Bradlee-McIntyre house while it was still in good repair in Altamonte Springs. The Queen Anne–style winter home built in 1885 in Altamonte Springs survives today as a museum in Longwood's downtown historic district at 130 Warren Avenue.

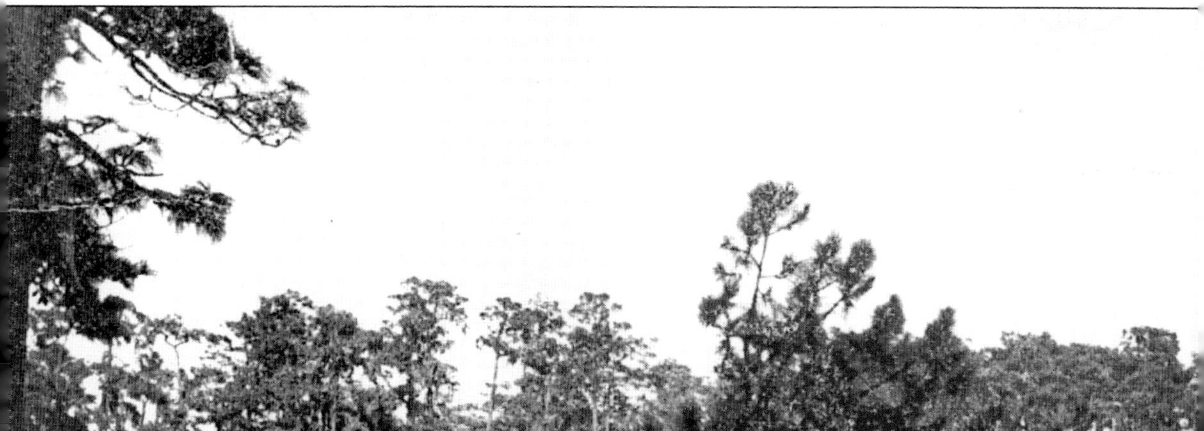

This is an early 1900s view looking across Lake Orienta toward the Altamonte Hotel property. It was used in a brochure of the Bates family. S. Maxwell McIntyre of New Hartford, New York, in 1906 bought much of the land originally developed by the Altamonte Land, Hotel, and

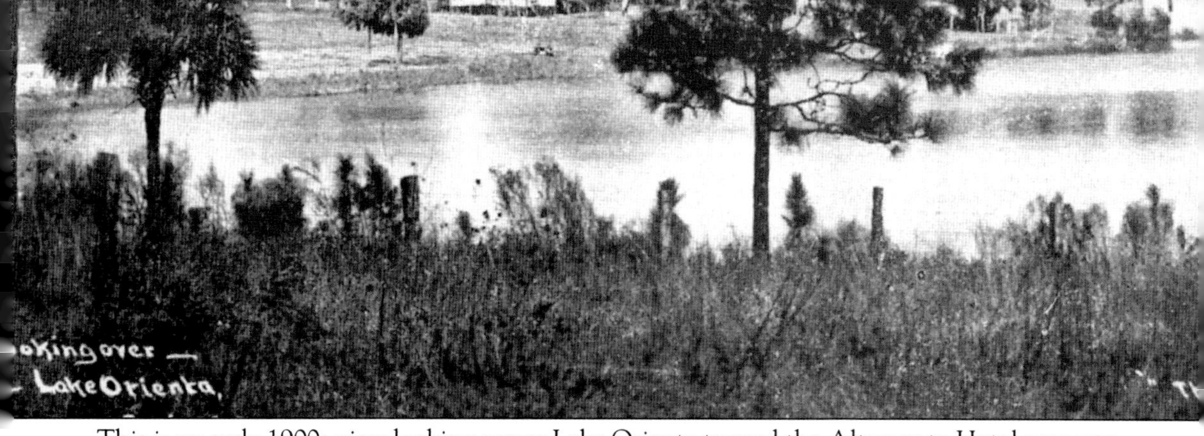

McIntyre in 1906 owned the hotel and its property, but the Bates remained proprieters through

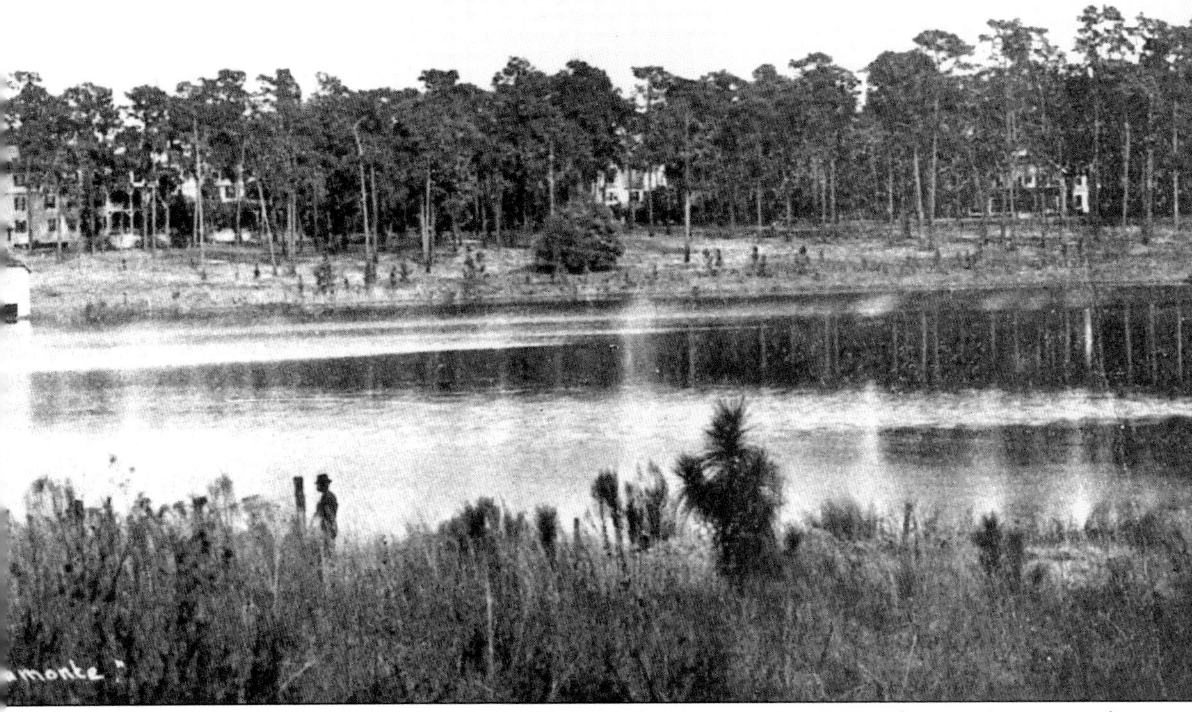

Navigation Company in 1882. In 1904 he bought the three acres at Massachusetts Avenue and Park Place including the mansion that would become the Bradlee-McIntyre House.

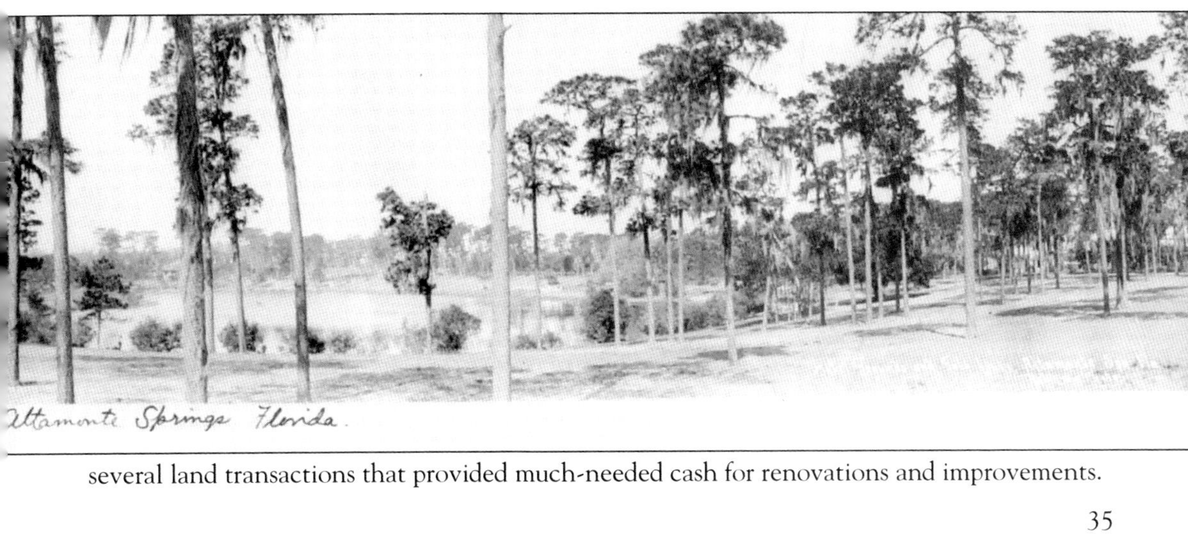

several land transactions that provided much-needed cash for renovations and improvements.

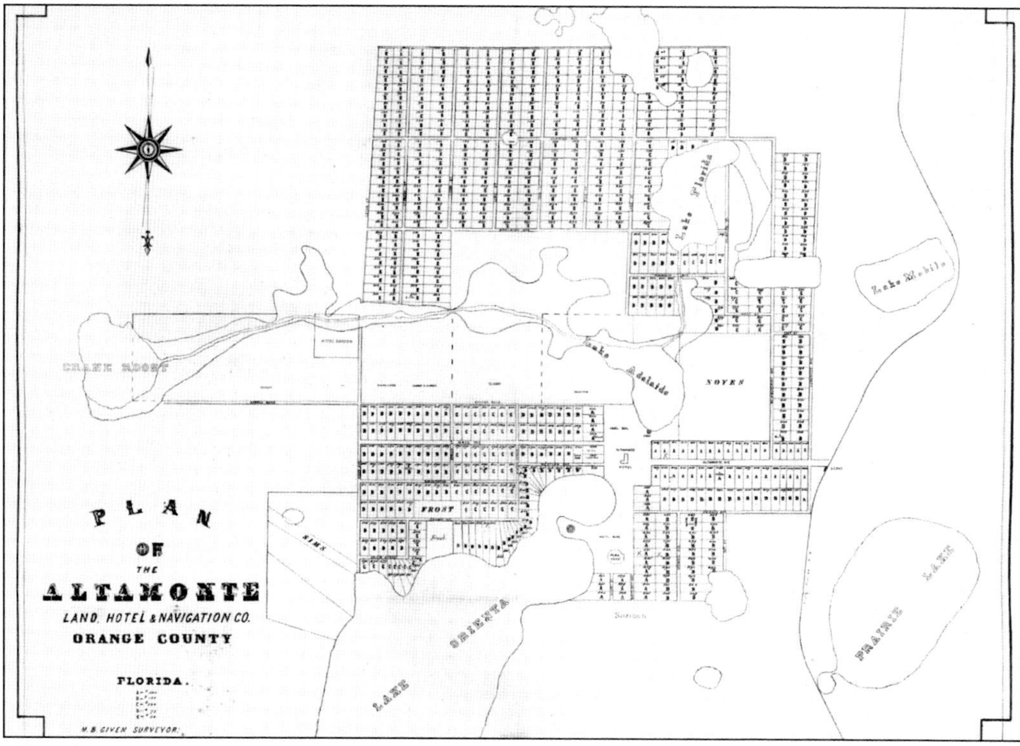

This plat shows the homesites and streets planned by the Altamonte Land, Hotel & Navigation Co. The plat was filed April 11, 1892.

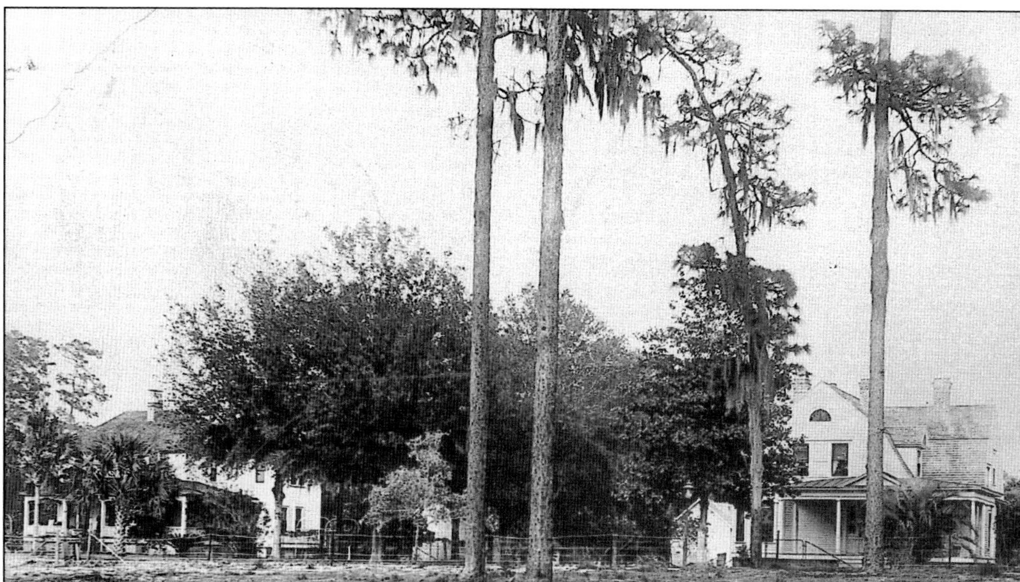

These are examples of some of the Altamonte cottages built for winter residents in the early 1900s. This photo was made from a postcard mailed December 26, 1910, from Altamonte Springs to Fairmont Springs, Pennsylvania. The postage was one penny. The note reads, "Arrived safely. Not rested yet. Eva doesn't feel very well, but we will be all right when rested. Will write."

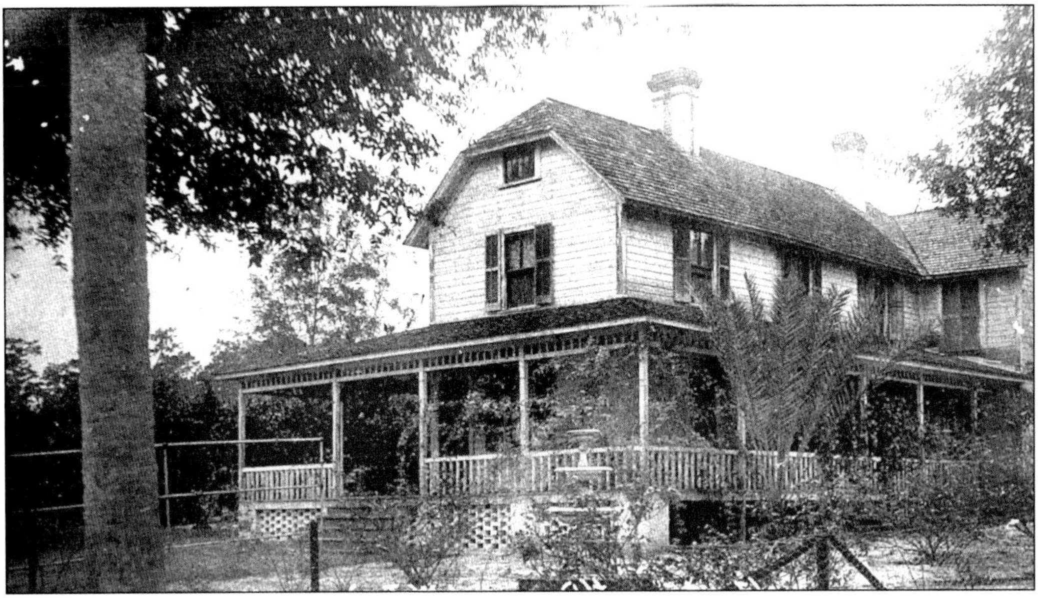

This house belonged to Joseph M. Lewis. Mr. Lewis was a building contractor who also cared for citrus groves.

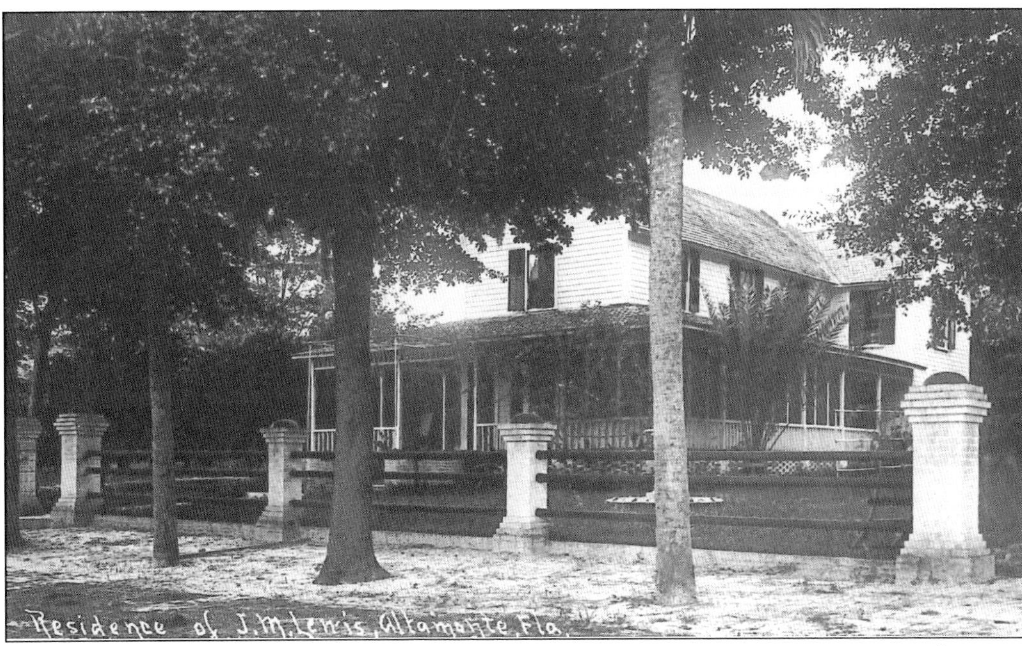

Joseph M. Lewis lived in this house, shown in about 1912. Lewis was a contractor who came to Florida from Boston in 1881 and built the first hotel. It opened in February 1883 at reduced prices for stockholders and patrons. The tram and the tracks west of the depot to the hotel were added in the summer of 1883. Lewis also planted citrus groves and took care of other groves whose owners lived most of the year in the North. When the Altamonte Chapel was moved from Lake Brantley to its current site, Lewis did some of the renovations.

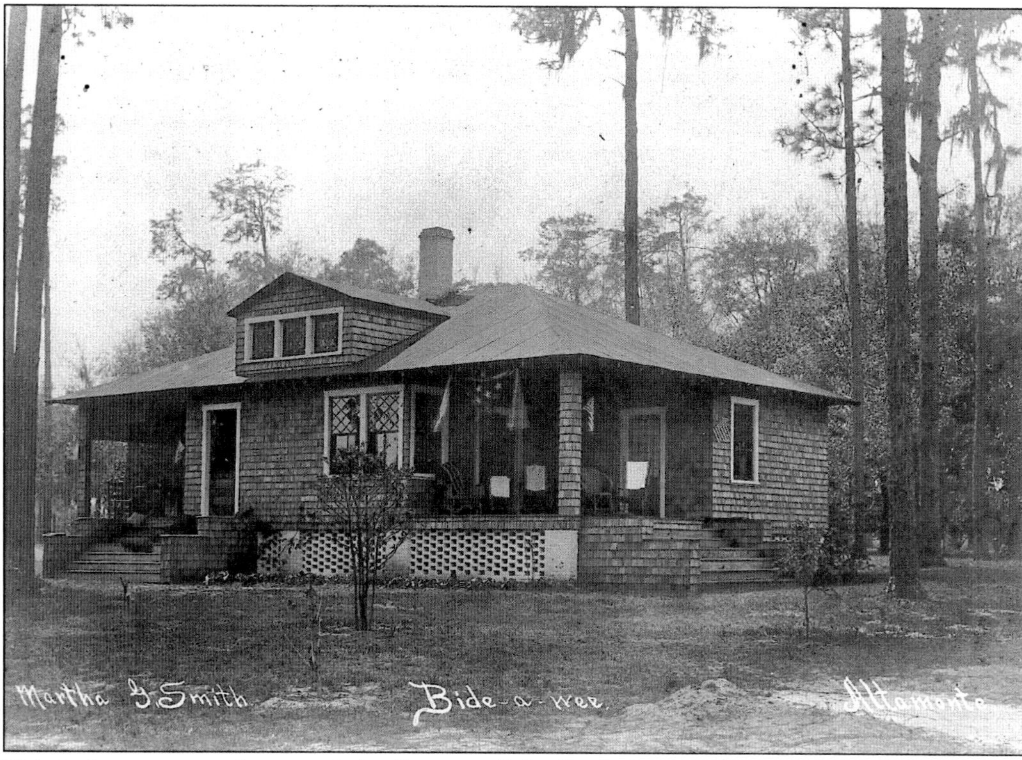

This is the winter residence on Lake Orienta of Martha G. Smith. She named it "Bide-a-Wee."

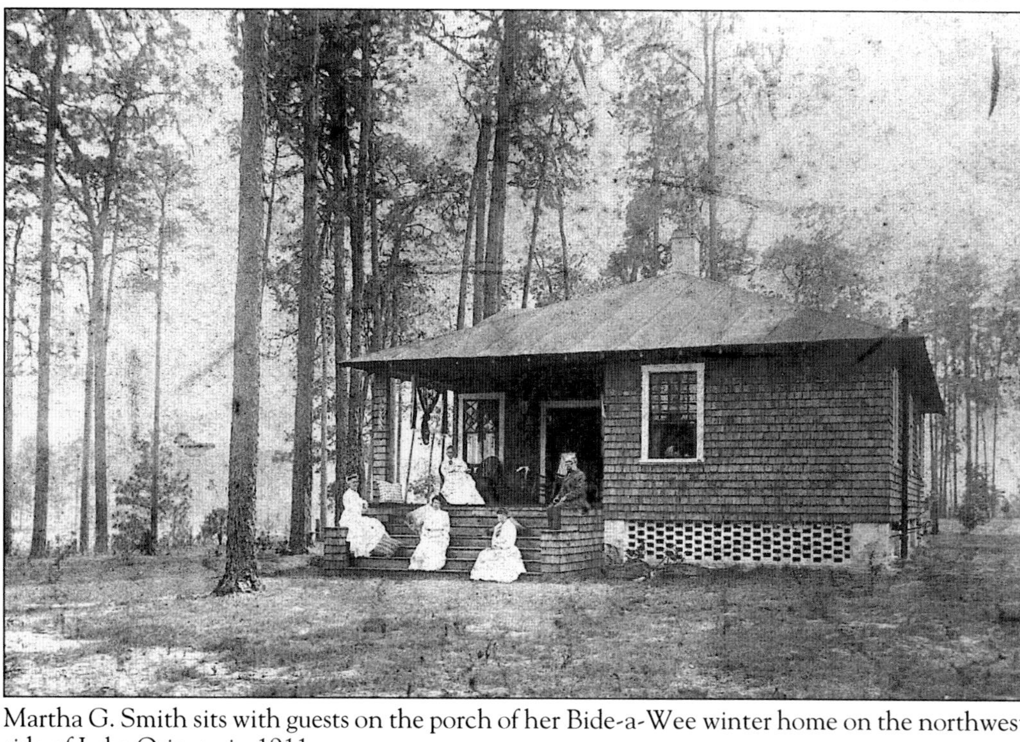

Martha G. Smith sits with guests on the porch of her Bide-a-Wee winter home on the northwest side of Lake Orienta in 1911.

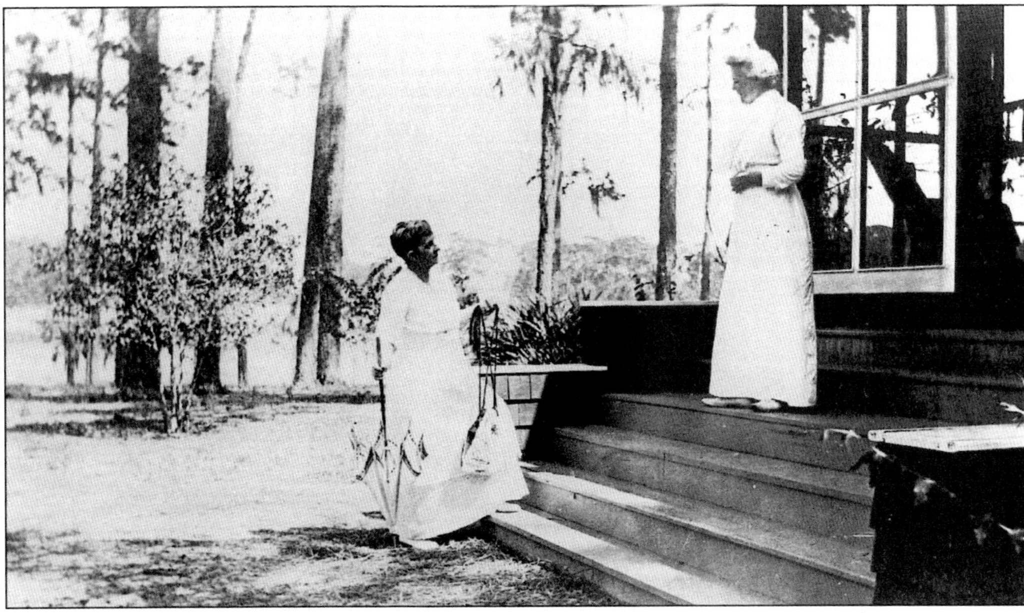

Martha G. Smith, standing on the steps of her home, greets actress Lucy Patch in 1912. Both women spent many winters in Altamonte Springs.

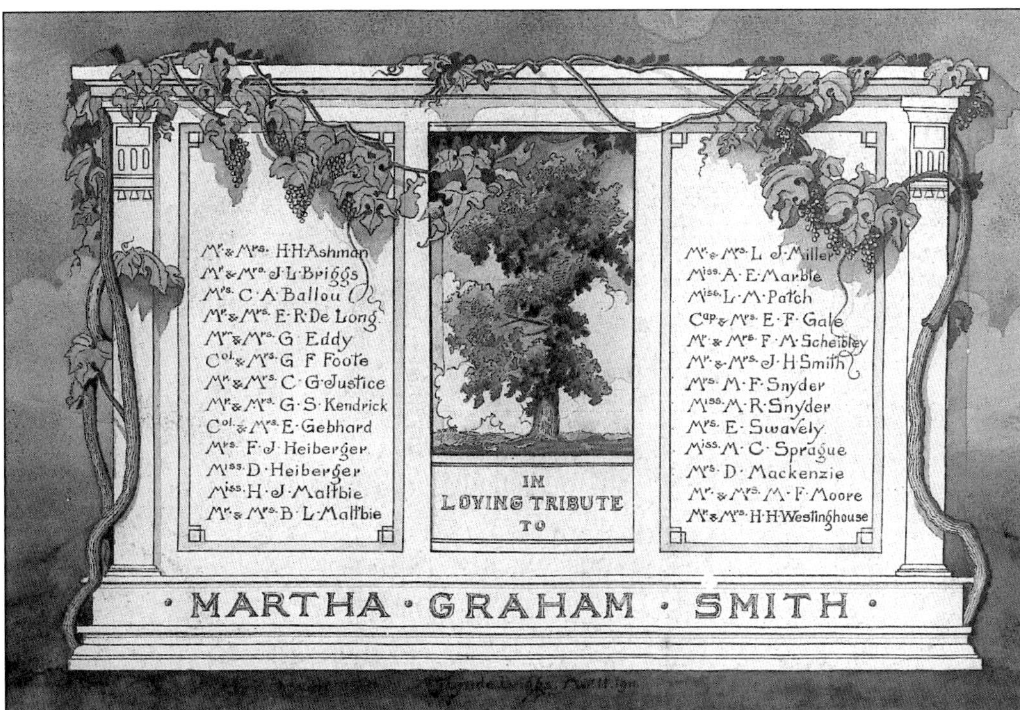

This memorial was a tribute to Martha Graham Smith, who spent her winters at the house she called Bide-a-Wee.

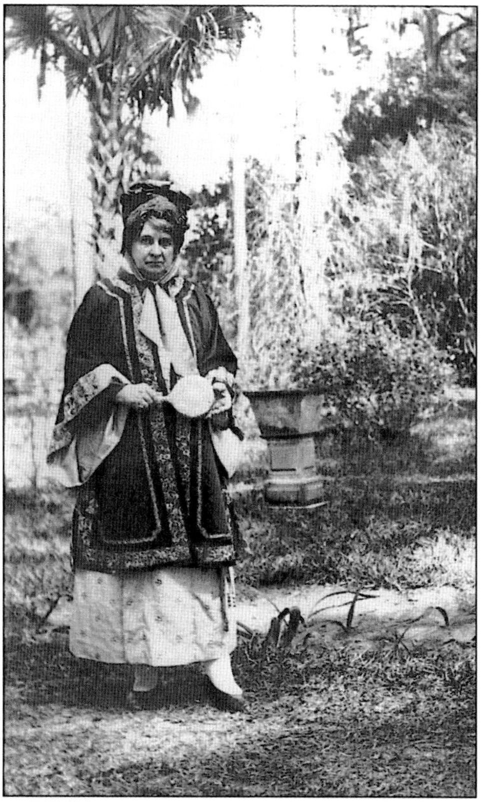

This is Lucy Patch, a well-known actress, shown in costume before a 1922 performance at the hotel. Stage performances were popular social gatherings at the hotel—the centerpiece of community life. Even before the hotel opened for the winter tourist season, guests arrived early and stayed with friends at their winter homes. As promoter Nathan Fogg wrote, "Winter in Altamonte Springs was 'one big happy family' and the hotel provided all their needs."

The Fuller family takes a row boat trip on Lake Orienta in the early 1900s.

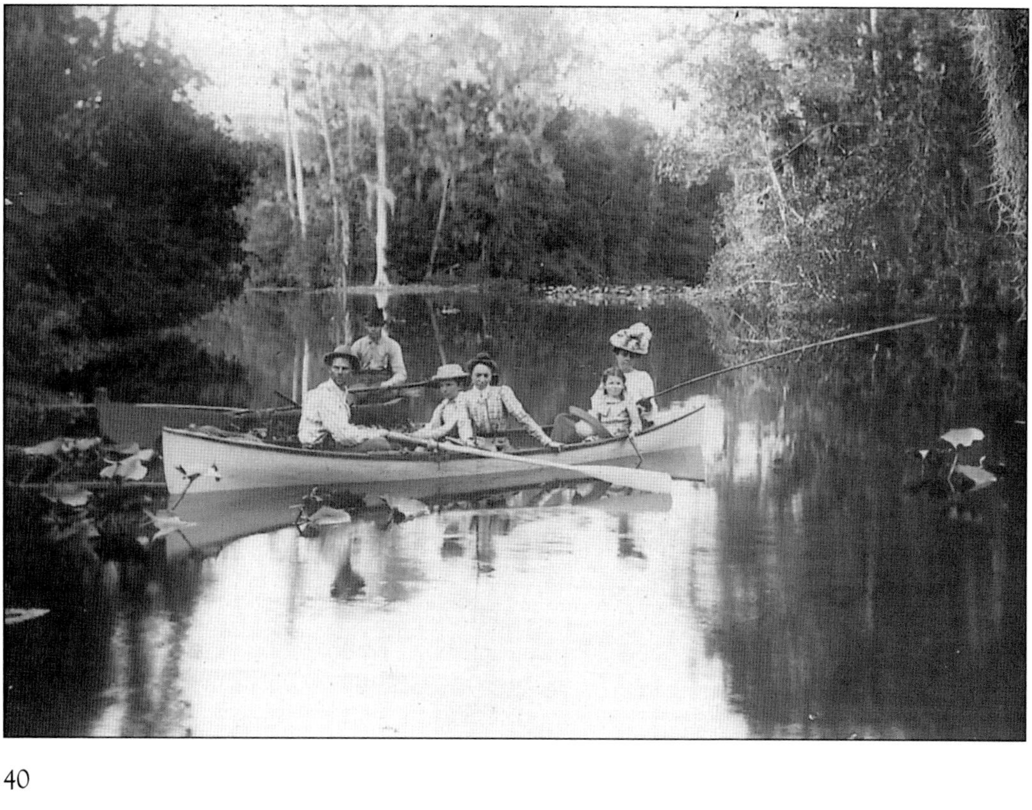

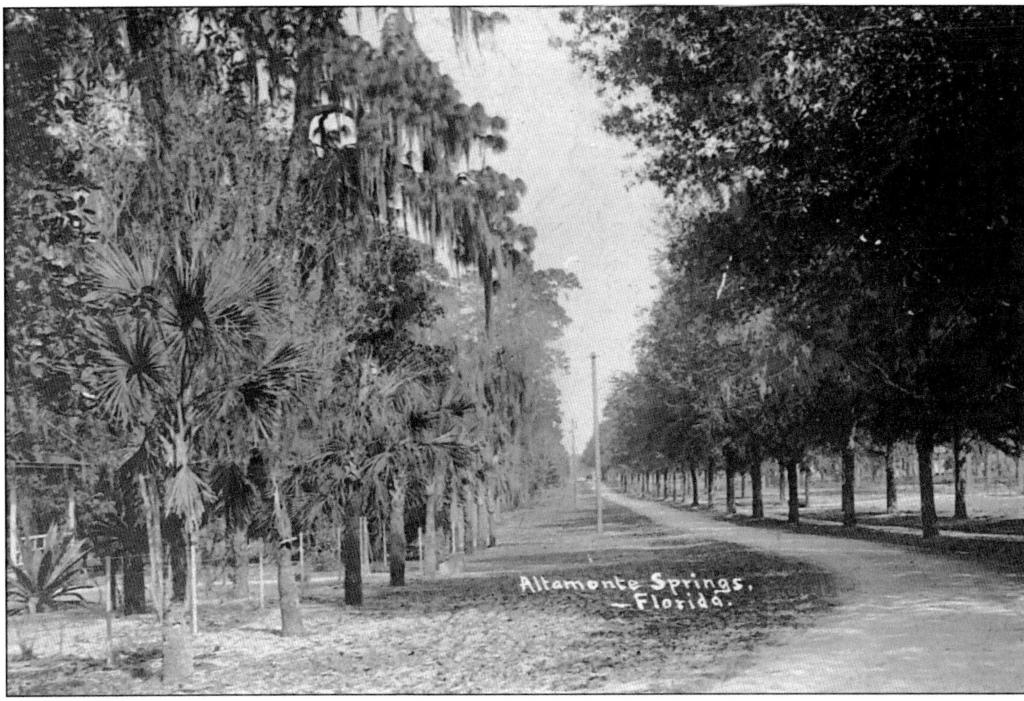

This shows Altamonte Avenue from the west in 1907. Note the trolley tracks between the tree lines.

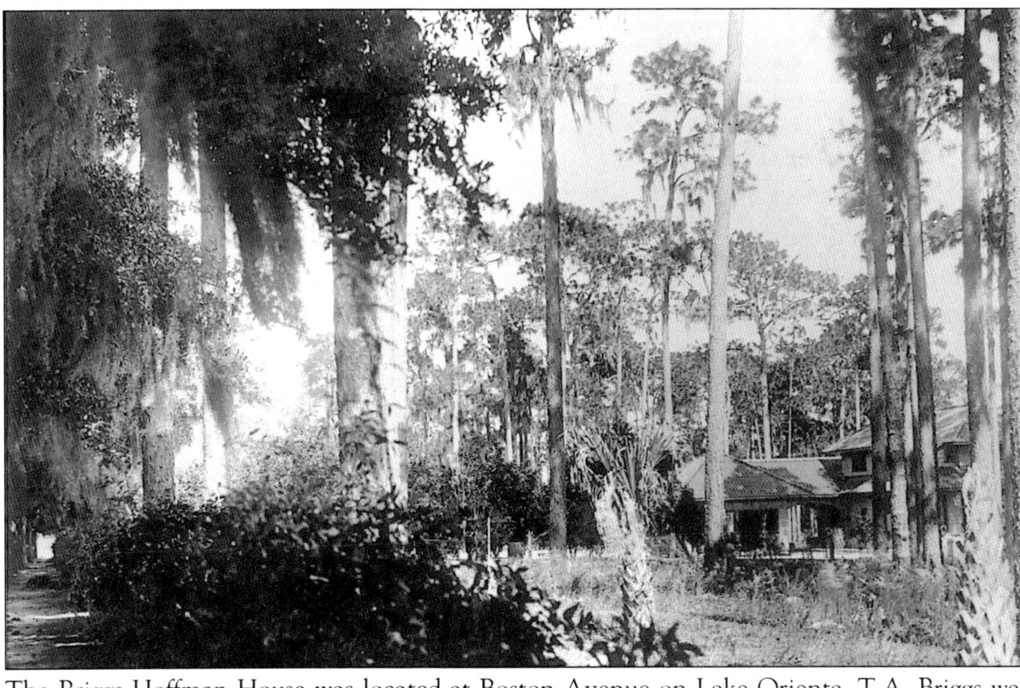

The Briggs-Hoffman House was located at Boston Avenue on Lake Orienta. T.A. Briggs was one of three partners in the Altamonte Springs Electric Company, which in 1931 won a 30-year franchise to provide electric power to the city. The Florida Public Service Company later bought its charter.

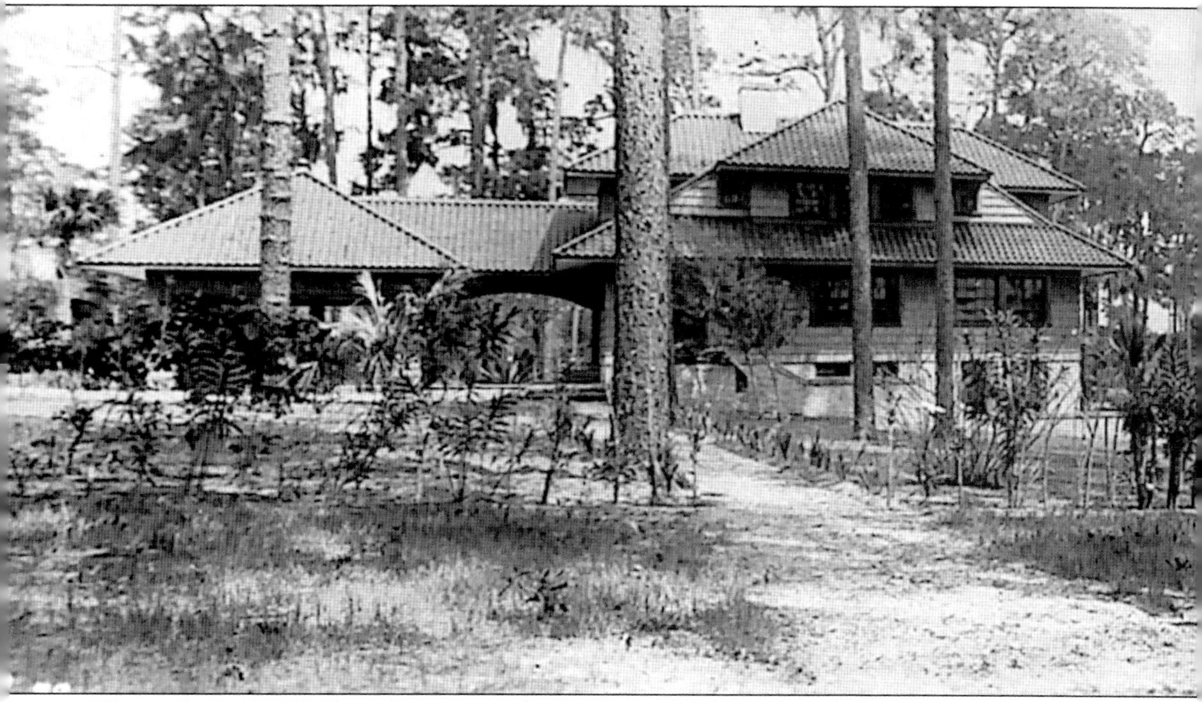

This is the Briggs-Hoffman house on Lake Orienta, and the Bide-a-wee house was nearby. Mr. and Mrs. R.E. Hoffman were among the 42 registered voters who on November 11, 1920, agreed to create a municipal government of Altamonte Springs and elected the mayor, aldermen, and

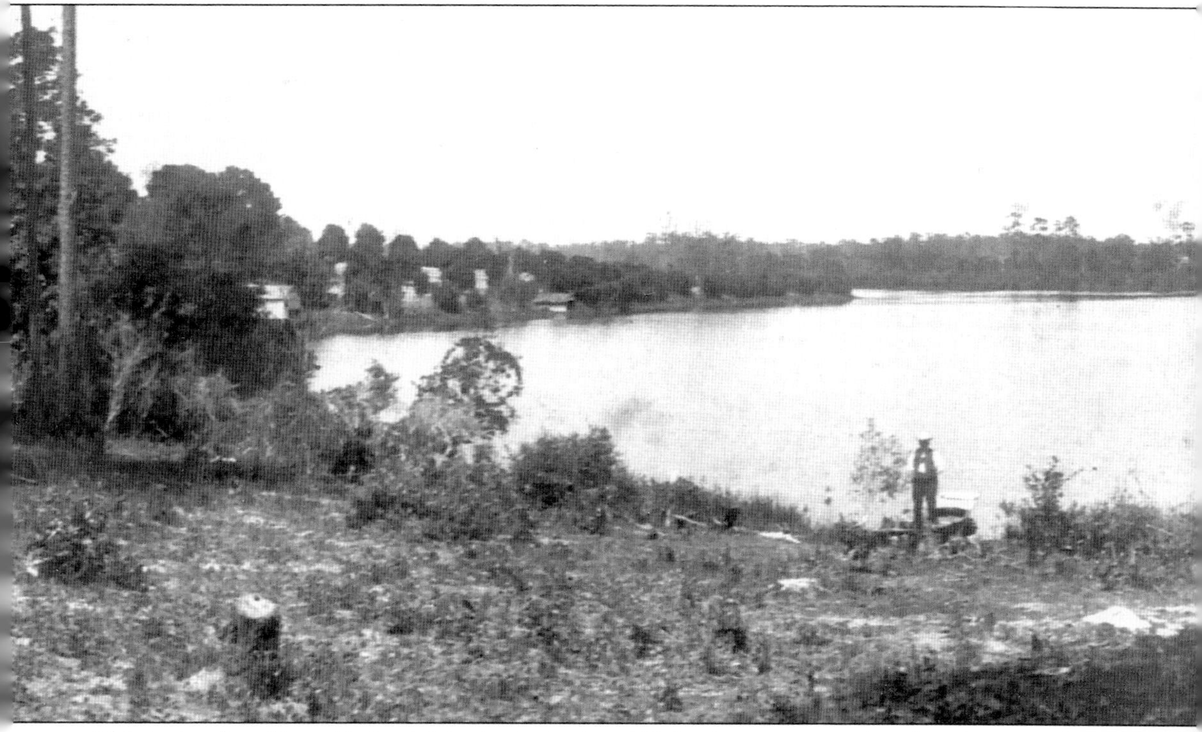

This is the shoreline of Lake Adelaide in the late 1800s. the site is now lined with a complex

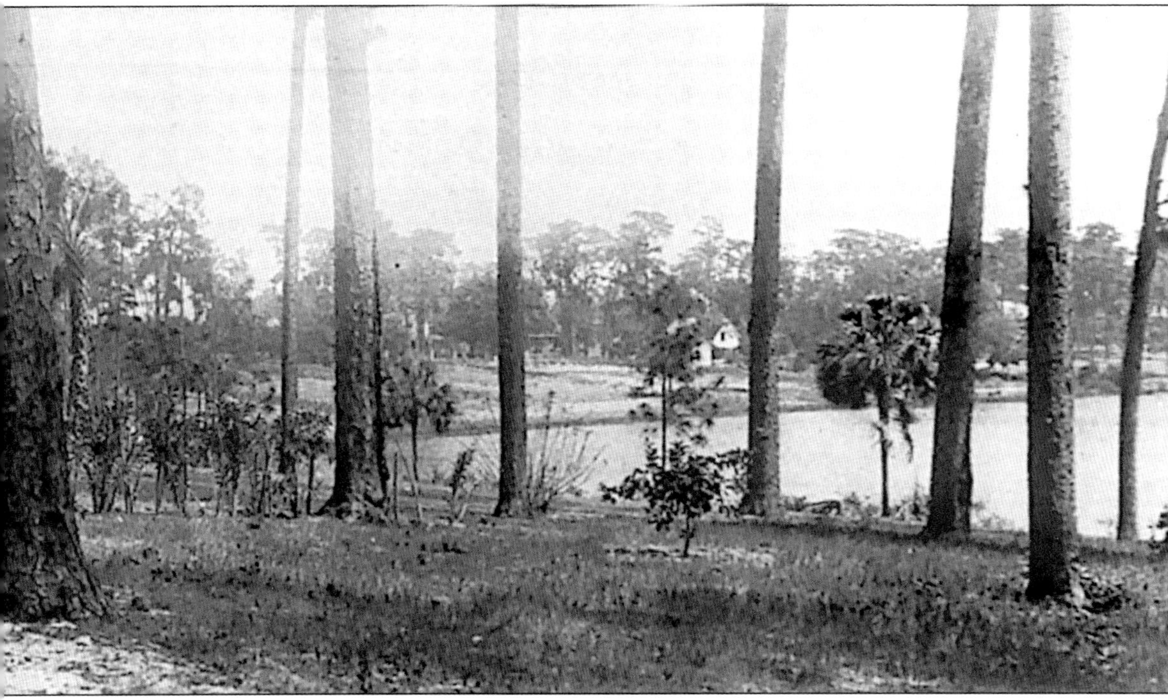

other officers. R.E. Hoffman was elected as one of the first seven aldermen and served the city from that date until World War II.

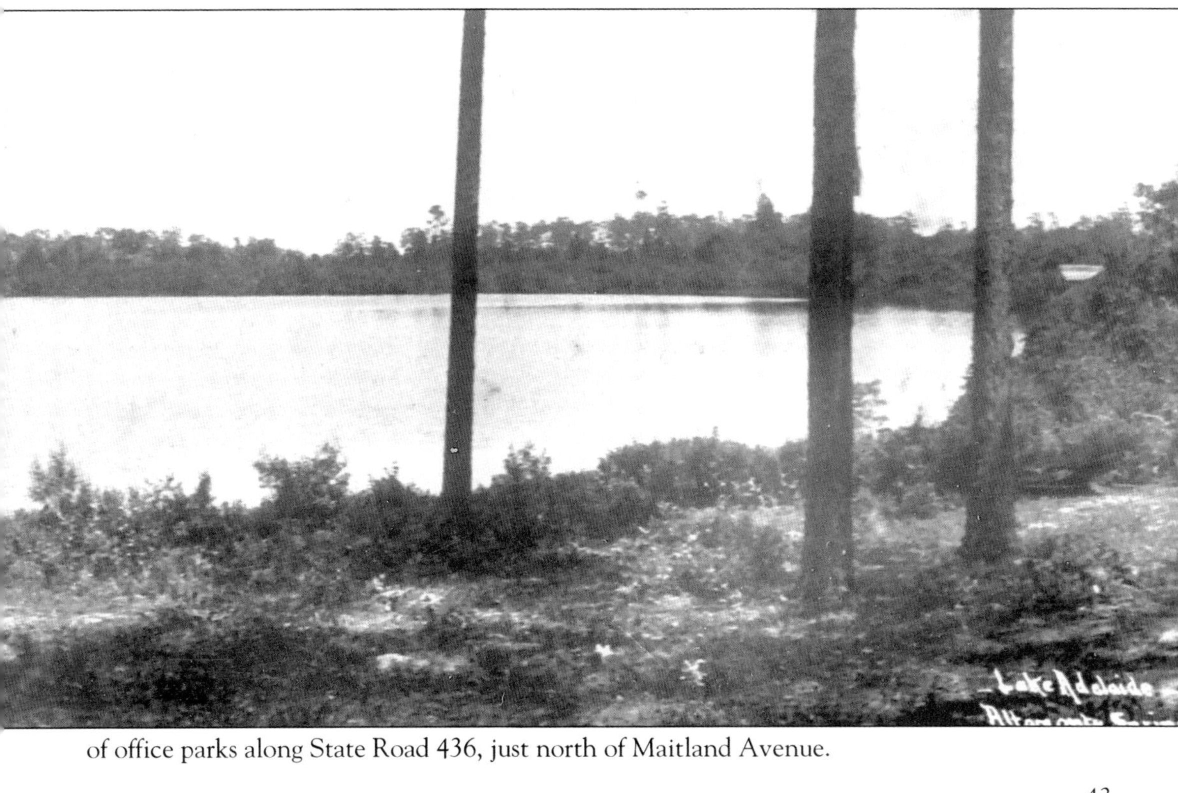

of office parks along State Road 436, just north of Maitland Avenue.

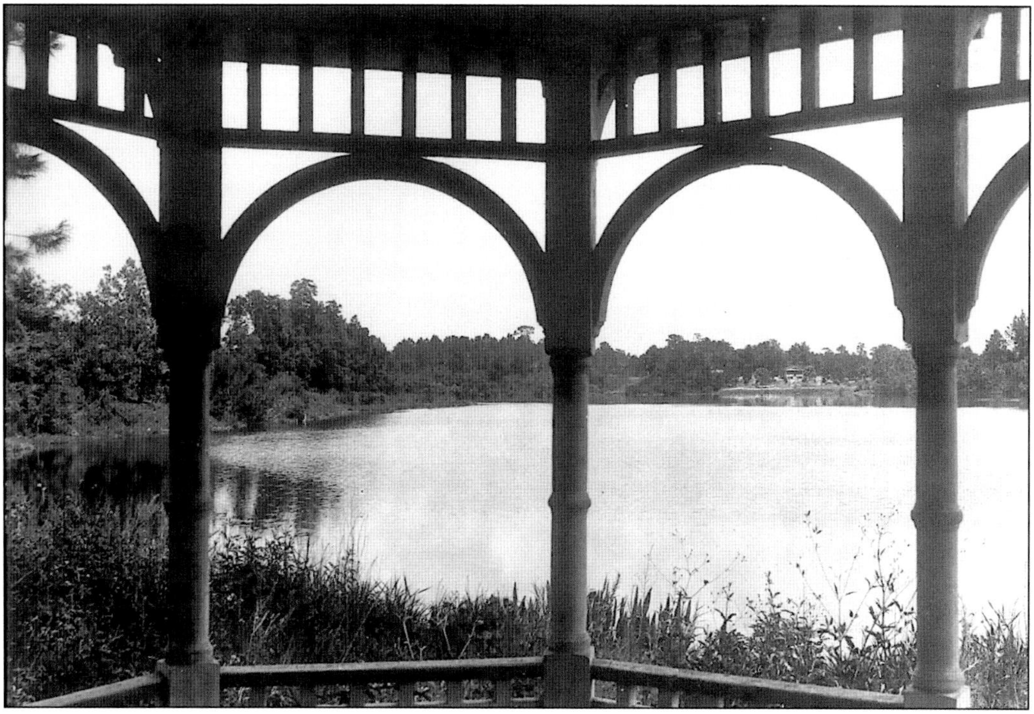

The shoreline of Lake Adelaide is shown looking through the hotel's springhouse in the 1920s.

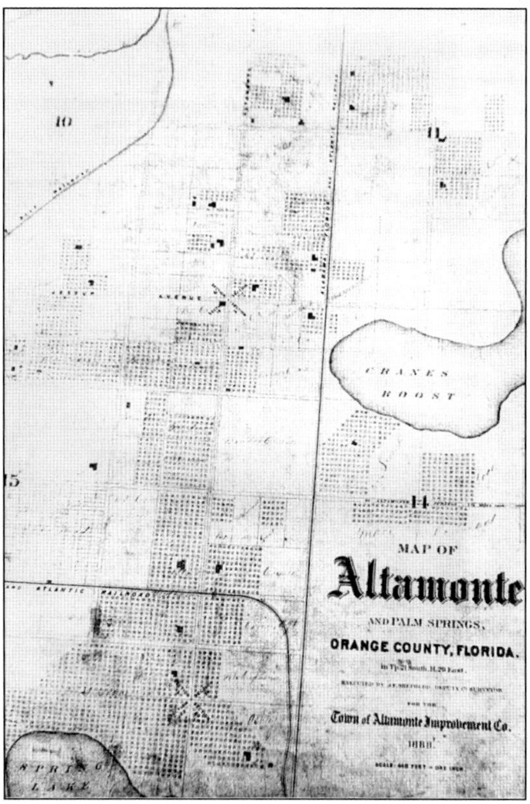

This 1888 map, labeled "Altamonte and Palm Springs," shows the railroad tracks and citrus groves between Spring Lake on the southwest corner and Cranes Roost on the northeast. The tracks running north-south follow the route of Interstate 4. The citrus groves south of Cranes Roost are now the Altamonte Mall.

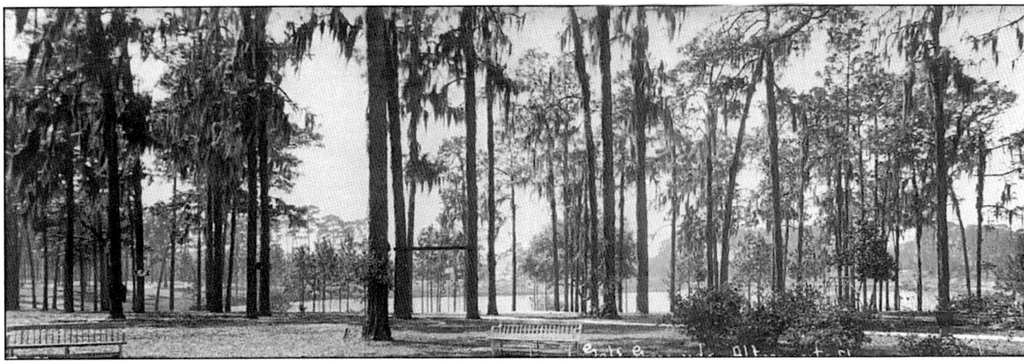

Many pines covered the hotel's golf course, dubbed the "damned trees" course by some guests. To help, the hotel provided a golf professional for the season.

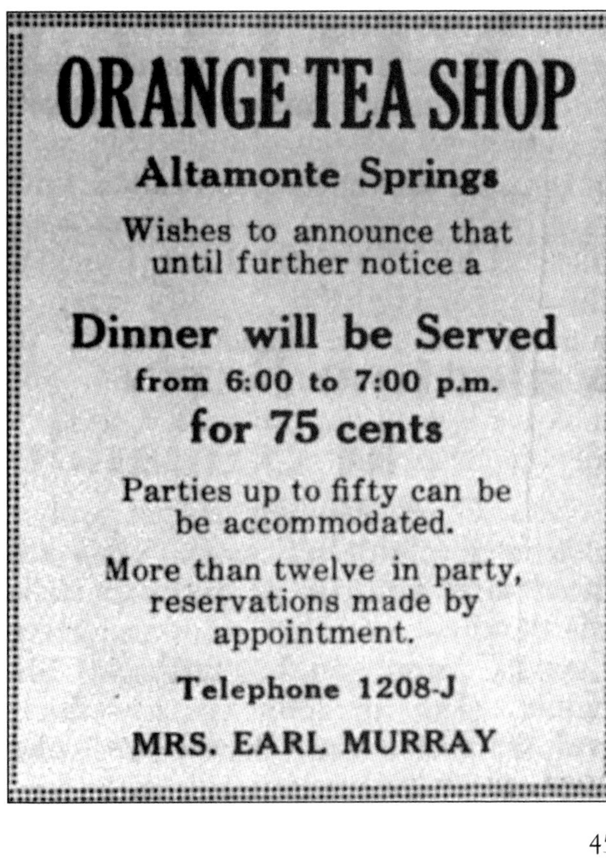

This newspaper advertisement for Orange Tea Shop in Altamonte Springs appears in *The Maitland News* in 1927. Mrs. Earl Murray, who spent her summers in North Carolina, opened the tea shop in Altamonte when she was living in one of the winter cottages built in the 1880s by H.H. Westinghouse.

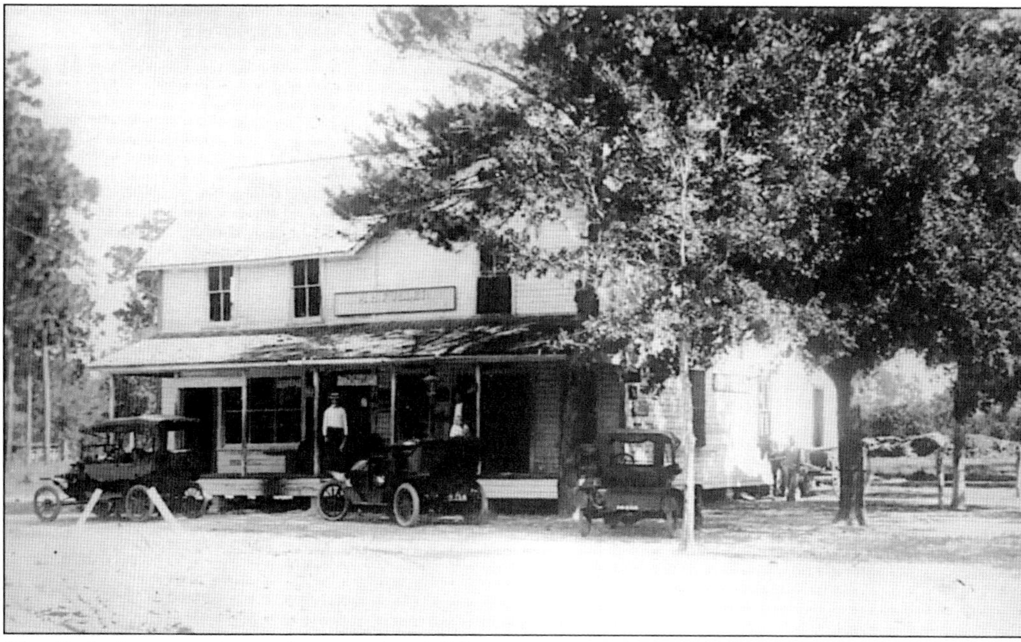

The Fuller's store, shown here in the 1920s, was a major part of the community. The Fullers were the postmasters, the store owners, the grove tenders, and the community builders.

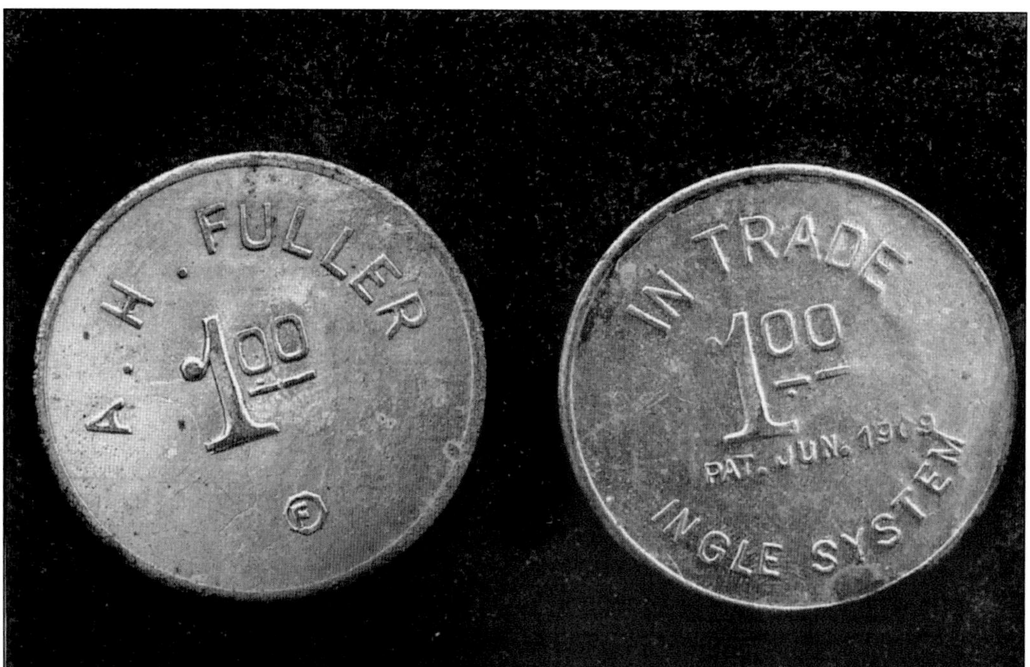

These $1 tokens were issued by the A.H. Fuller store from 1909. The store was in the center of commerce in the early 1900s when the area was becoming the world's leading fern grower.

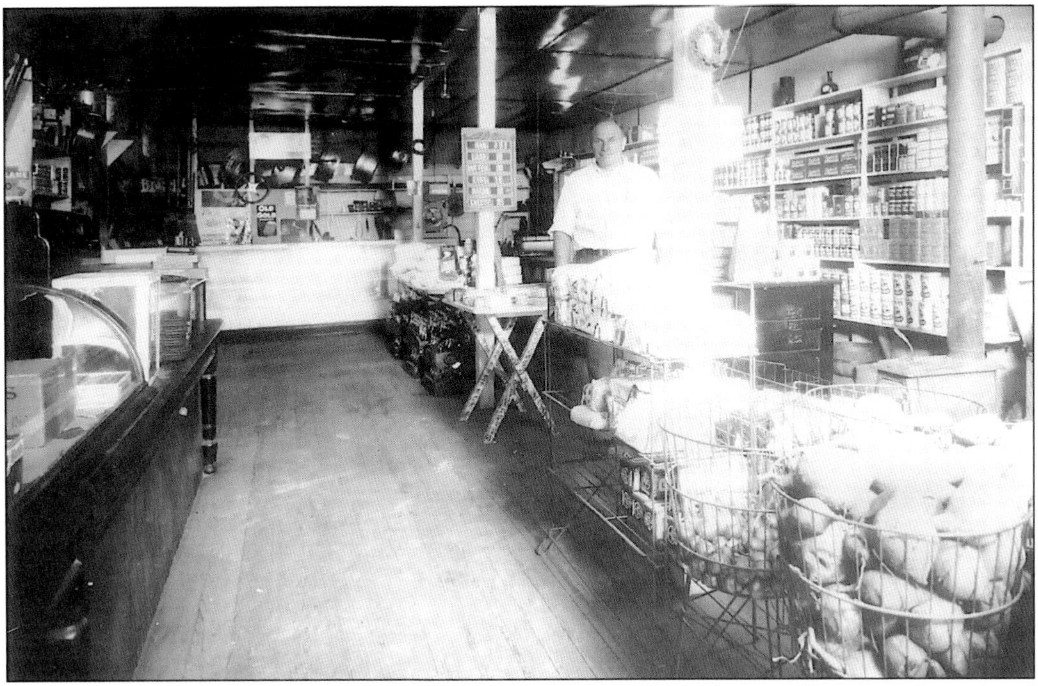

Shown is the interior of the Fuller family's store. The store and post office near the railroad depot was one of the few establishments that remained open year-round.

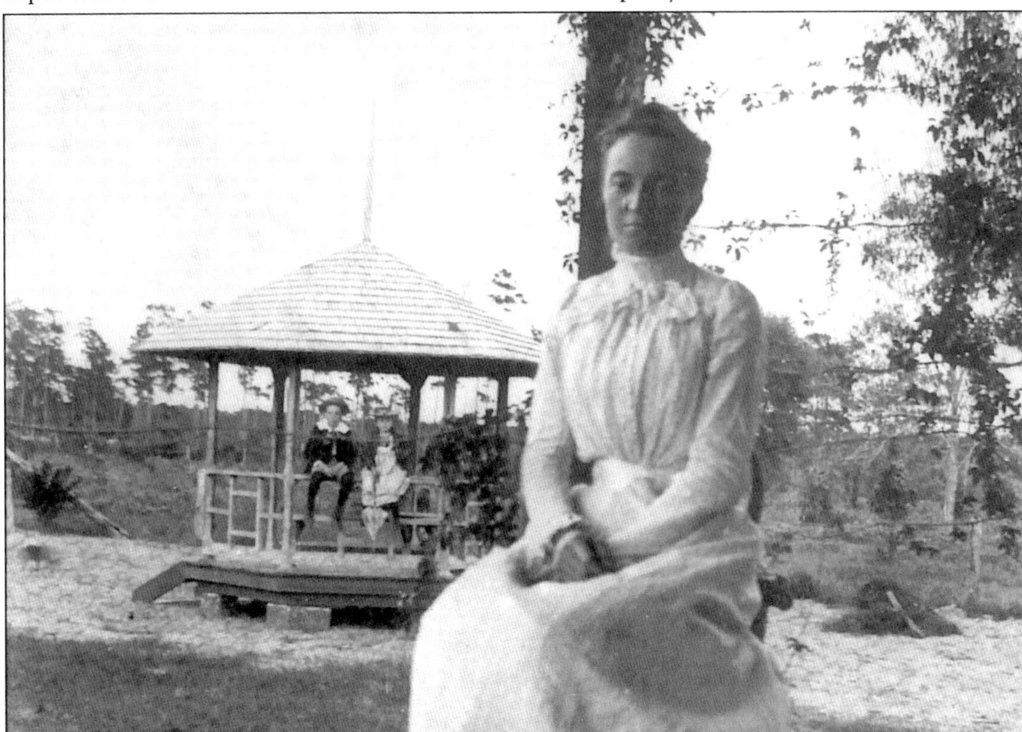

Mary Fuller poses for this 1920s photo. In the background are Herbert and Irene Fuller at the gazebo.

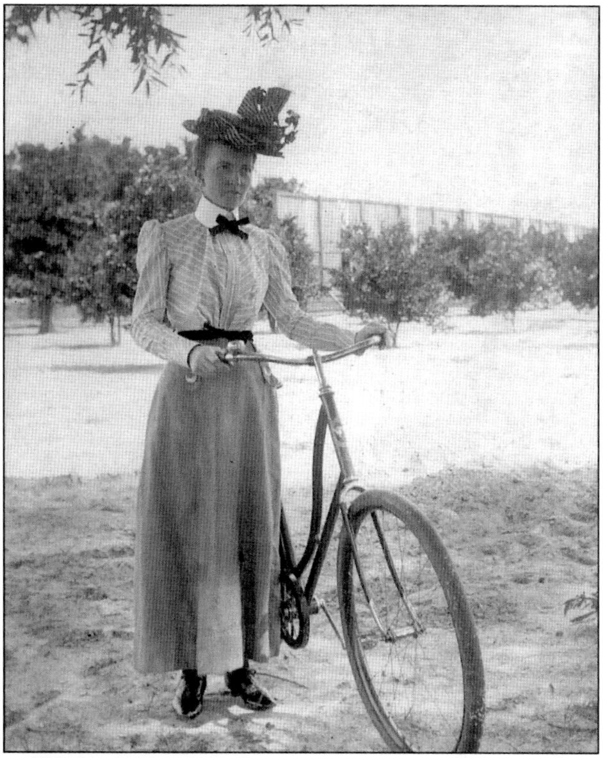

Mamie Fuller poses in this image with her bicycle at the family groves at Spring Lake.

Arthur Fuller prepares to take a bicycle ride, a growing pastime in the late 1890s and into the early 1900s at Spring Lake.

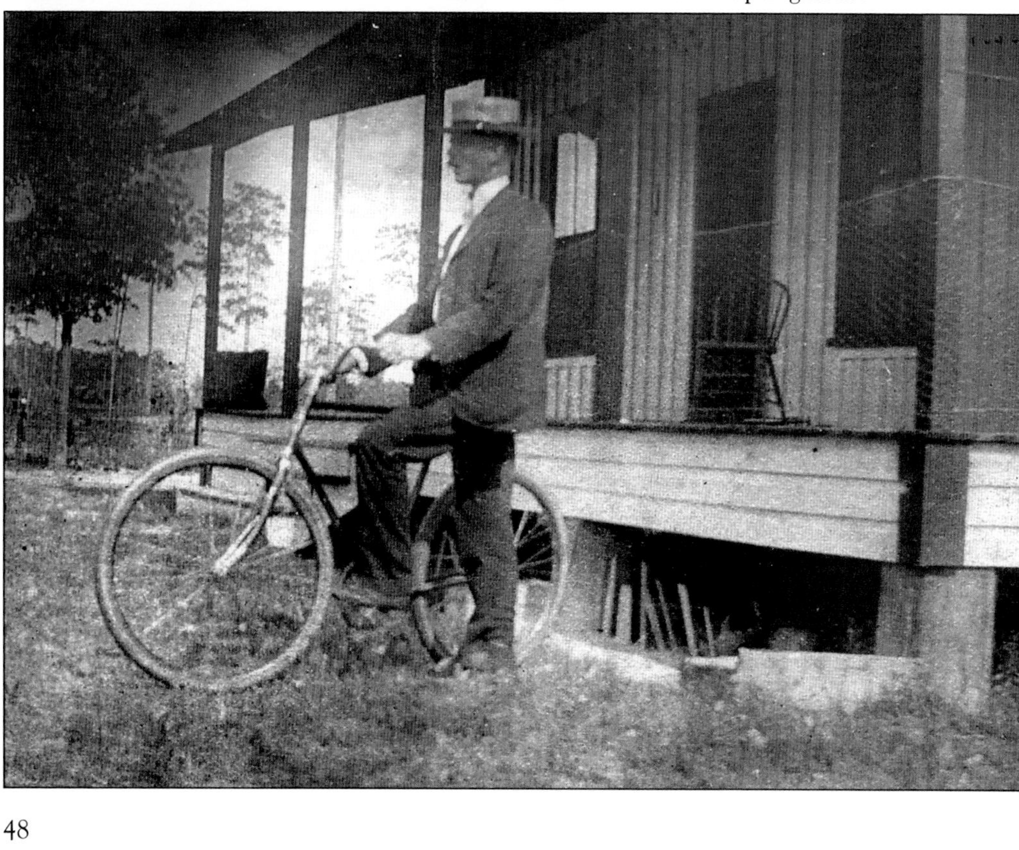

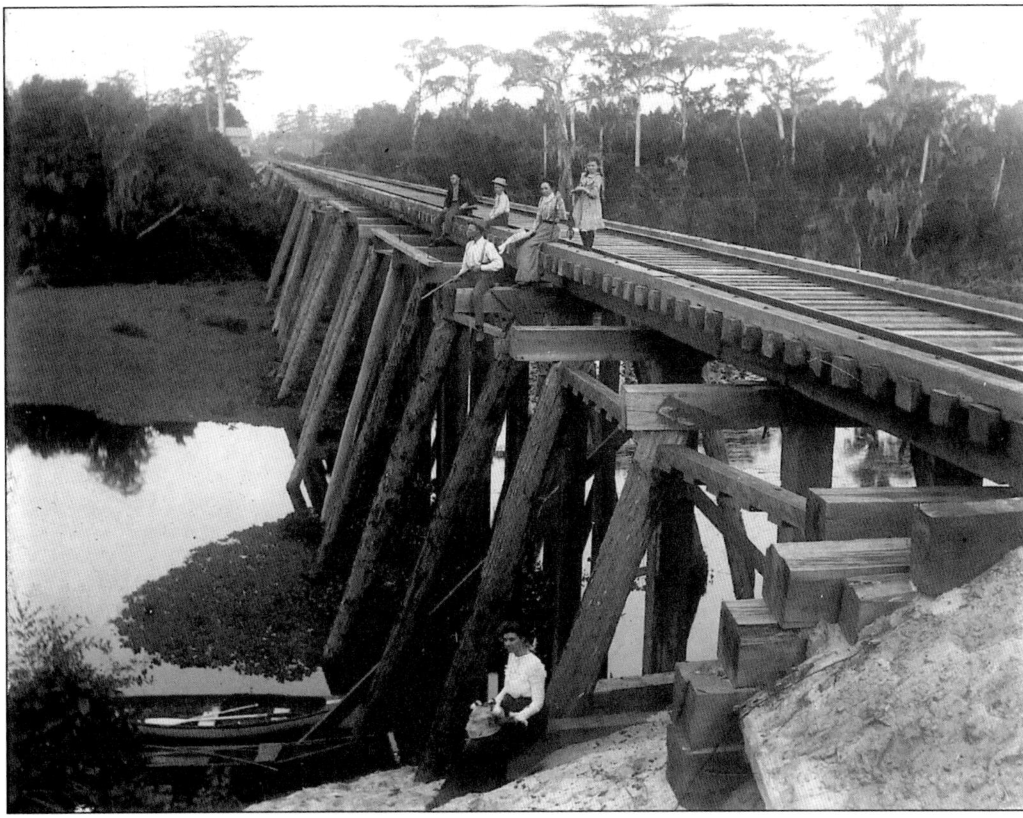

The first bridge over the Wekiva River was built for the railroad, but automobile travel would soon end the railroad era. Note that the Fuller men hold rifles as protection again rattlesnakes. The young woman standing holds a small alligator likely shot by the men.

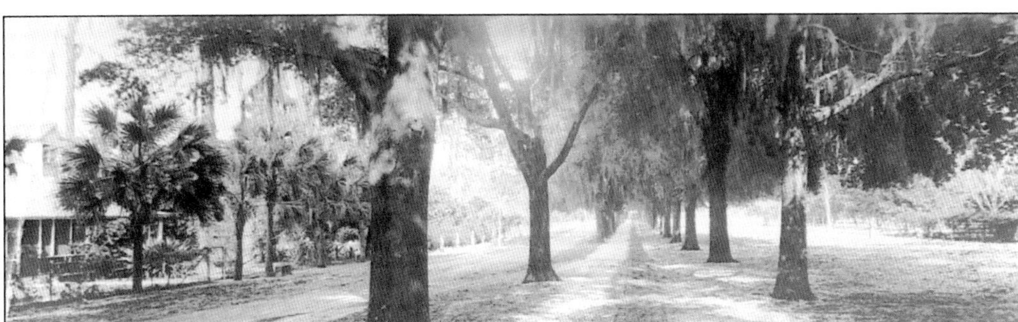

This 1916 postcard shows the Altamonte Hotel's trolley tracks between two rows of trees along Altamonte Avenue, which today is State Road 436. The postcard's message reads, "Saturday, April 1, 1916—We'll soon be going down in the tram over this road en route for "home." Even Mrs. C. says that it seems lonely here now—so many have gone. It's warm and lovely today. I have bought Kreisler's "Venetian Caprice" to give Everett on my departure. He always does so much for us girls." Everett Bates was the manager of the hotel.

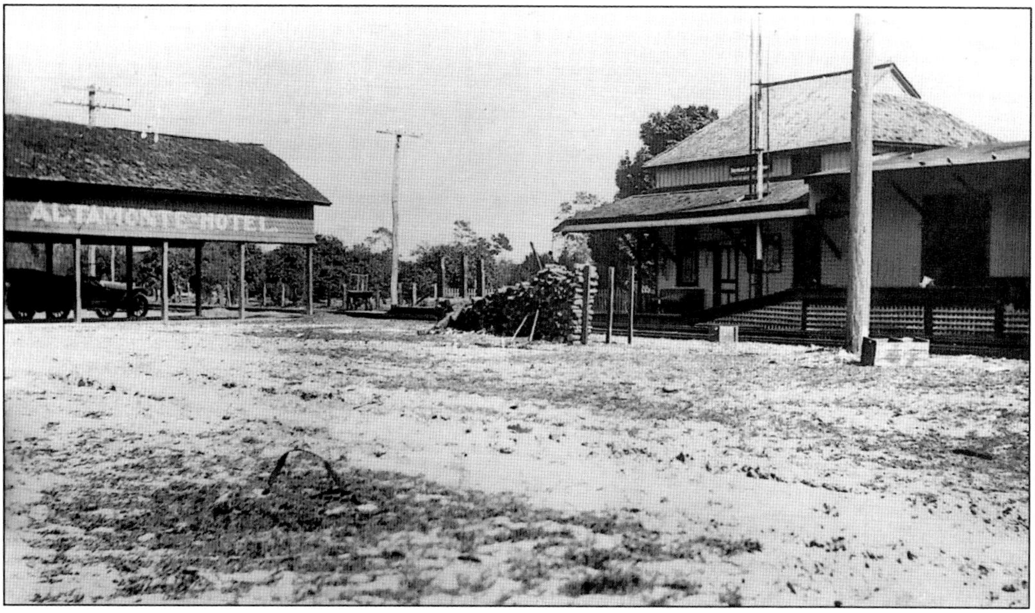

This is the Atlantic Coast Line station at Altamonte in the 1920s. Note the car parked in the tram's shelter.

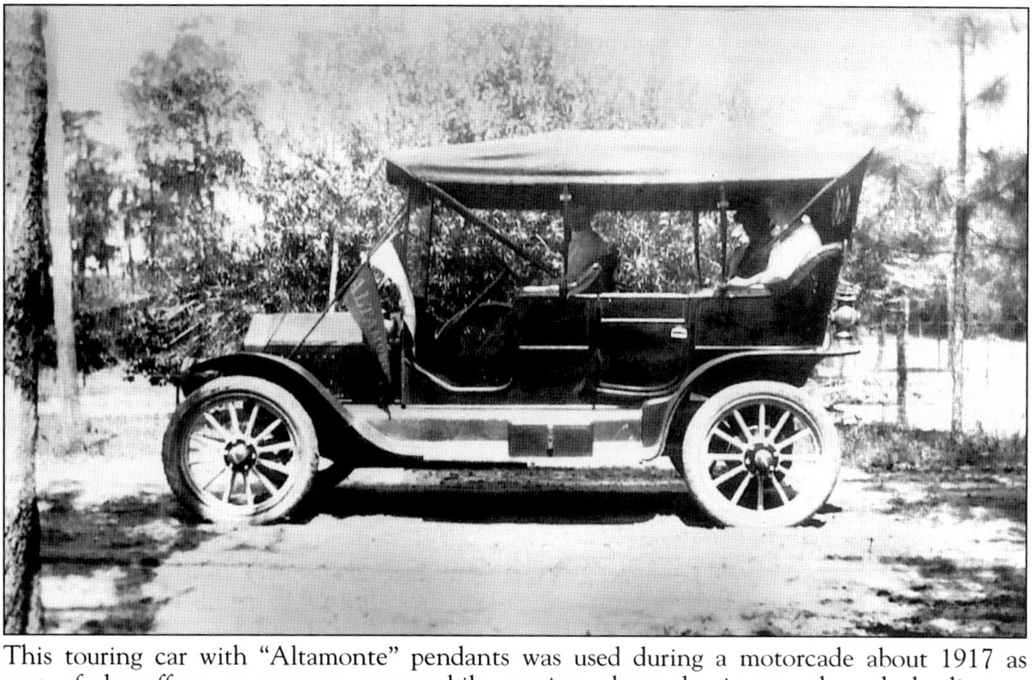

This touring car with "Altamonte" pendants was used during a motorcade about 1917 as part of the efforts to promote automobile tourism along the improved roads leading to Altamonte Springs.

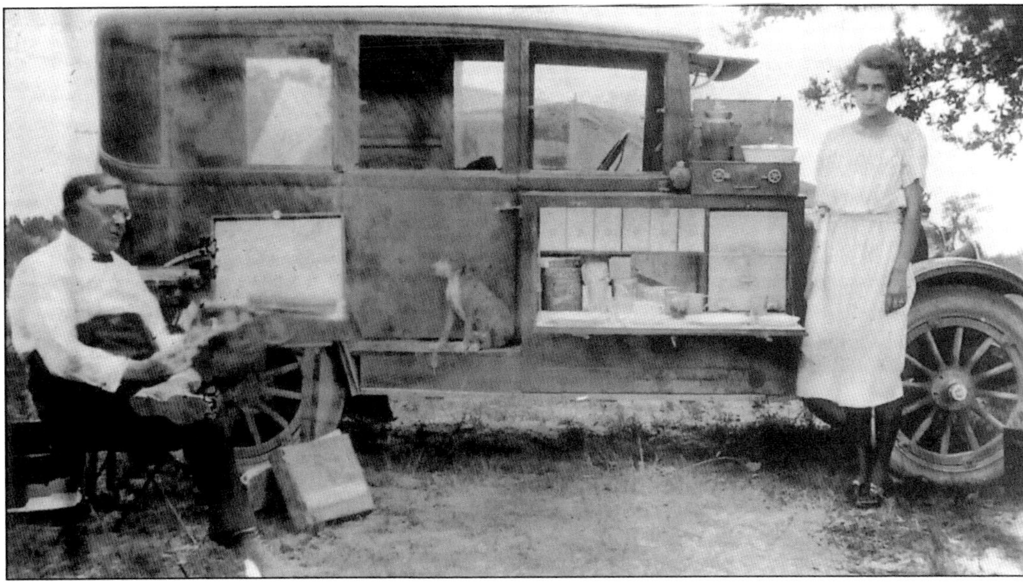

They are tin-can tourists. Their cars are now antiques. Their roads no longer exist, except for a few rare miles of abandoned stretches. Named for the canned food they hauled in their makeshift trailers, Americans with moderate incomes discovered they could afford a Florida vacation by loading up their Fords with tents and camping and cooking gear. Their destination was never Palm Beach. They could never afford to travel in the luxury railroad coaches that carried the wealthy to Florida winter resorts along the coast. Instead, they found comfort from the sunshine at scattered inland auto camps.

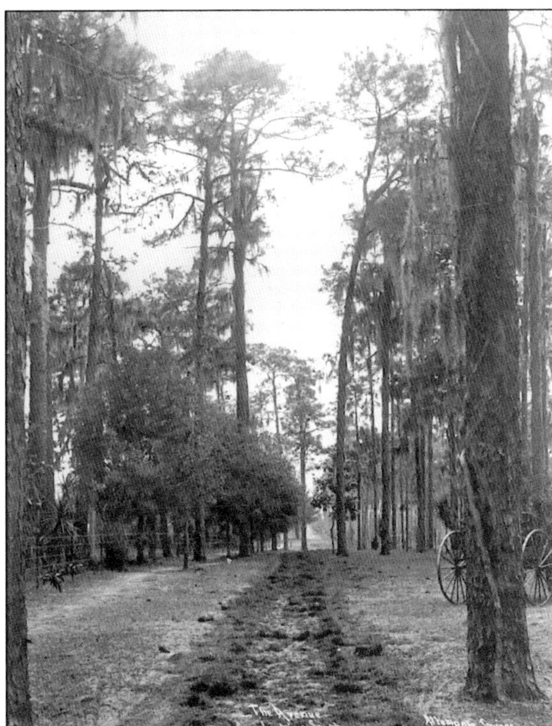

This is Maitland Avenue then called The Avenue, looking south with a carriage in view on the right. This is the condition of most of the roads in Florida when the tourists arrived in the first automobiles. Tin Can Tourists descended on Florida in such numbers that cities created municipal campgrounds to accommodate the influx. These tourists were the first to combine the idea of home and auto, mobility and bedrooms, into a single entity. With canvas and wood, they converted their cars into crude travel campers, using their back seats for beds and their radiators for cooking.

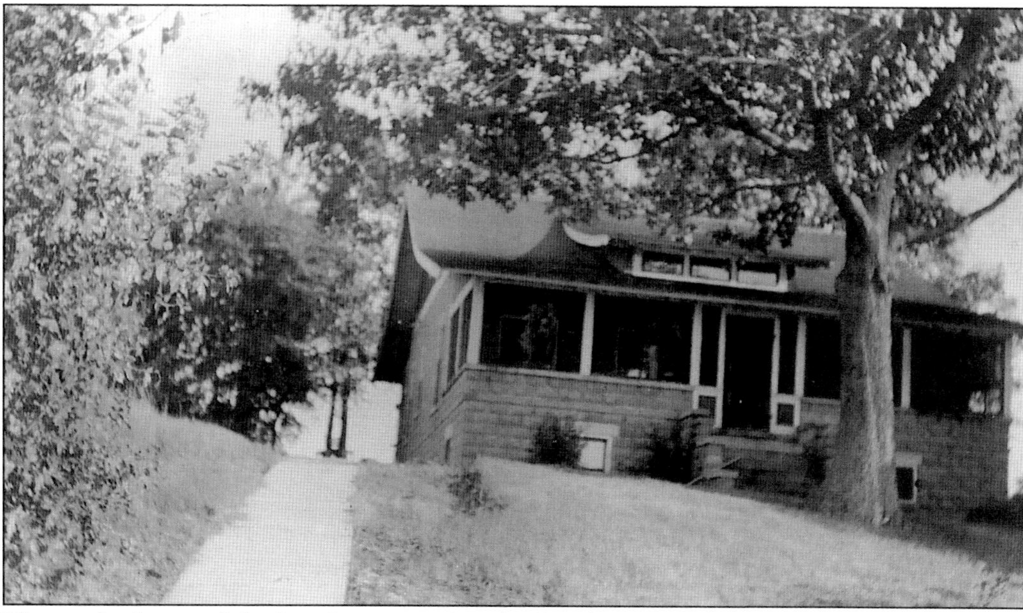

This is the home of the Landmans on Apopka Road near Little Wekiva River about 1917. Nina Landman would marry Everett Bates, who took over running the Altamonte Hotel from his father.

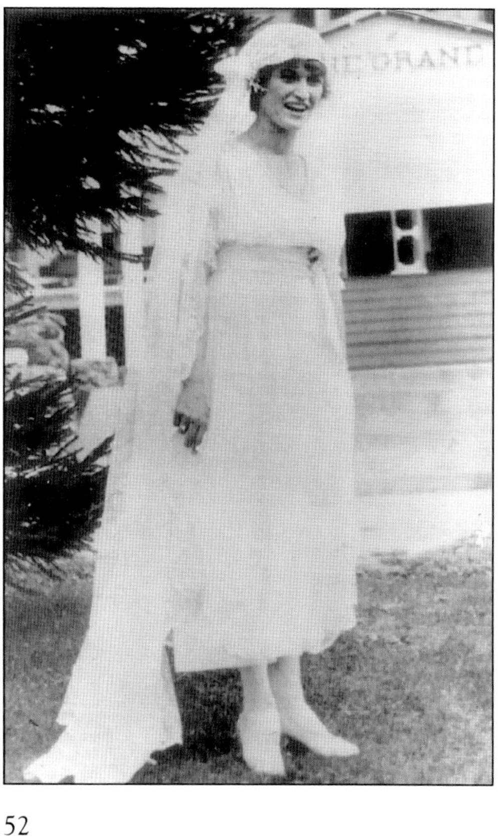

Nina Landman Bates, shown in her wedding gown, married Everett Bates at Grand Hotel in Mount Vernon, New Hampshire in 1917. Nina and Everett Bates ran the hotel in New Hampshire during the summers, opening the Altamonte Hotel in the winters. They lived in a two-and-a-half-story, Queen Anne residence across Maitland Avenue from the hotel for 30 years.

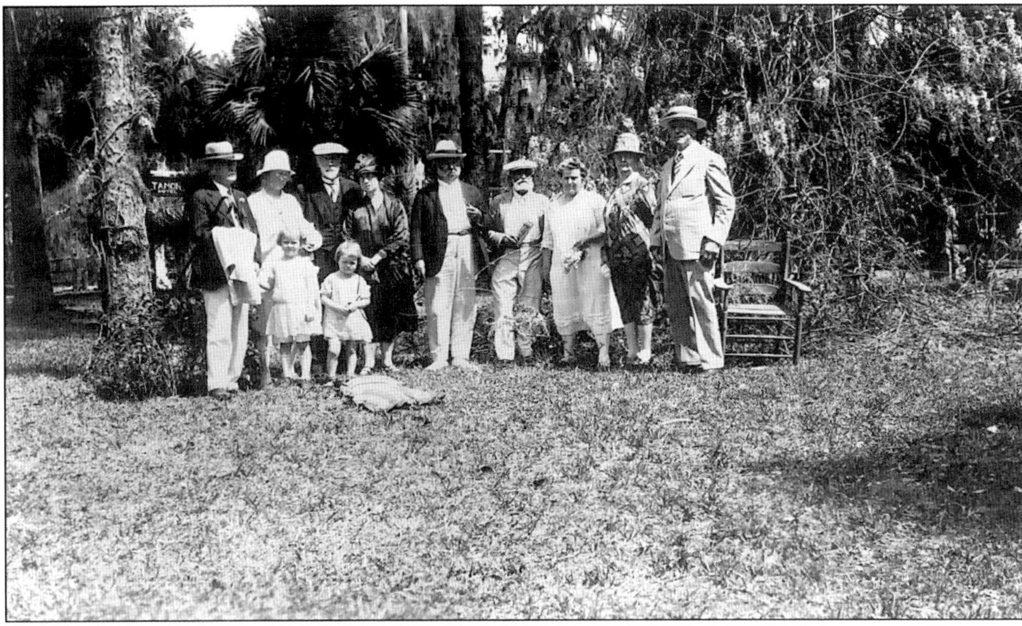

The Bates family gathers for a group portrait about 1927. Lillian and George Bates are third and fourth from the right. George Bates was the Altamonte Hotel's proprieter from 1901 until his death in 1931, when his son took over. The Bates enjoyed the loyalty of their staff and guests. Many among the staff and guests followed the family in the summers to its grand hotel in Mount Vernon, New Hampshire.

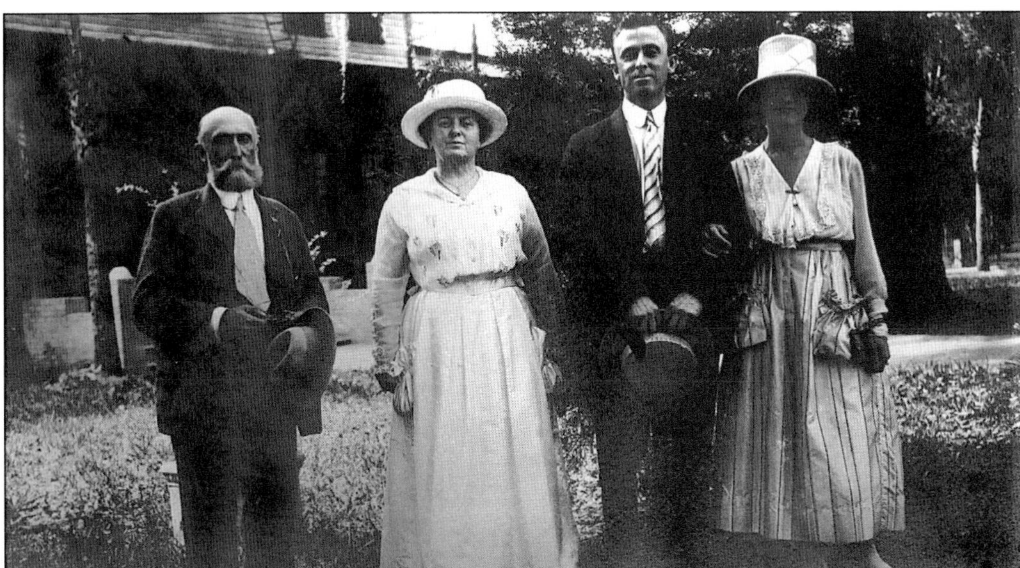

George E. and Lillian Bates pose with their son, Everett C. Bates, and his wife, Nina Landman Bates, in 1920 in front of the Altamonte Hotel.

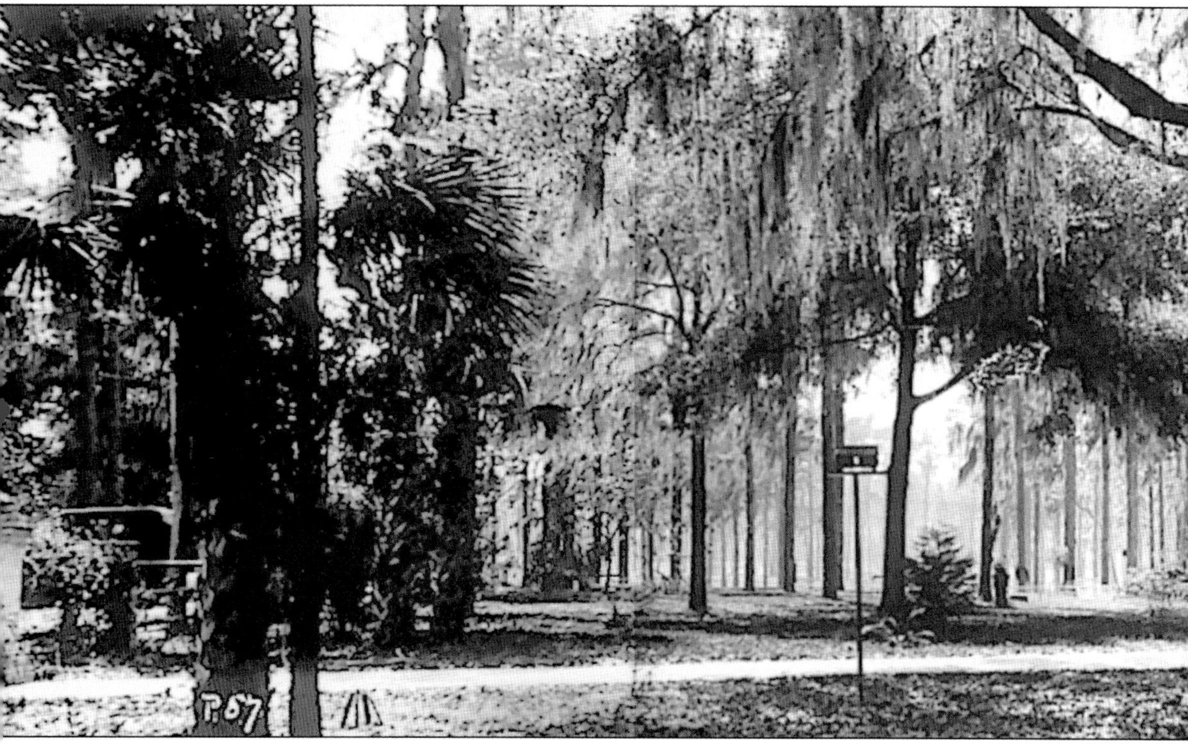

This wide view shows the steps to the porch of the Altamonte Hotel from the lakefront side.

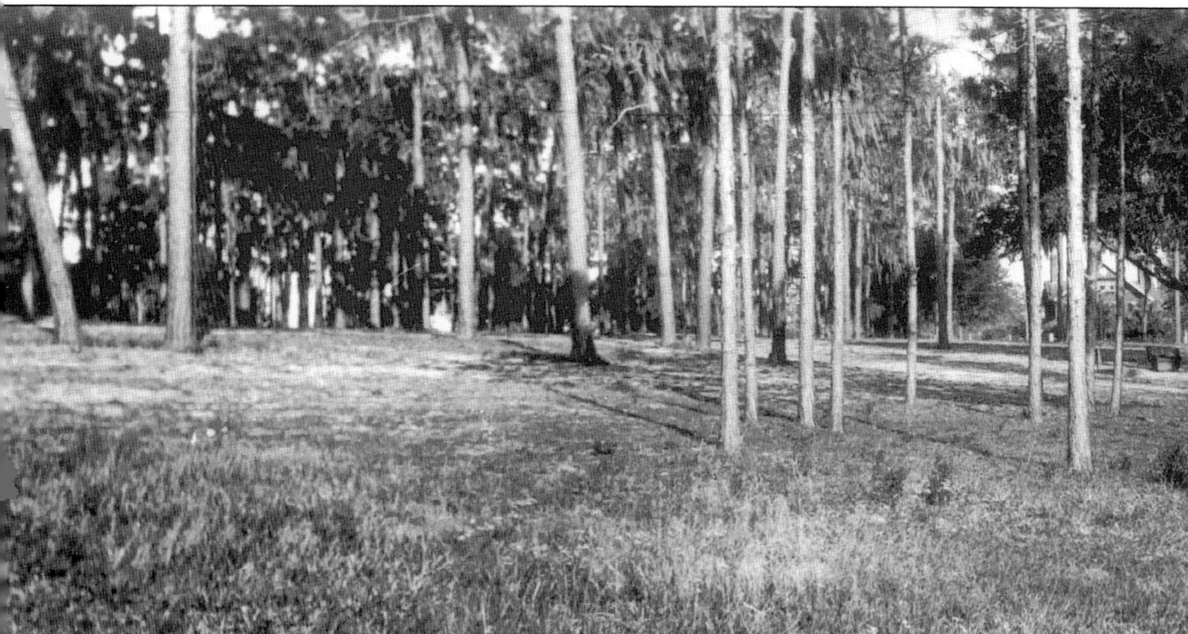

This view of the hotel's boating shows some of the rowboats made available to guests. The hotel grounds provided quiet, peaceful areas for guests when they were not joining some of the more

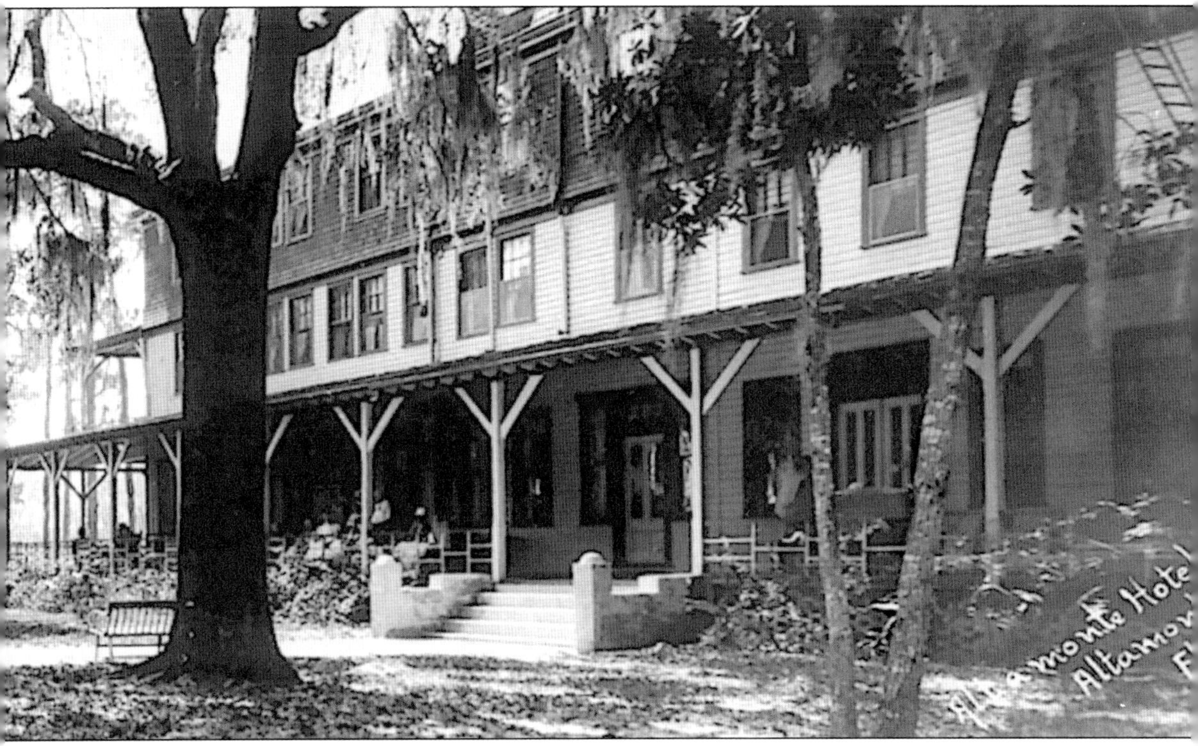

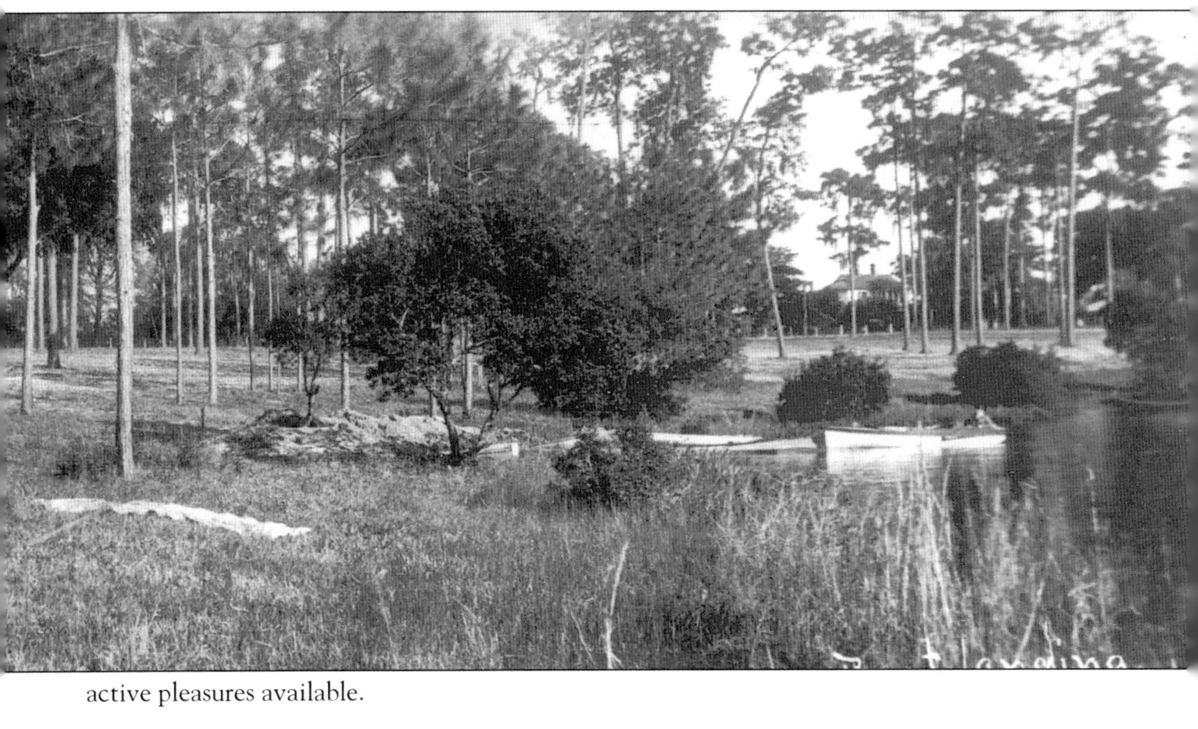

active pleasures available.

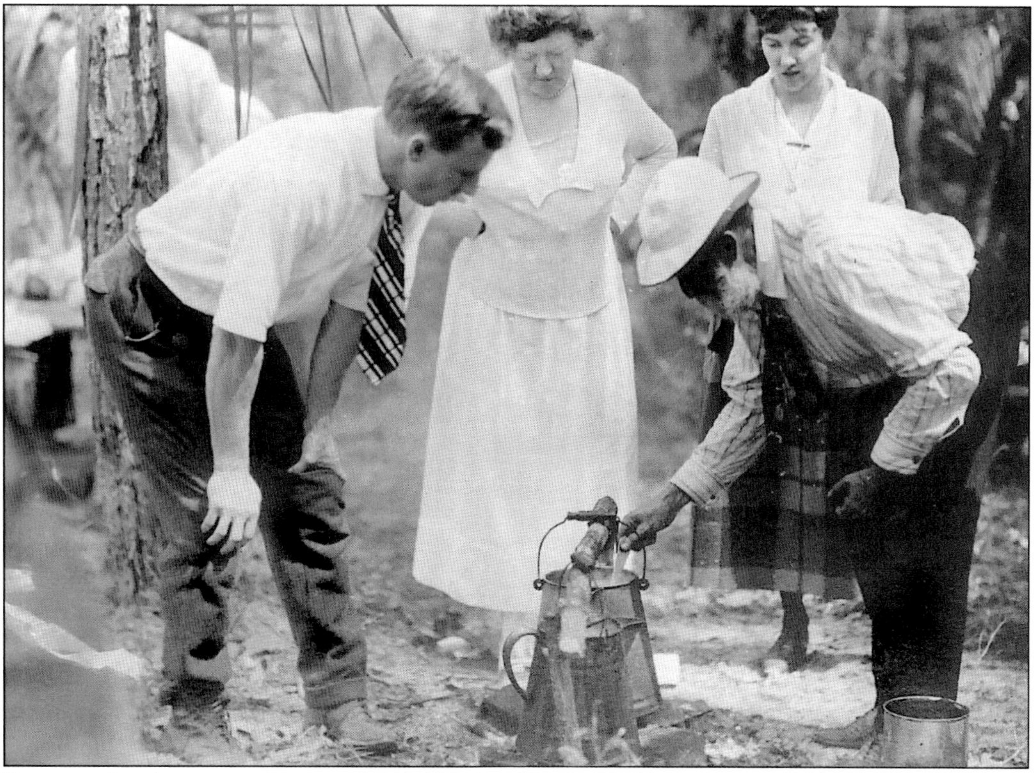

During a family camping trip at Good Shepherd Springs about 1910, Everett Bates bends over to look into the pot of boiling coffee stirred by his father, George E. Bates. Keeping watch are Lillian and Nina Bates.

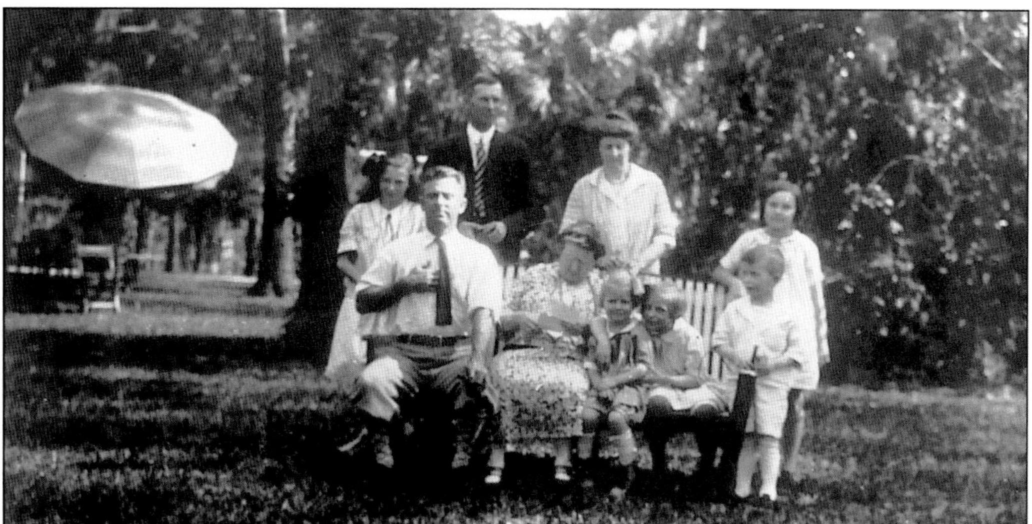

Everett C. Bates, with his right hand under his tie, poses with others in the Bates family for this 1928 photo. He is seated next to his mother, Lillian Bates, who is reading a letter. Sitting next to her are Virginia Bates Wyman and Violet Wilkins. Standing next to her is Vernon Wilkins. Standing in the back, from left to right, are Lillian Wilkins and Harold and Violet Bates. The girl with them is unidentified.

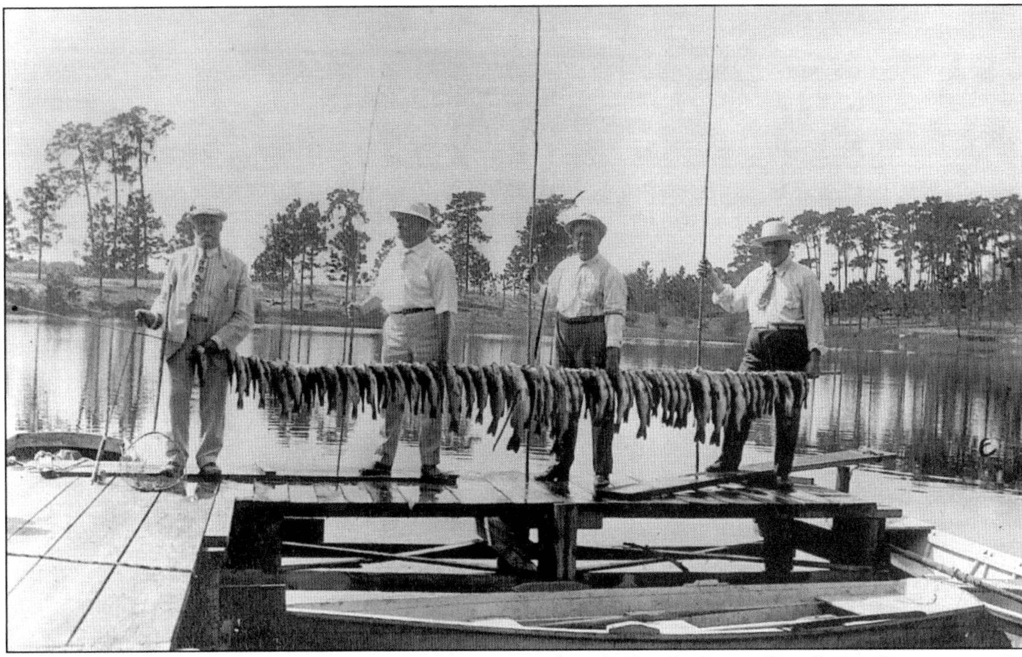

George Emelius Bates and his fishing partners stand with the day's catch at Lake Orienta on the hotel's dock sometime between 1910 and 1912.

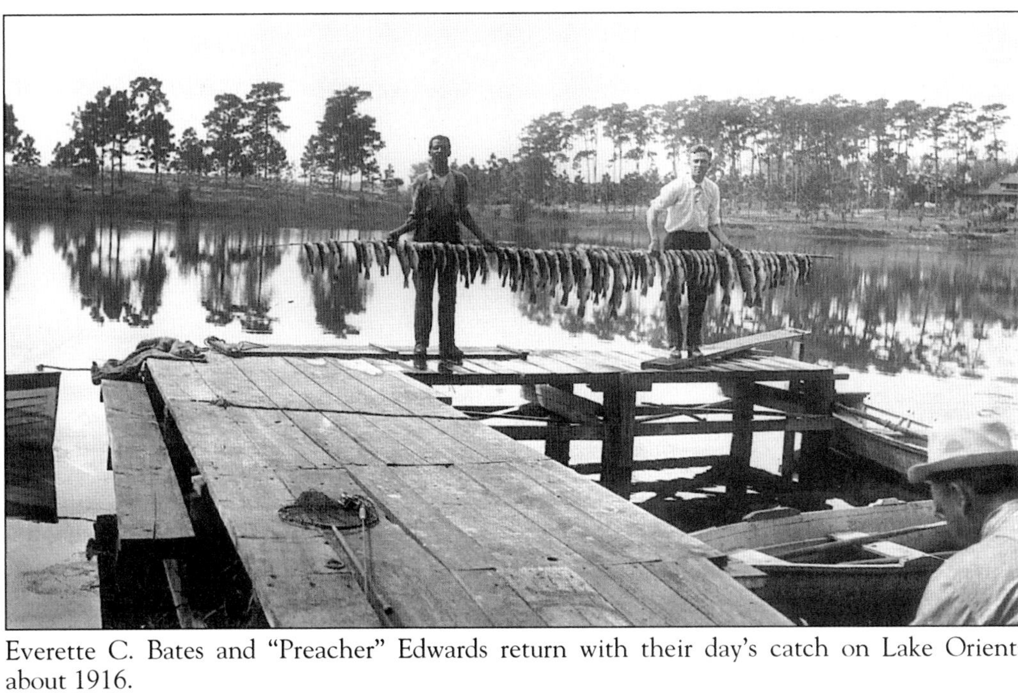

Everette C. Bates and "Preacher" Edwards return with their day's catch on Lake Orienta about 1916.

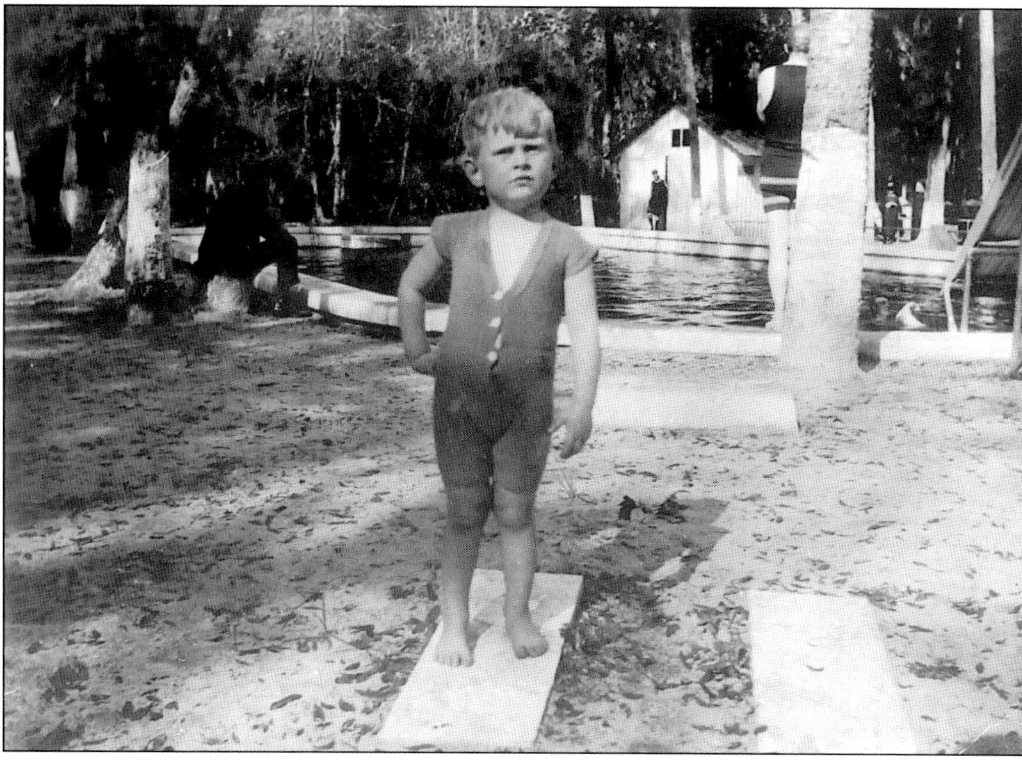

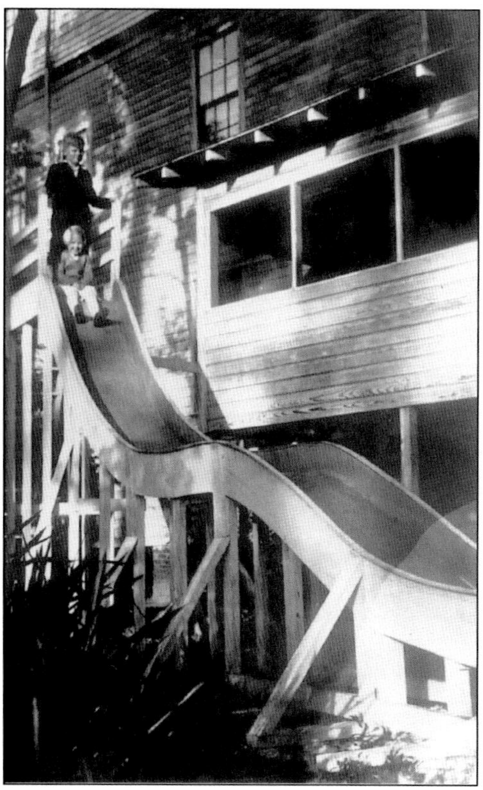

George Everett Bates is shown in his bathing suit at Palm Springs in 1924.

George and Virginia Bates play on a slide next to their home on Maitland Avenue. The slide was built for the Bates children by one of the carpenters at the Altamonte Hotel, which was owned and managed by their father.

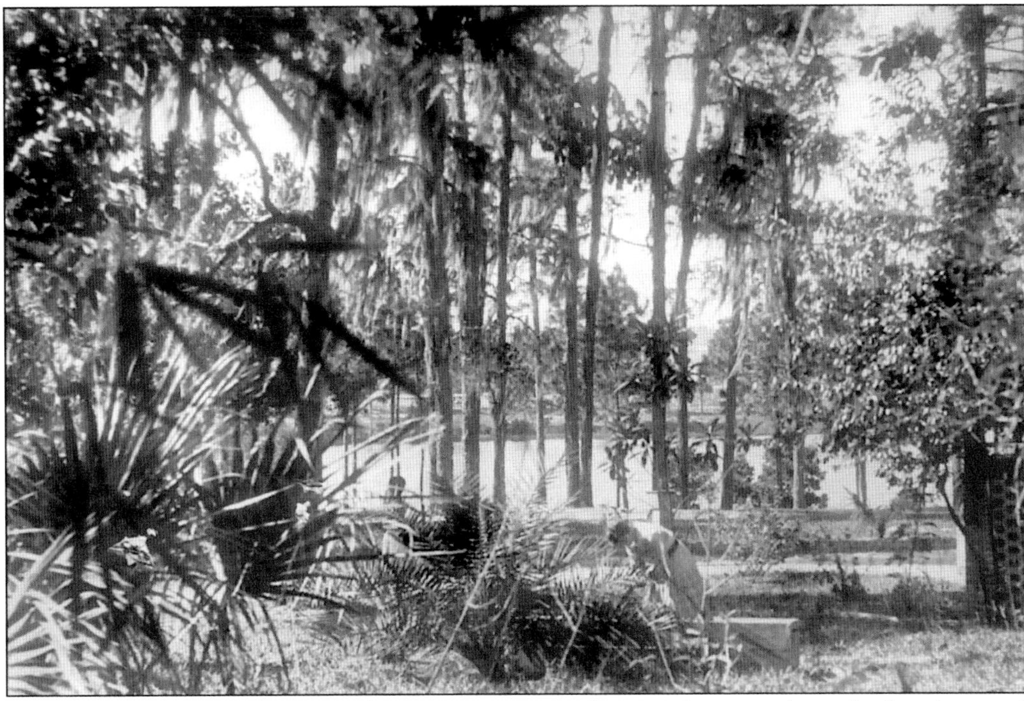

Nina Landman Bates, shown in the center next to palmetto plants, works at the hotel grounds near Lake Orienta in 1930.

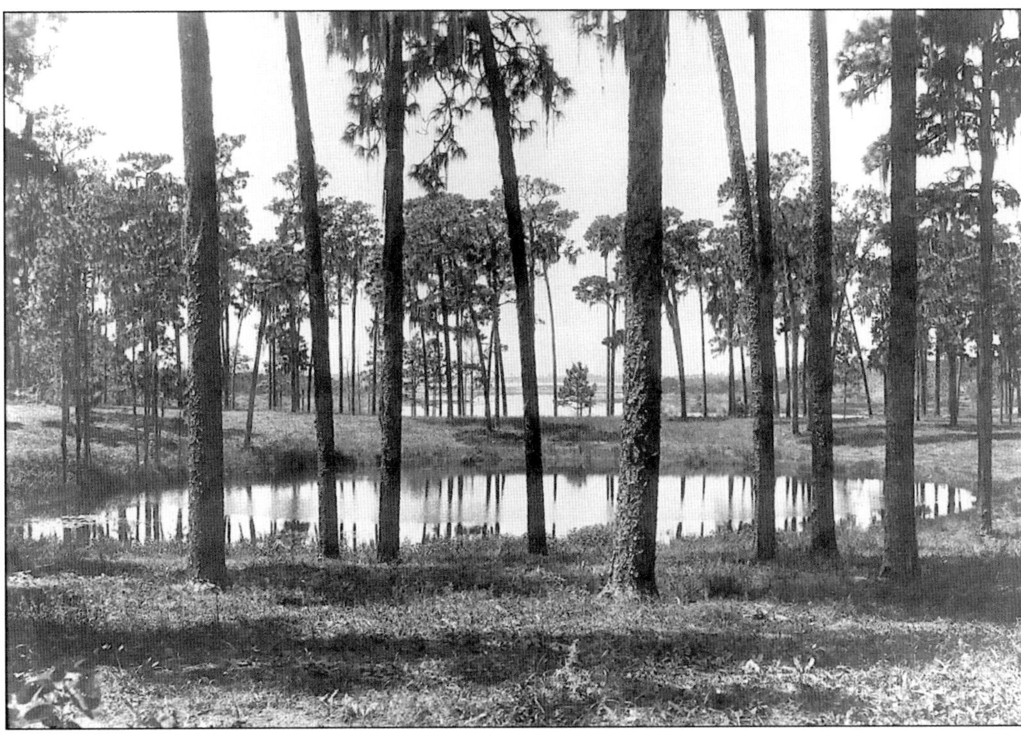

This 1923 view shows a sinkhole that filled with water, which was located behind the hotel. Lake Orienta is in the background.

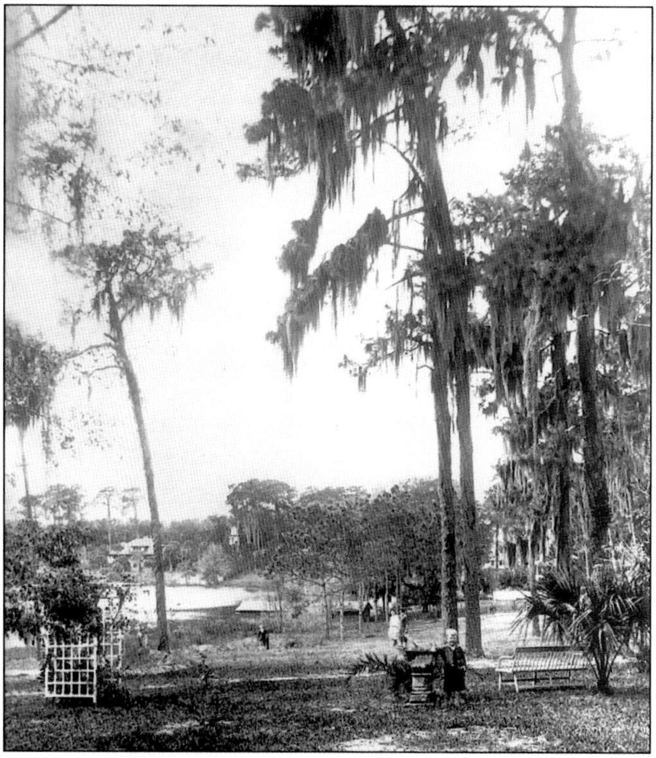

George Everett Bates was three years old when this photo was taken in 1922 at the hotel's golf course. Across the lake is the water tower at the house of R.E. Hoffman.

Nina and Everett Bates wait to tee off at the hotel's golf course.

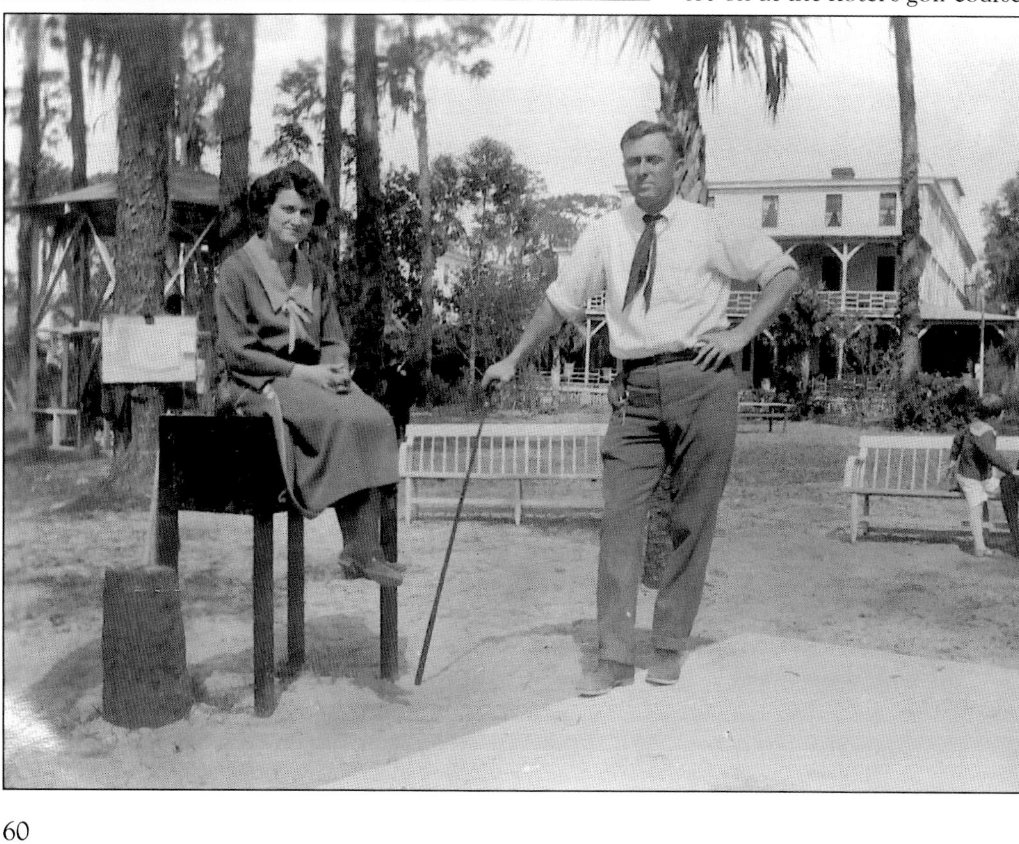

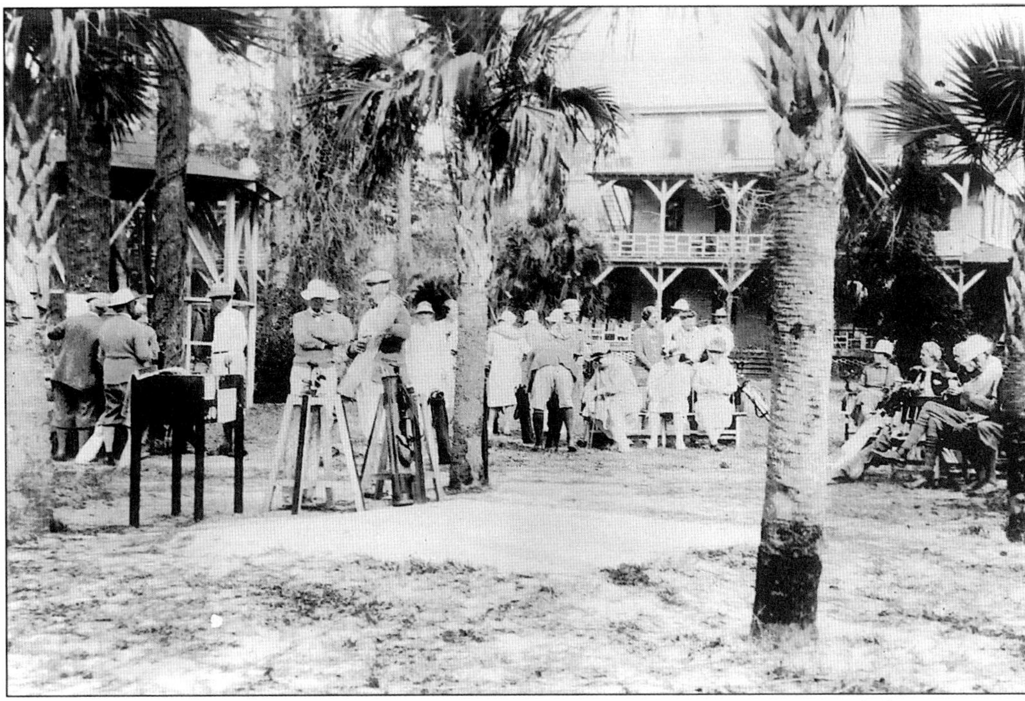

Hotel guests assemble for a golf tournament in 1925. Tournaments provided competition between communities. The *Sanford Herald* in February 1925 reported that a team led by Sanford Mayor Forrest Cake defeated the Altamonte team led by Mayor B.L. Maltbie. The Altamonte team won on its own course the next week.

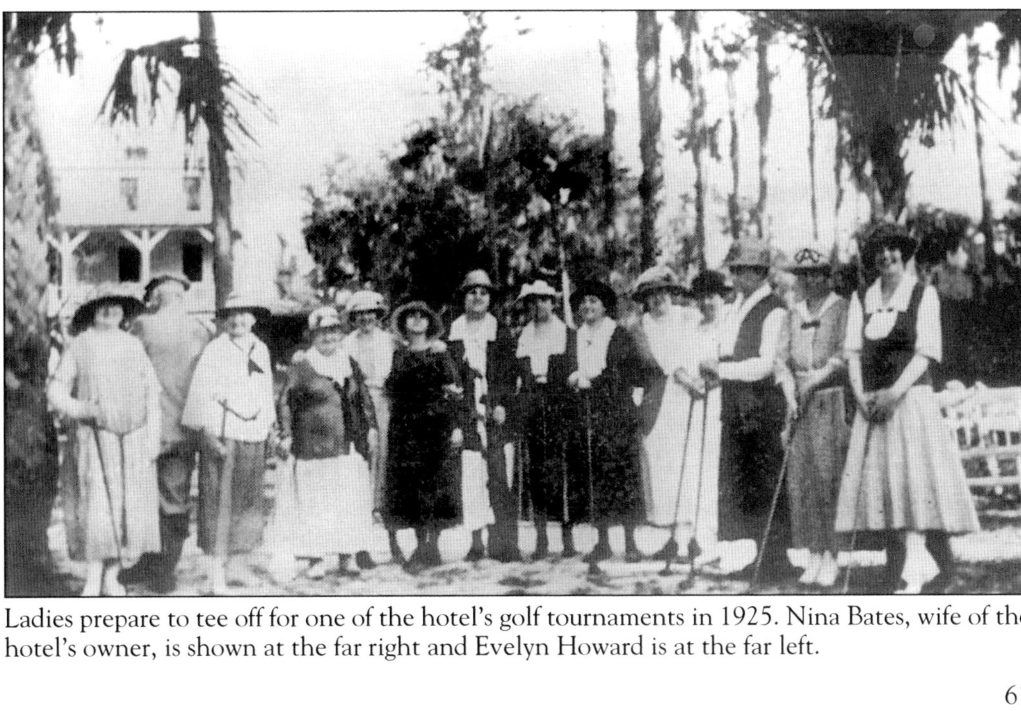

Ladies prepare to tee off for one of the hotel's golf tournaments in 1925. Nina Bates, wife of the hotel's owner, is shown at the far right and Evelyn Howard is at the far left.

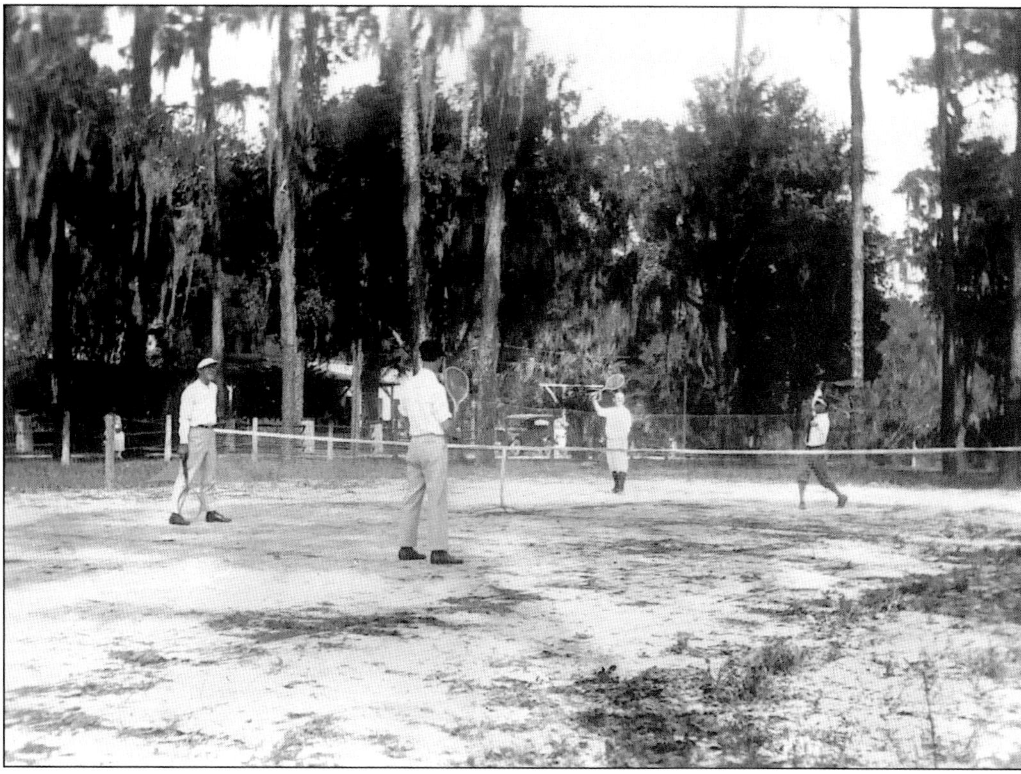

Besides golfing, tennis was a popular recreational activity at the hotel. This 1928 photo shows guests enjoying the courts at the southeast corner of Altamonte Avenue (now state Road 436) and Maitland Avenue.

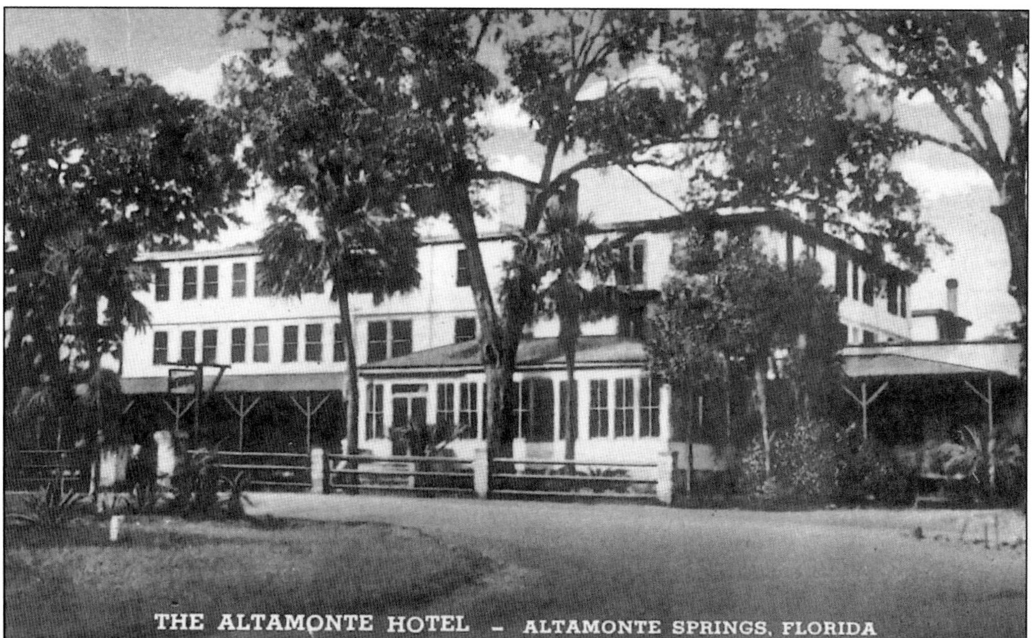

The Altamonte Hotel is shown in the 1940s.

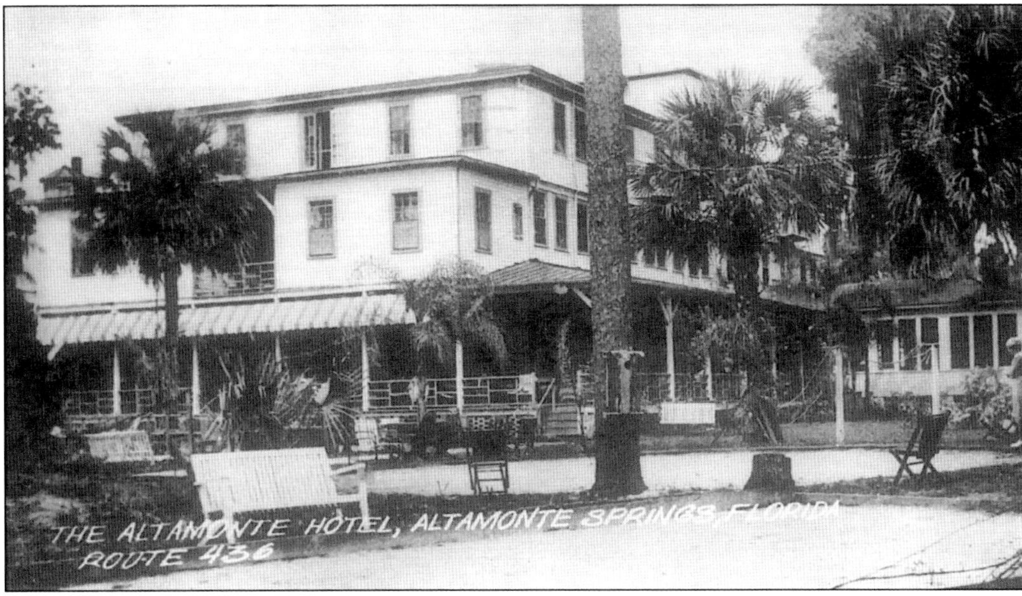

This side view of the hotel was taken in the 1940s. The hotel's American plan included a room and bath at $55 to $85 a week for two guests.

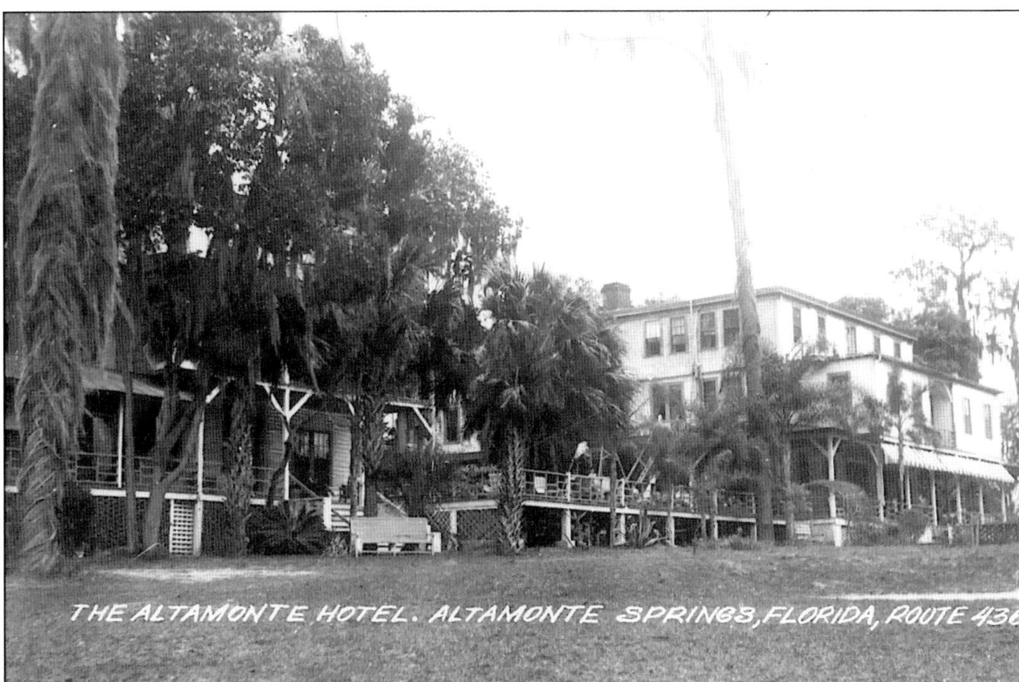

This view shows the raised walkway between the south patio of the hotel and bungalows in the 1940s.

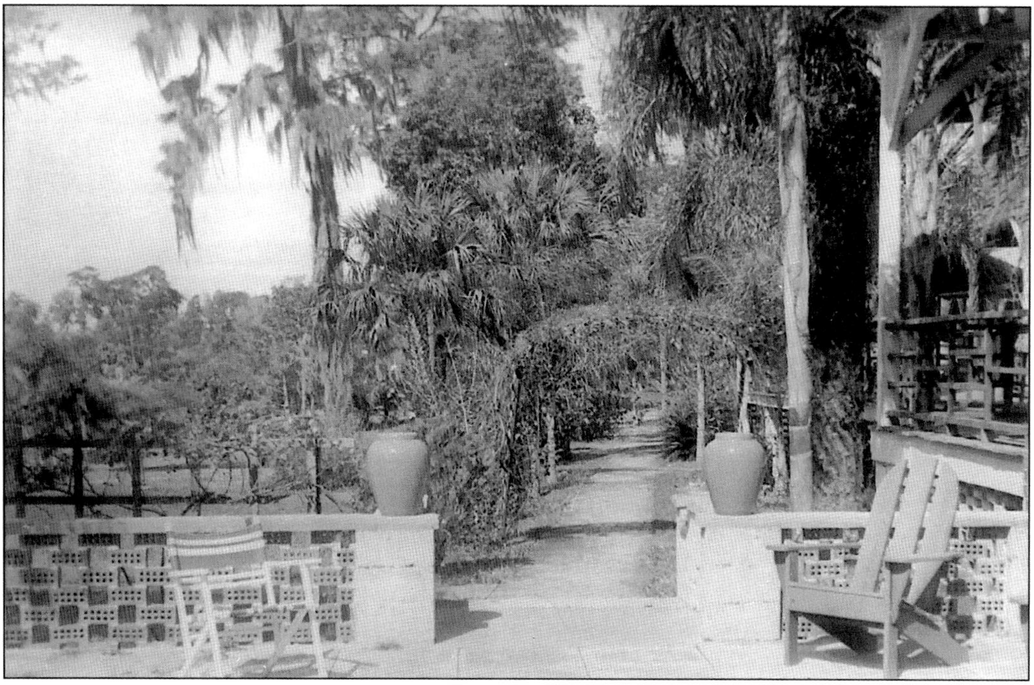

Altamonte Hotel's south patio and sidewalks to bungalows are shown in about 1940.

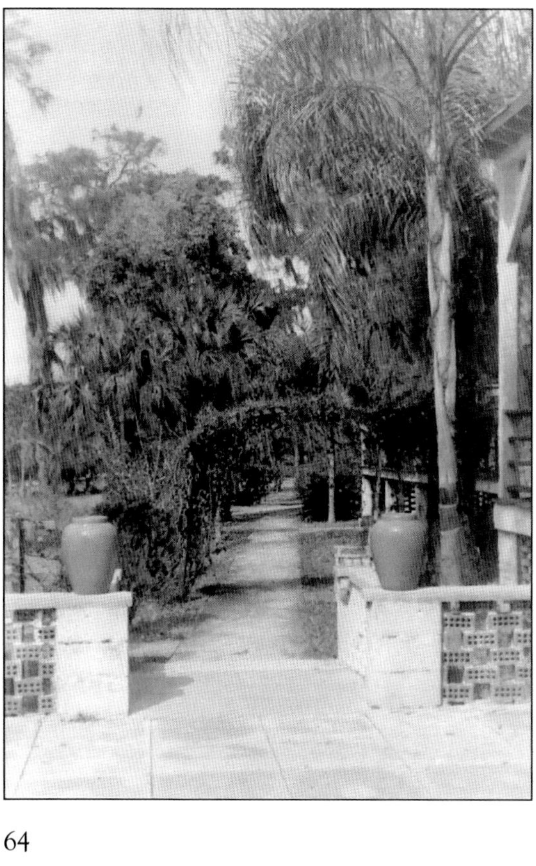

This sidewalk, pictured in the 1940s from the hotel's south patio, leads to the bungalows. Besides the main house, the hotel complex included a three-story annex connected to the main house. The annex also included a link to a lodge. Sixteen room were in two rows of connected bungalows.

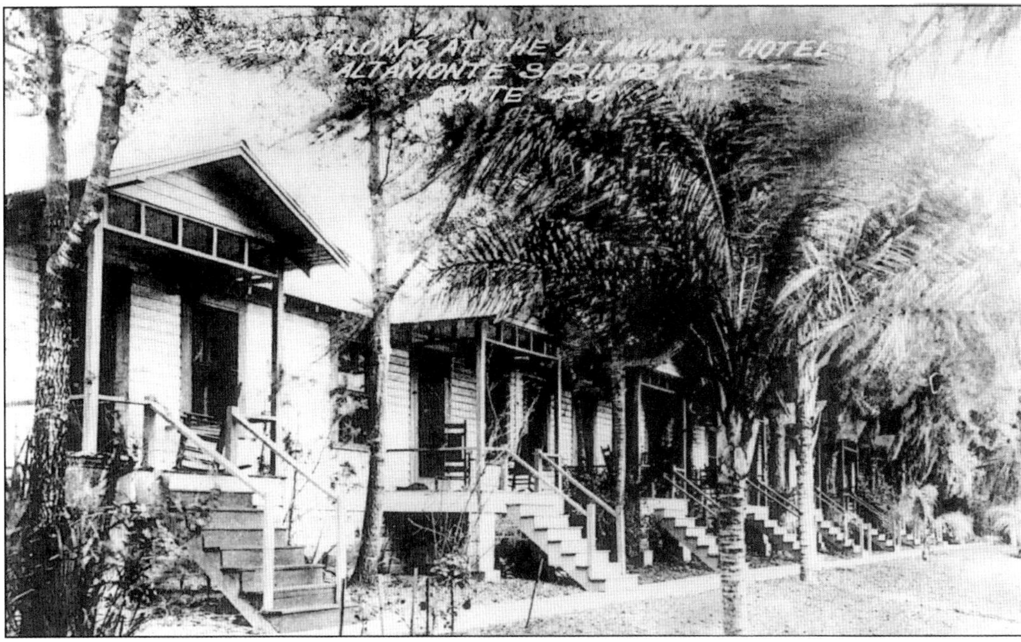

These are the hotel's bungalows shown in the 1940s. Guests came to enjoy golfing, hunting, and fishing. The hotel was a short drive from the dog and horse racing tracks at Longwood and Casselberry.

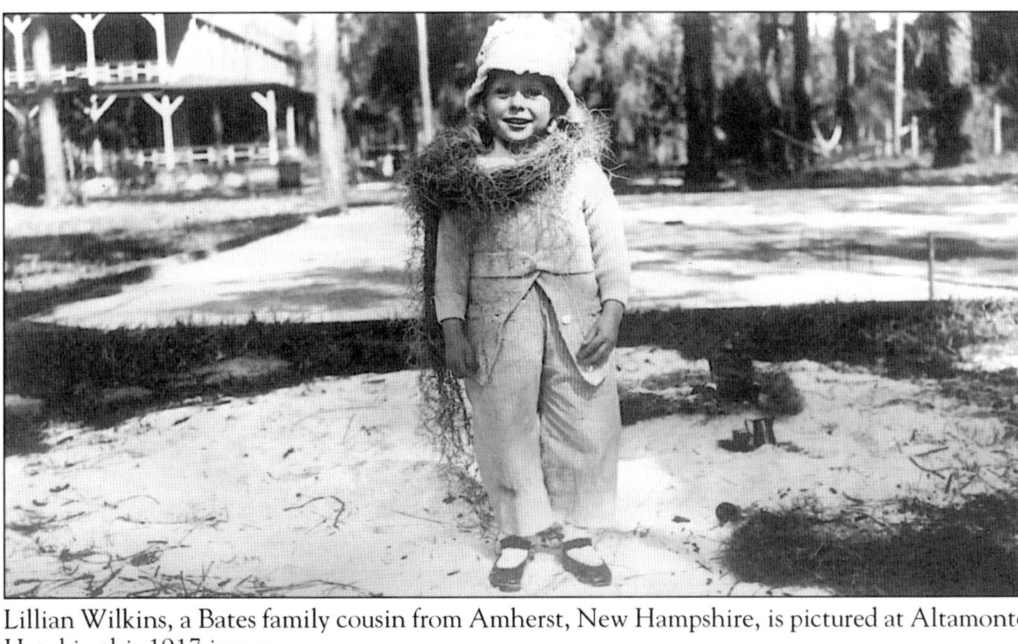

Lillian Wilkins, a Bates family cousin from Amherst, New Hampshire, is pictured at Altamonte Hotel in this 1917 image.

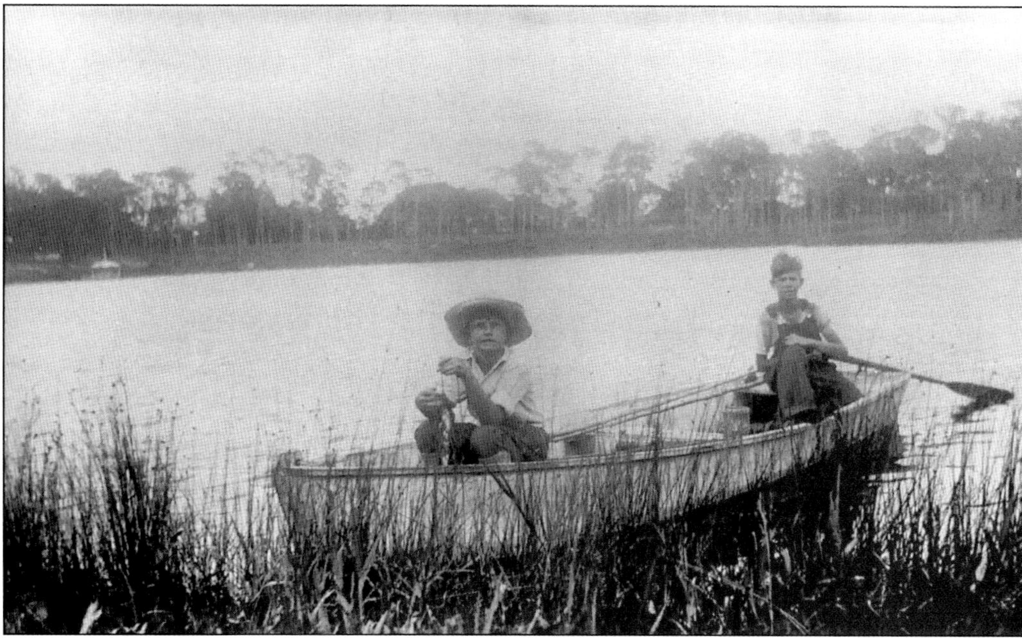

Herbert Graham Fuller and his friend "Had" return to the shoreline after a day of fishing on Lake Orienta in the 1930s.

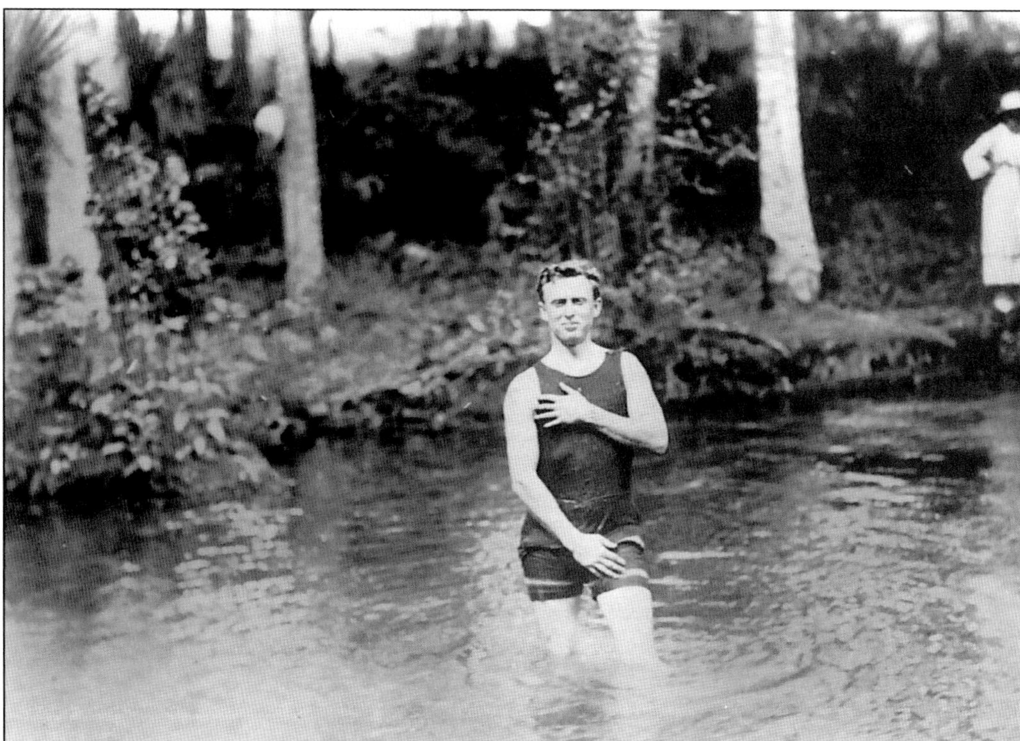

Everett Bates enjoys a day at Palm Springs in 1915.

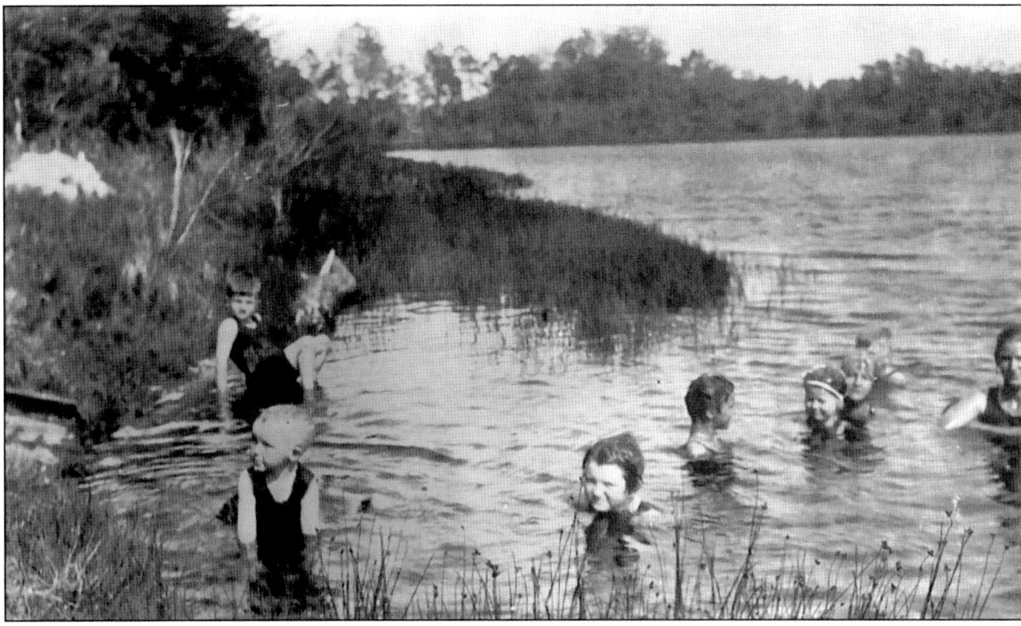

This 1927 photograph was taken at a Sunday School picnic at Lake Florida. Nina Bates, far right, swims with the children.

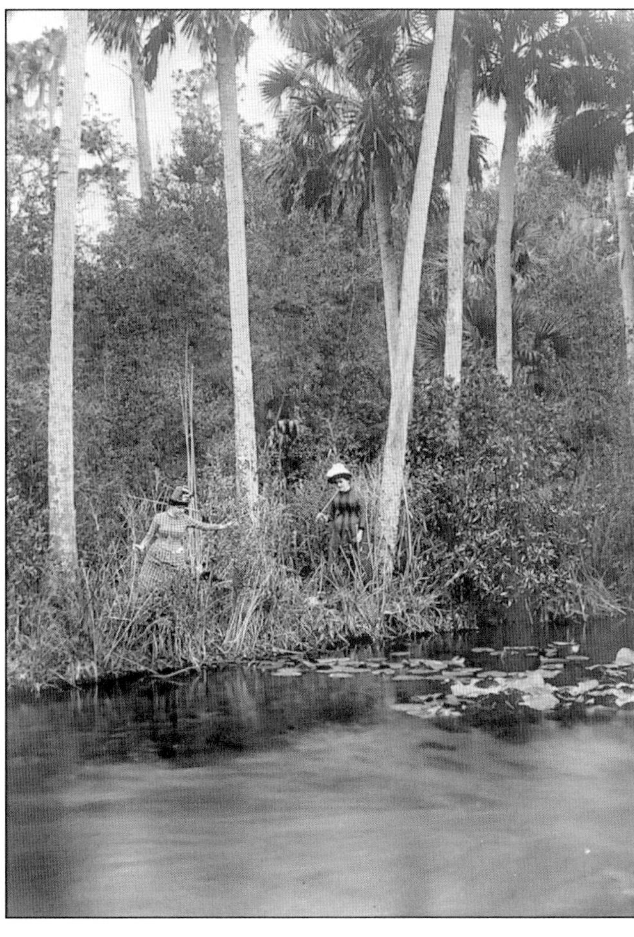

The springs scattered throughout the region had been the area's major tourism draws. Here, Martha and Nellie Graham are photographed at Shepherd Springs in 1888.

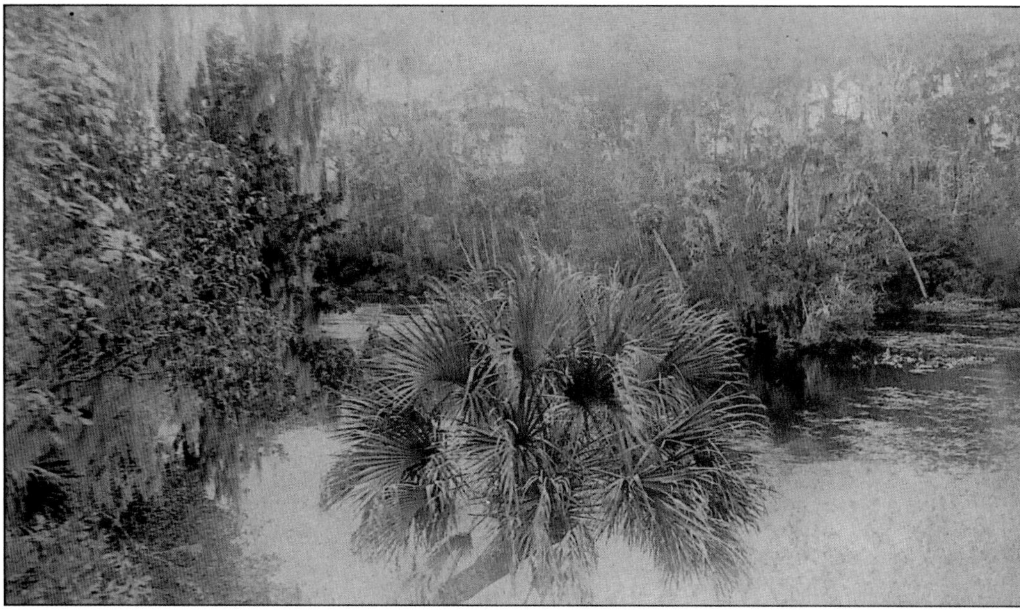

The narrow, winding Wekiva River, shown here in 1885, flows from springs west of Altamonte Springs to the St. Johns River. Early developers of Altamonte wanted to cut a canal to the river and open the wild river to the commerce on the St. Johns. That goal was never accomplished.

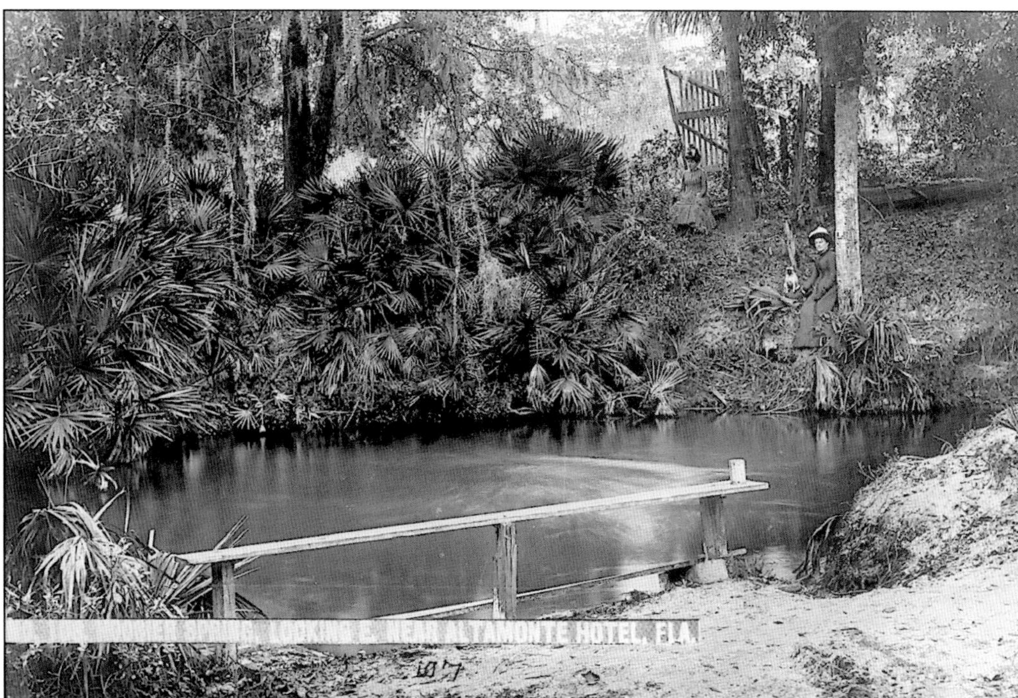

Sanlando Springs was called Hoosier Springs until renamed in the 1920s.

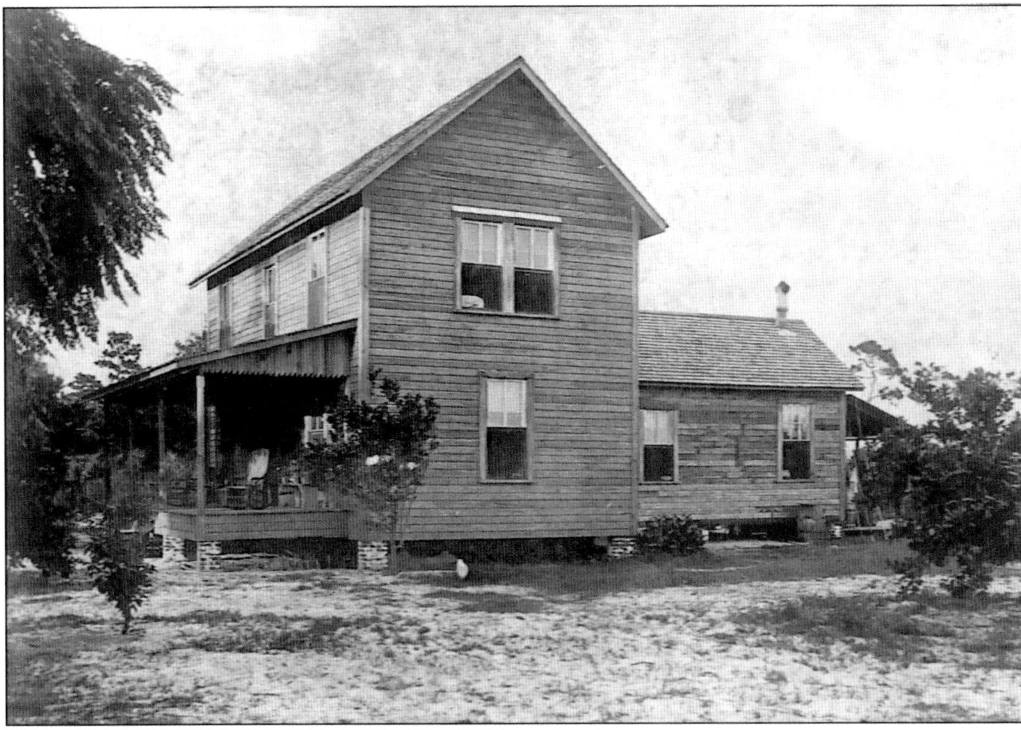

The Caldwell House, shown here *c.* 1900, stood near the railroad tracks east of Longwood Avenue (today's County Road 427) at Altamonte Avenue (now State Road 436).

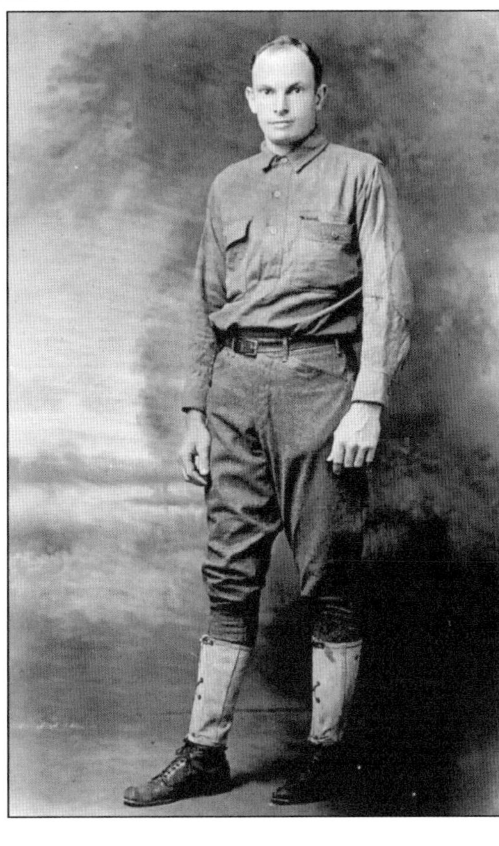

Herbert E. Fuller is shown here on June 15, 1917. He took over running the family store from his father in the 1920s.

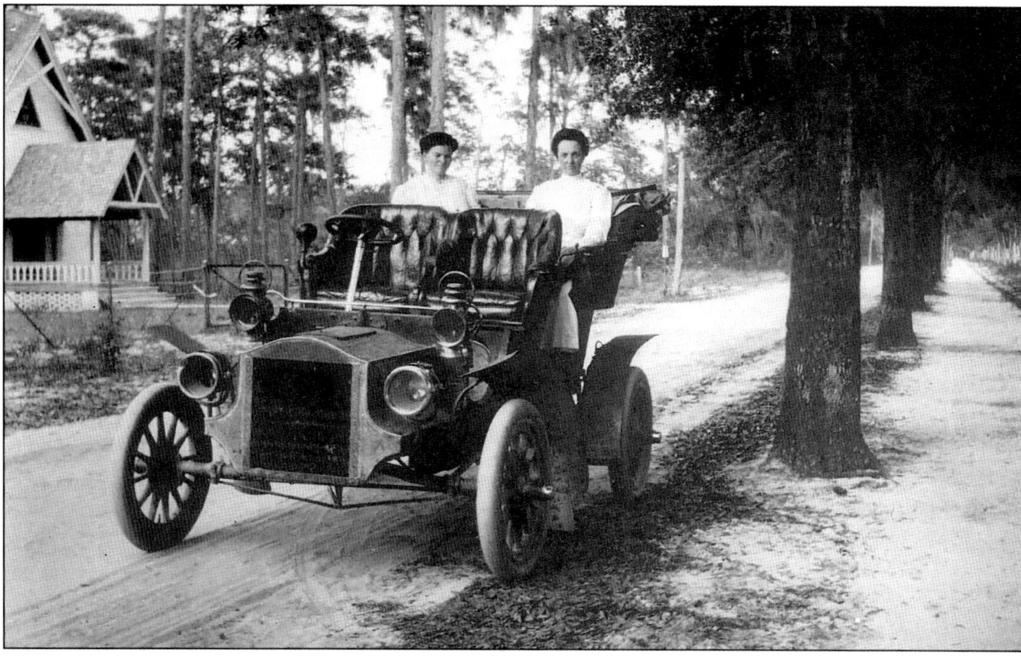

Irene Fuller, at the steering wheel, and Mamie Fuller set out for a drive along Altamonte Avenue about 1914. They are shown passing in front of the chapel and the Fuller home. Dirt roads were replaced with nine-foot brick roads in the early 1900s.

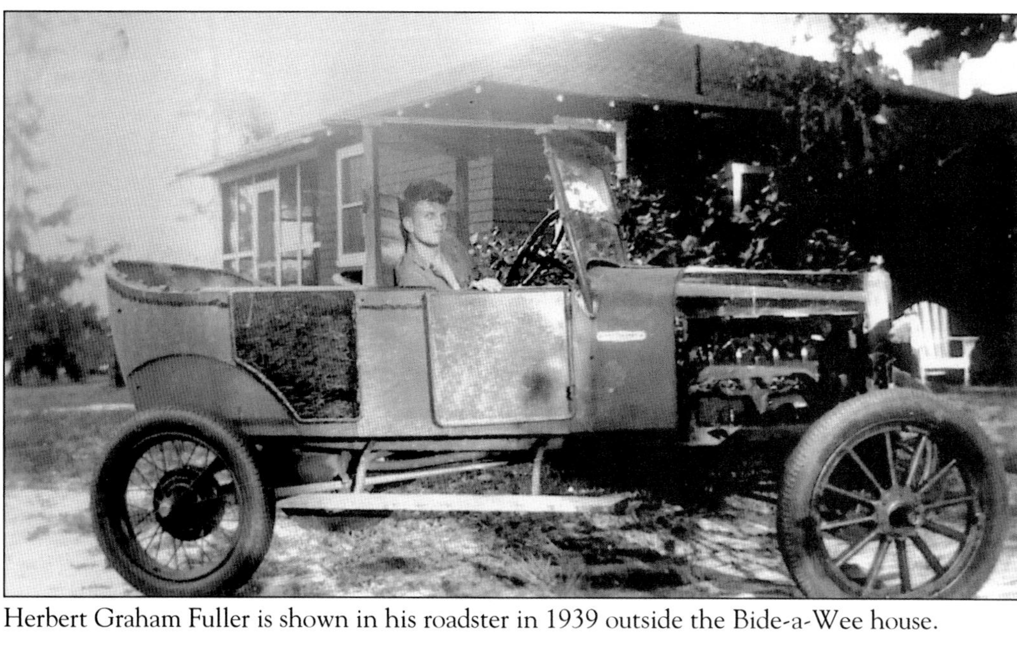

Herbert Graham Fuller is shown in his roadster in 1939 outside the Bide-a-Wee house.

Mr. and Mrs. A.H. Fuller are shown in 1931 near the porch of their home. A basket of cut gladioli is at their feet. The Fullers touched every era of Altamonte Springs from the days when the first groves were planted at Old Altamonte to today's efforts to preserve in photography the images of yesterday. The Fullers were the postmasters, storeowners, grove tenders, and community builders.

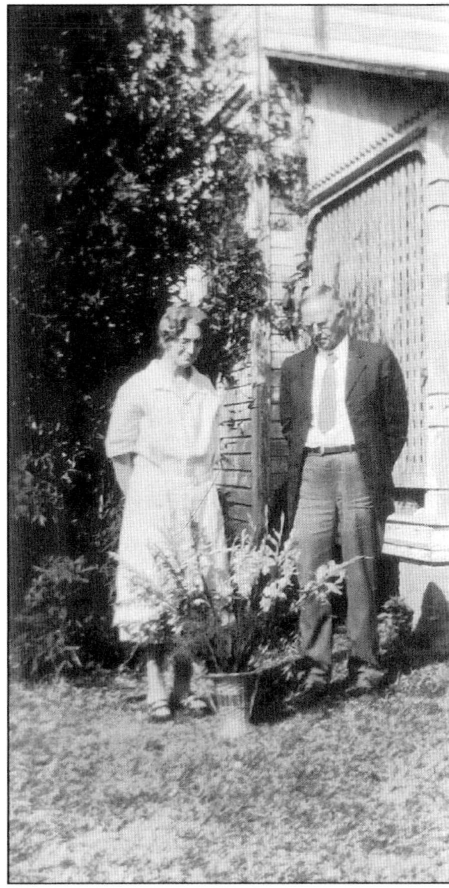

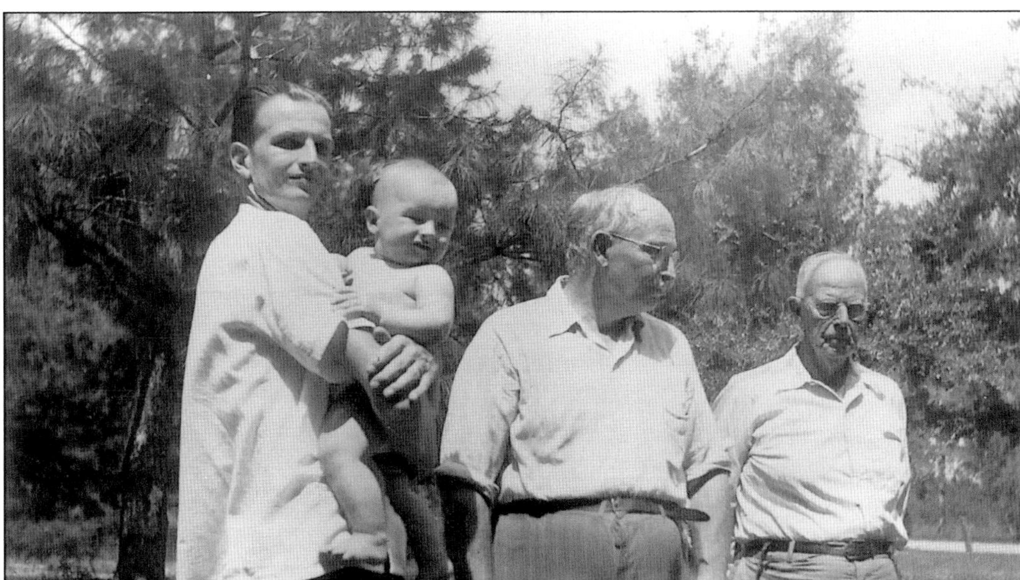

Shown here from left to right in 1948 are four generations of the Fullers: Graham G., Kent, Herbert E., and Arthur H. Fuller.

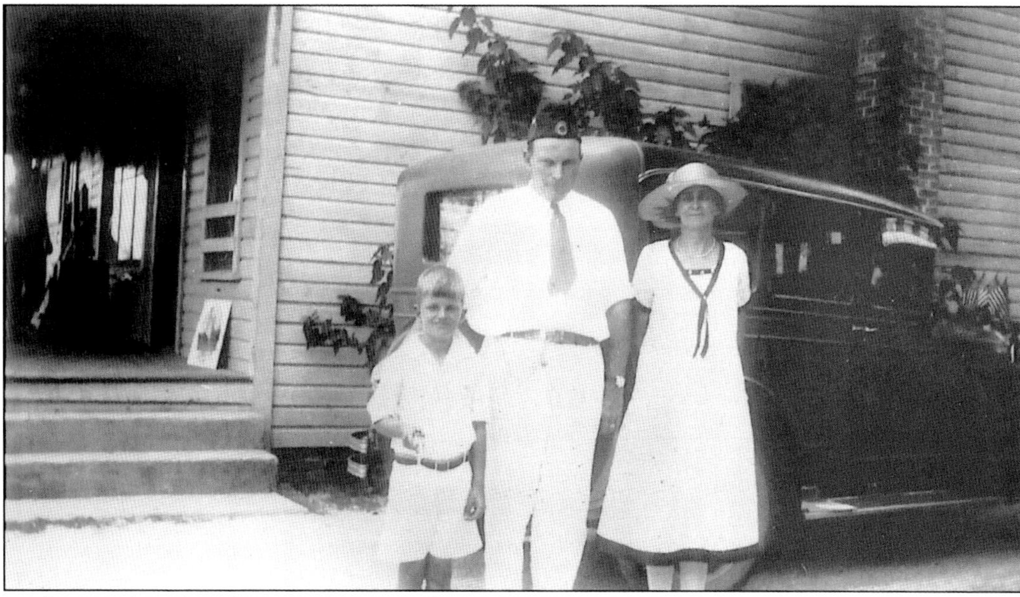

Herbert and Ruth Fuller are shown with their son, Graham, in 1929 outside the Fuller Store. The Fuller's store, while still selling general merchandise, began selling gasoline and oil in the 1920s. During the Great Depression Herbert Fuller was one of the Altamonte aldermen who helped identify families in need and provided work for them. Herbert and Ruth Fuller also volunteered to take care of the Community House.

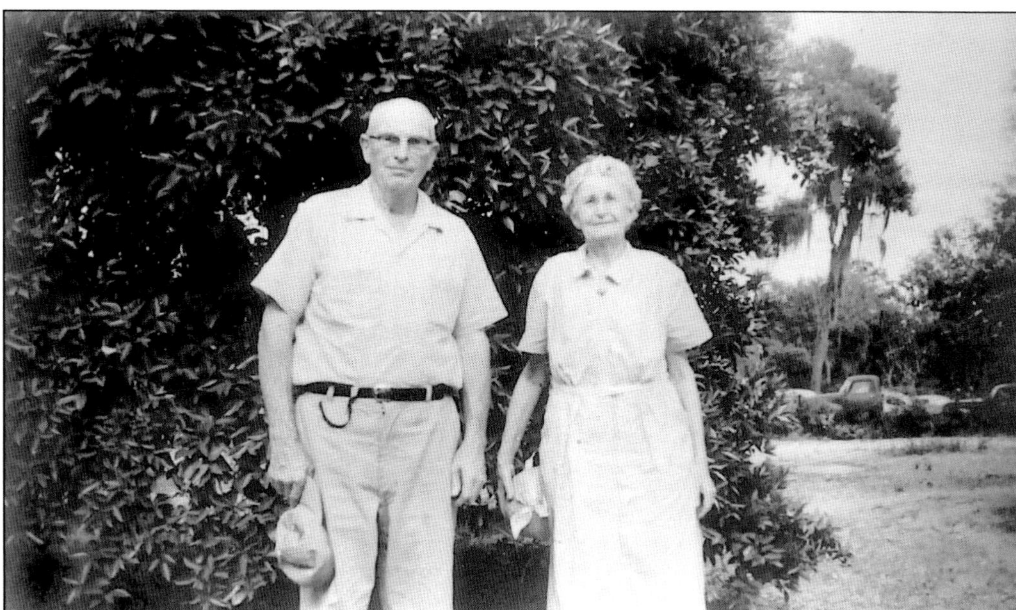

Pictured here are Herbert E. Fuller and Ruth G. Fuller in 1956. Herbert Fuller helped expand the Chamber of Commerce membership.

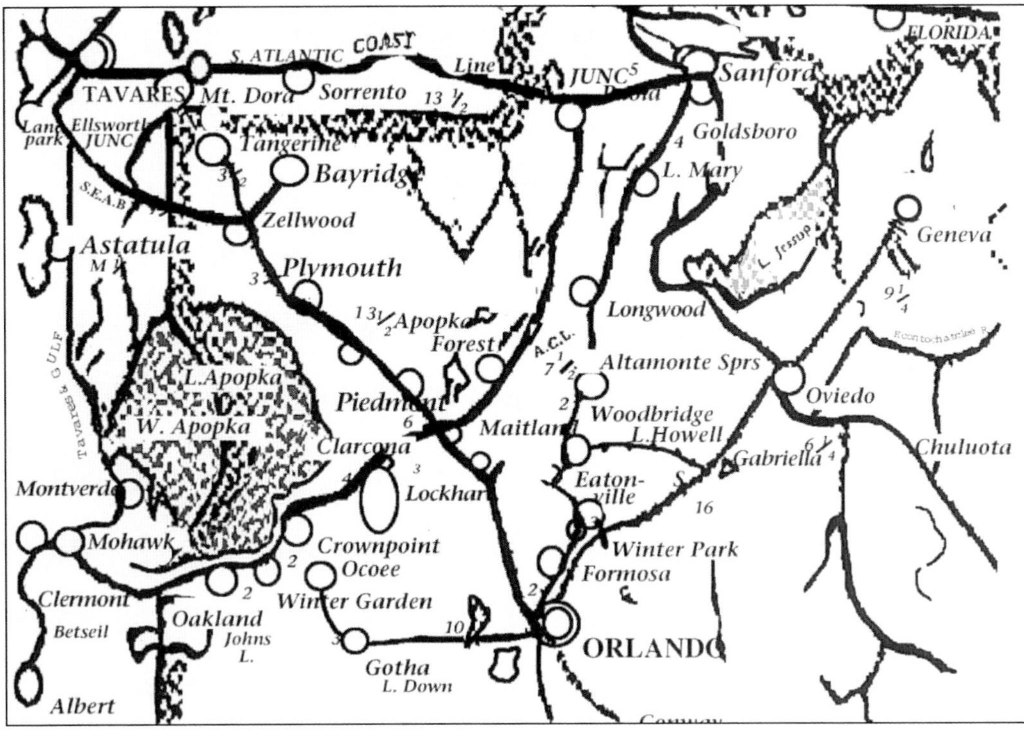

This is the Central Florida section of the postal route map in 1911. Altamonte Springs is shown in the middle.

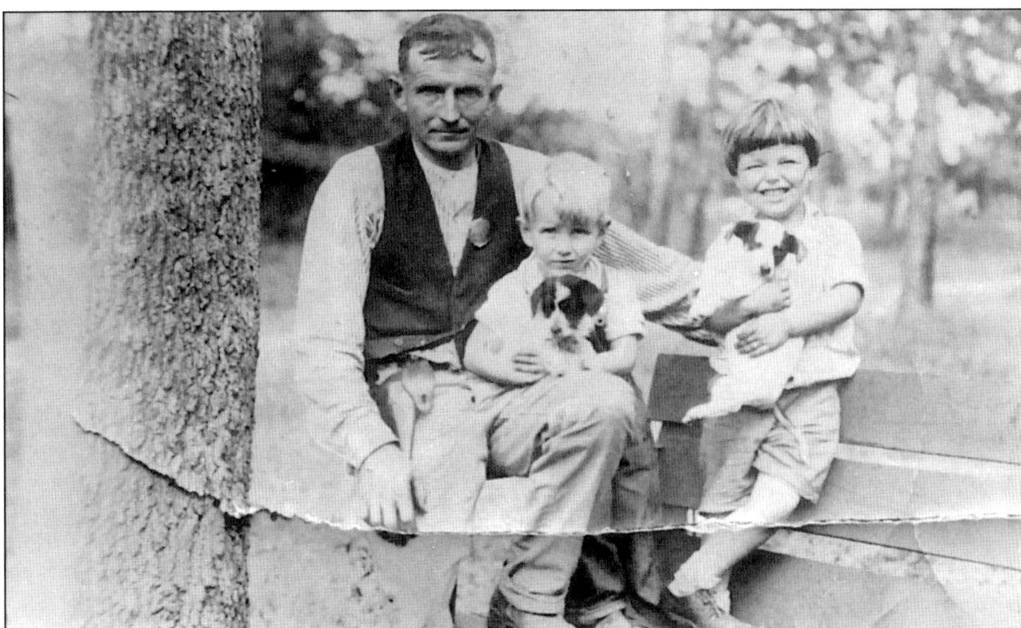

Town Marshal Charles Martin Hogg Sr. is shown here in 1927 with his son, Charles Martin Hogg Jr., at his side, and friend Robert "Bobby" Wright Jr. Besides his duties as marshal, Hogg was the town's road foreman. He was paid $85 a month to dig up clay at Sanlando Springs and other sites and repair streets.

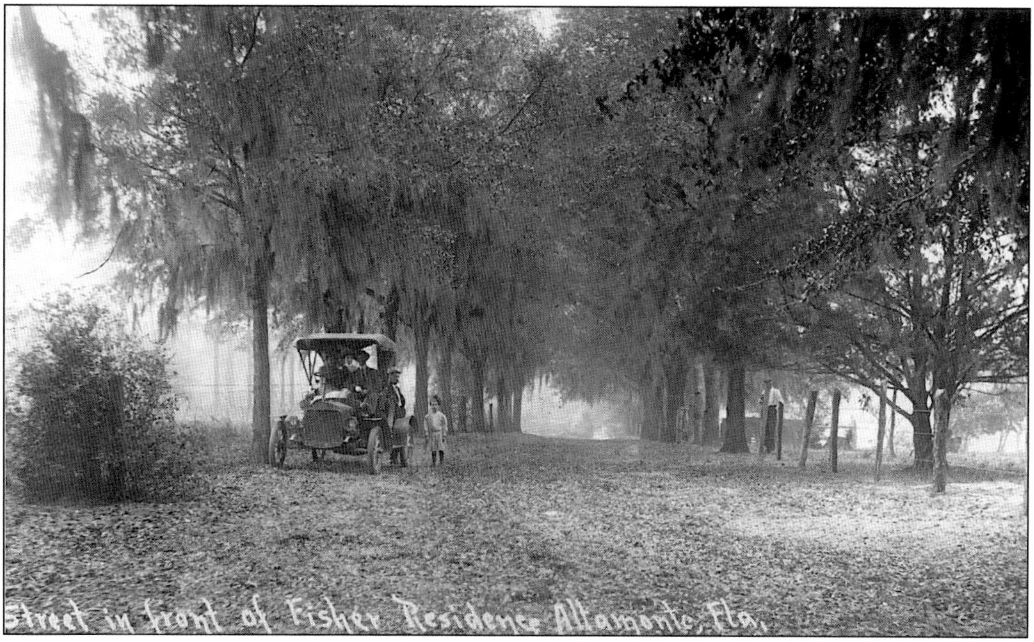

The Fullers prepare for a drive. Their car is shown along Salem Street in front of the Fisher residence.

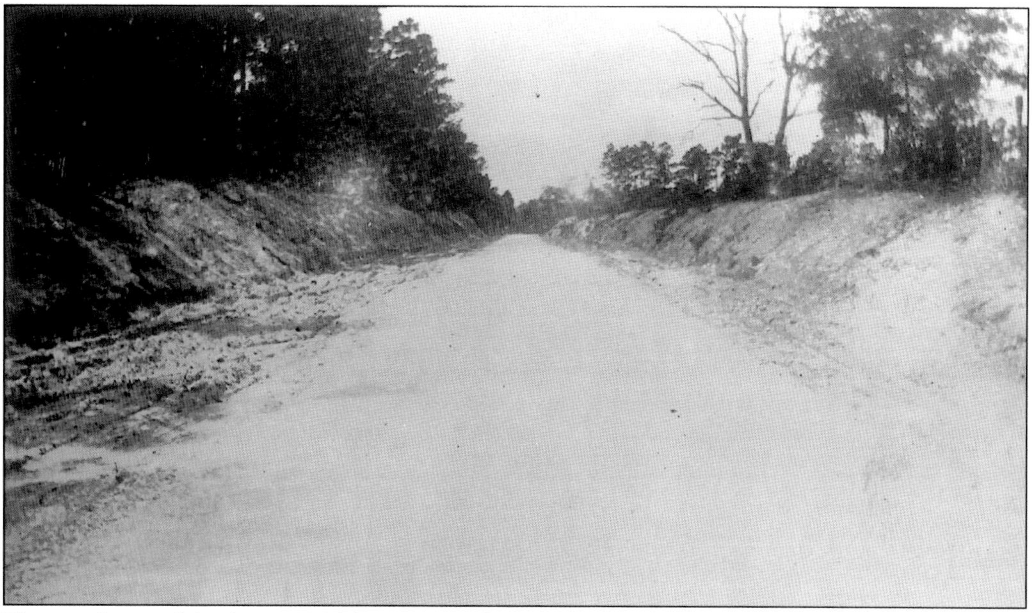
This is the road built in 1926 between Palm Springs and Longwood to Sanlando Springs. James Haithcox gave Calvin O. Black of Cleveland 400 lots to build an 18-hole golf course and clubhouse. Rollins College President Hamilton Holt joined the club, and Rollins students played on the golf course. Many new homes were built in the area of Sanlando Golf and Country Club and Sanlando Springs. The road followed the route of what today is State Road 434.

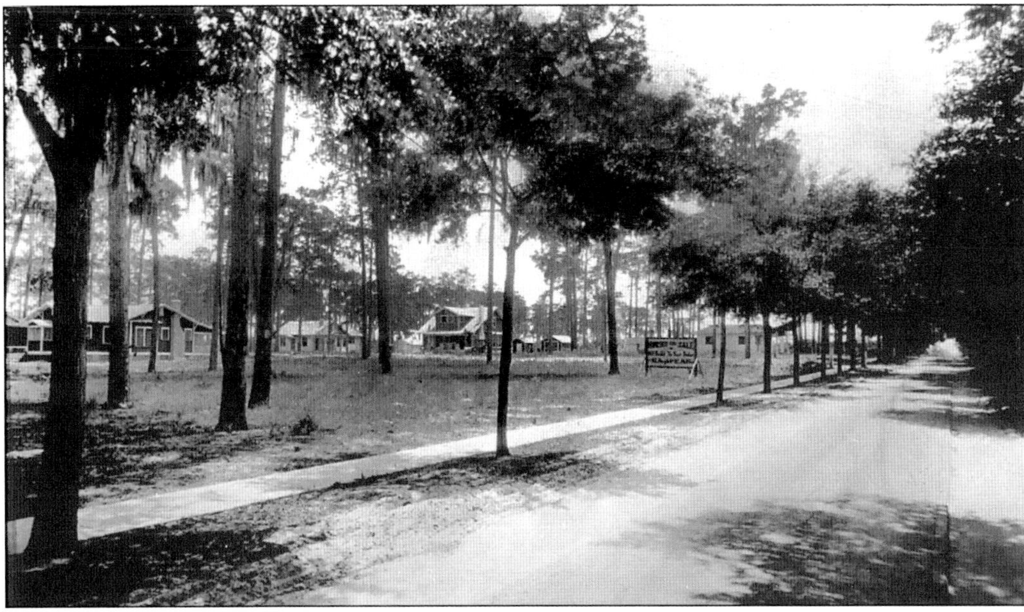

This property along the east side of Maitland Avenue, looking to the south toward Maitland in the 1920s, is now the Altamonte Springs City Library and Cultural Center.

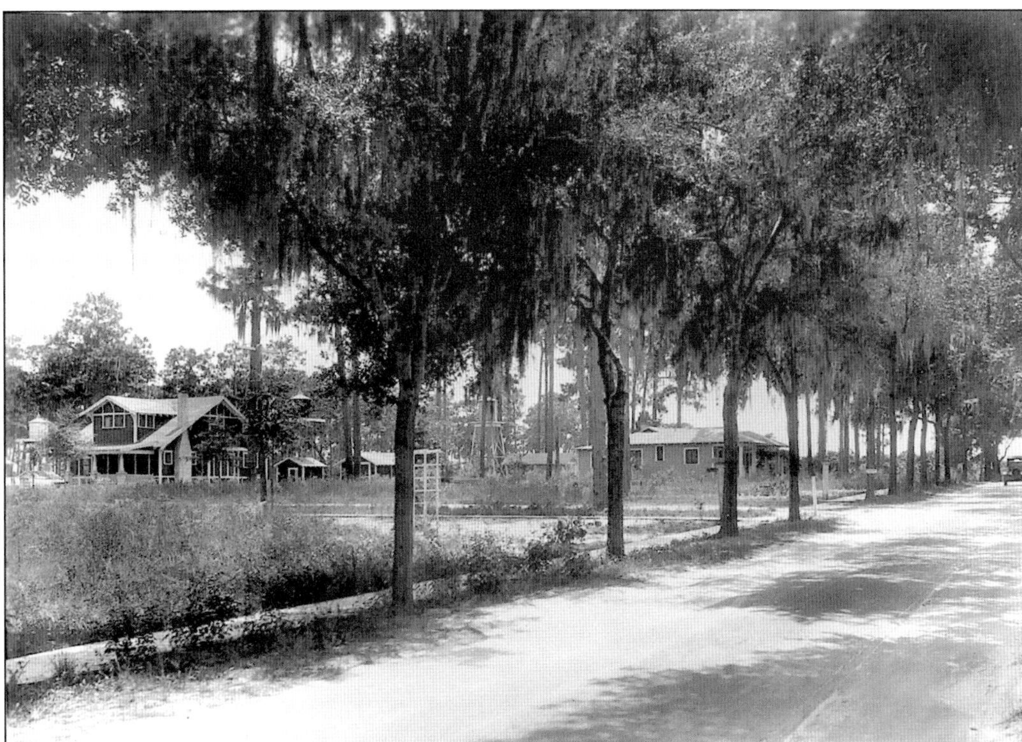

This is Maitland Avenue, looking south from Magnolia, in the 1920s.

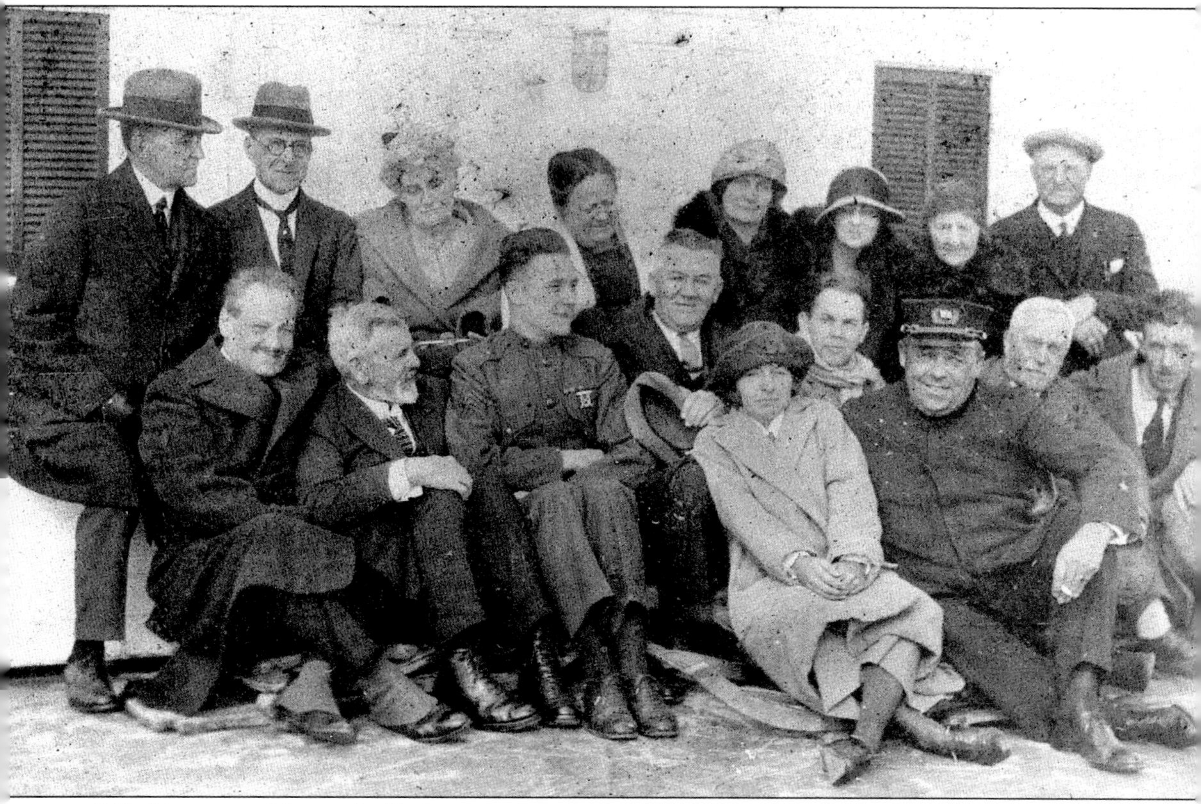

C.D. Haines and his wife, Katherine, shown second and third from the left on the top row, gather with others after the captain of their steamboat arrived in Sanford.

Three

A CONGRESSMAN'S WINTER HOME

Charles D. Haines, the son of a skilled cobbler, was born at Medusa in Albany County, New York, on June 9, 1856. He studied the telegraph as a child. It helped him win his first job as a train dispatcher. Promotions followed, and he became assistant superintendent, then railroad superintendent. Later, he joined his brothers and a sister in building and owning streetcar and railroad lines in the United States, Mexico, and Canada. In 1893, as the owner of the Kinderhook & Hudson Railroad, Haines won election to Congress as a Democrat. A re-election campaign failed, and Haines turned his interests to Florida. He joined the cluster of wealthy families who built fine winter homes among the tall pines and mossy oaks and along the spring-fed lakes.

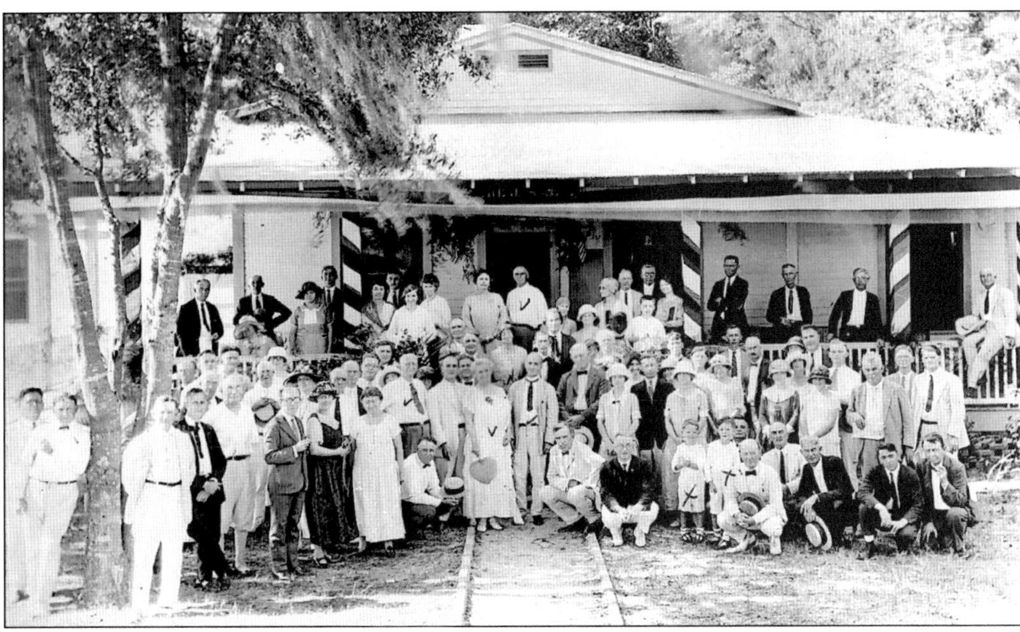

This large crowd gathered in 1923 in front of the Jasmine Theater during William Jennings Bryan's visit to the Haines winter home on Lake Orienta. Bryan stands in center on the back row in front of door.

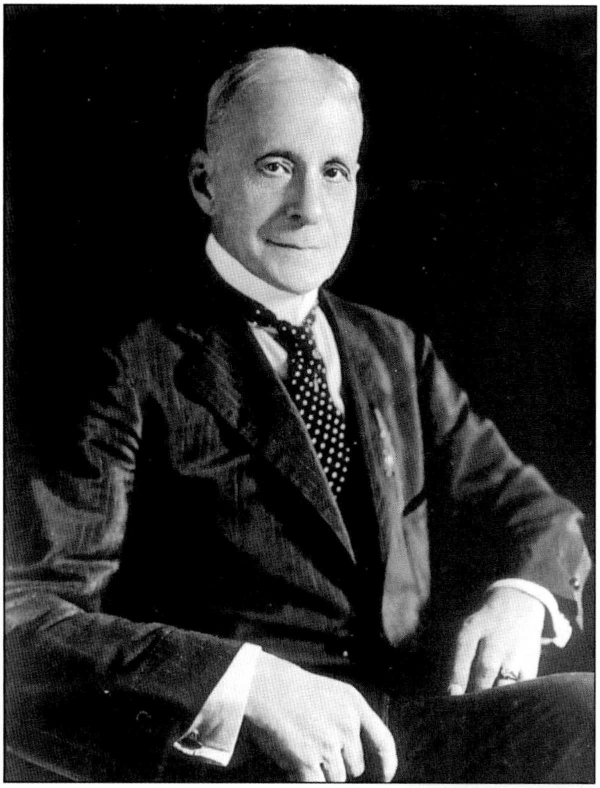

C.D. Haines was a wealthy man when he arrived in Altamonte Springs, and he enriched the community he helped to build. Haines came to Florida to relax at Altamonte Springs, a winter retreat on the South Florida Railroad where northerners with wealth came to soak up the sun and bathe in Florida's springs. The family rail business and their Altamonte ferneries were just a sample of his ventures. When a gambling win landed him ownership of property in Santo Domingo forested with mahogany, Haines had the trees cut down and shipped to Tampa, where he started a furniture business. His first visits to Florida were winter vacations in the 1890s. During a stay in Leesburg, he invested in kaolin mining in northwest Lake County. A geologist from the Massachusetts Institute of Technology had discovered the white clay used in manufacturing fine porcelain.

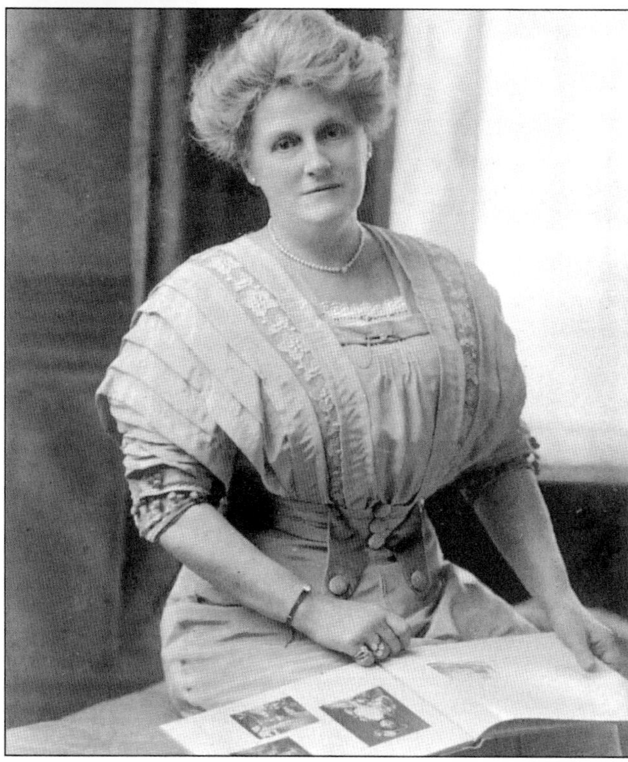

By the early 1900s, Former New York Congressman Charles Delemere "C.D." and his second wife, Katherine Haines, shown here, were spending their winters in Altamonte Springs. On the north shore of Lake Orienta, Haines built a winter home within a 200-acre orange grove. It was at the site of Lakepointe Apartments' Lake Meade Court. He named his retreat along Lake Orienta "The Ferns," a nod to the thriving fern-growing industry he helped bring to the winter resort town on the South Florida Railroad.

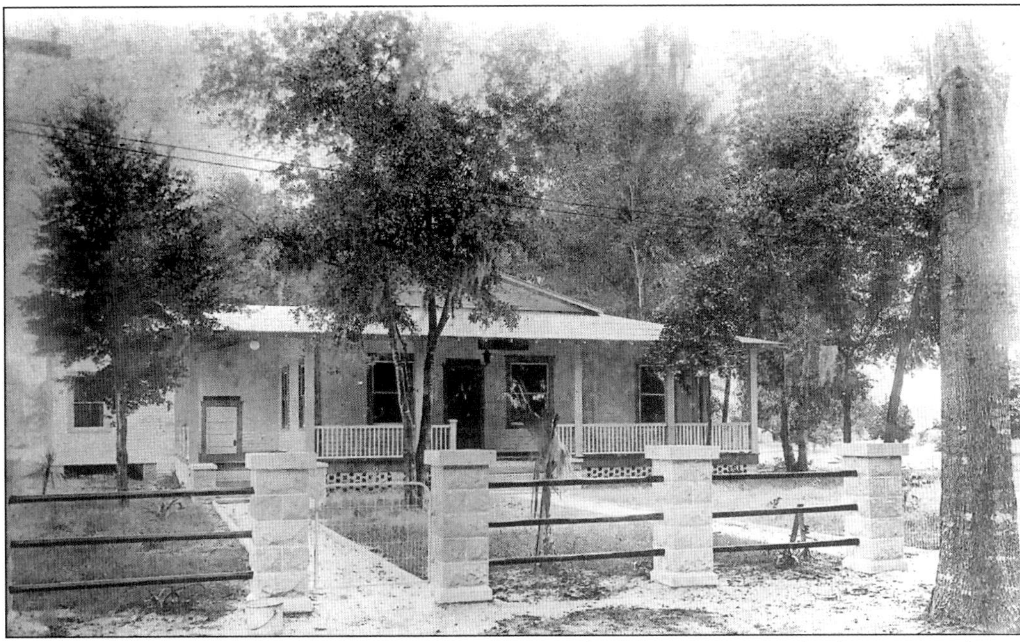

Across Orange Drive from the entrance to his winter home, C.D. Haines built a private theater for his wife, and named it the Jasmine, which survives today as one of Altamonte's architectural treasures. The Jasmine Theater was renovated as a residence in the 1930s. Haines built the Jasmine for social gatherings hosted by his wife.

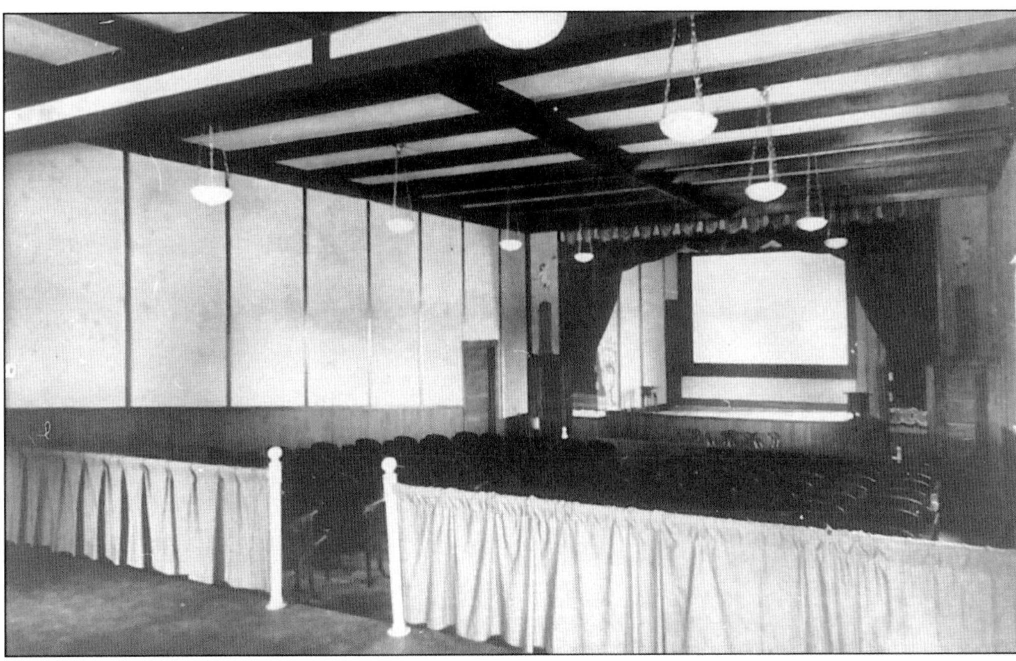

Shown here is the interior of the Jasmine before the theater was renovated as a residence. The Jasmine was the center of Altamonte's social circle. Each winter, Haines set aside one week to entertain guests from nearby towns at the theater and enjoy a tour of the lake aboard his party boat.

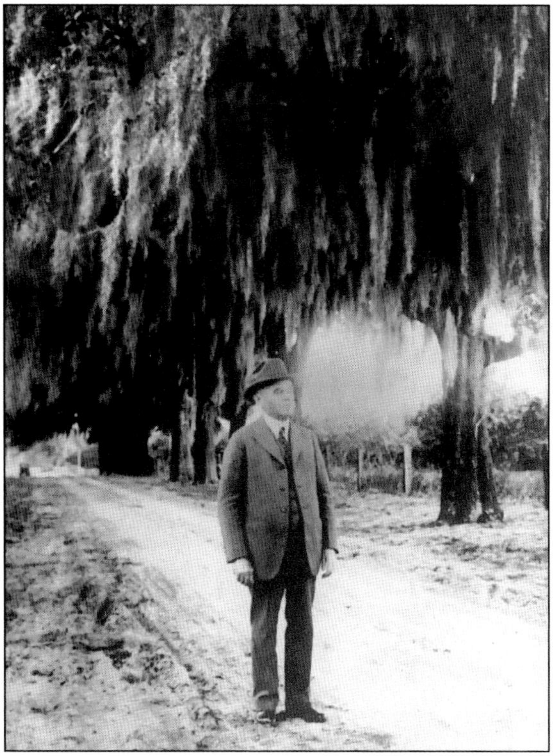

This is believed to be William Jennings Bryan standing at the entrance to the C.D. Haines home on Lake Orienta. Bryan had served in Congress with Haines and was a frequent guest in Altamonte Springs.

The Haines and guests gather for a dinner at the Jasmine during the 1923 visit of William Jennings Bryan, shown at the head of the table.

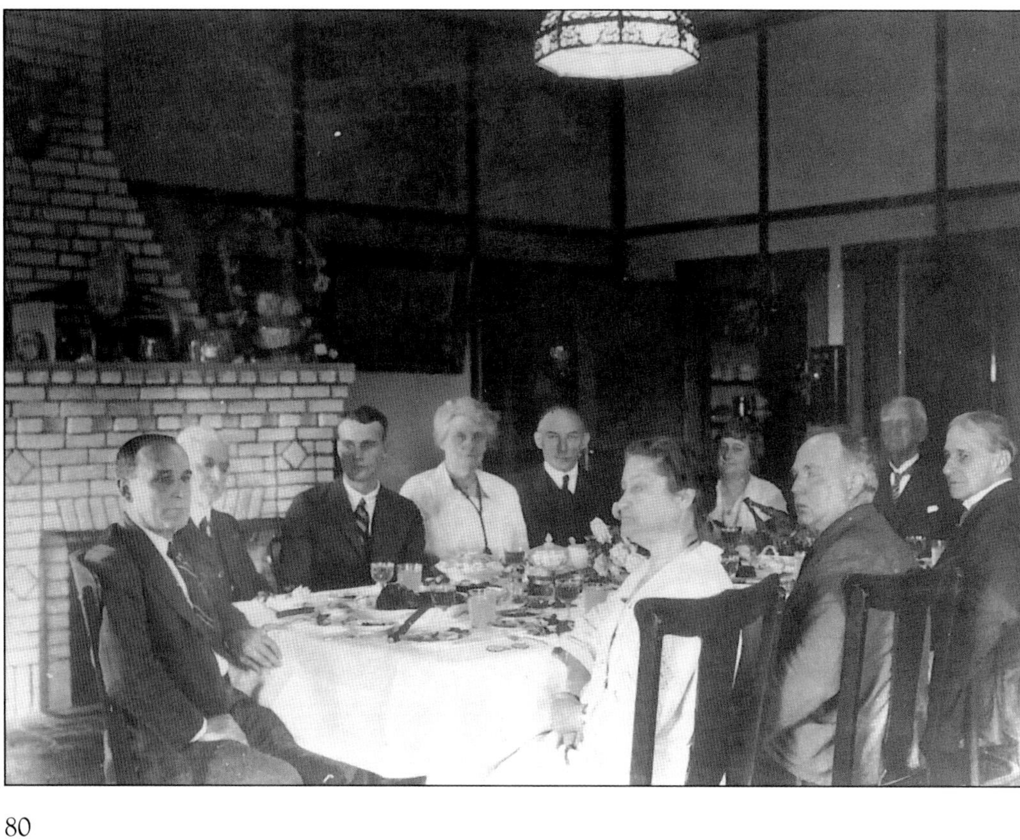

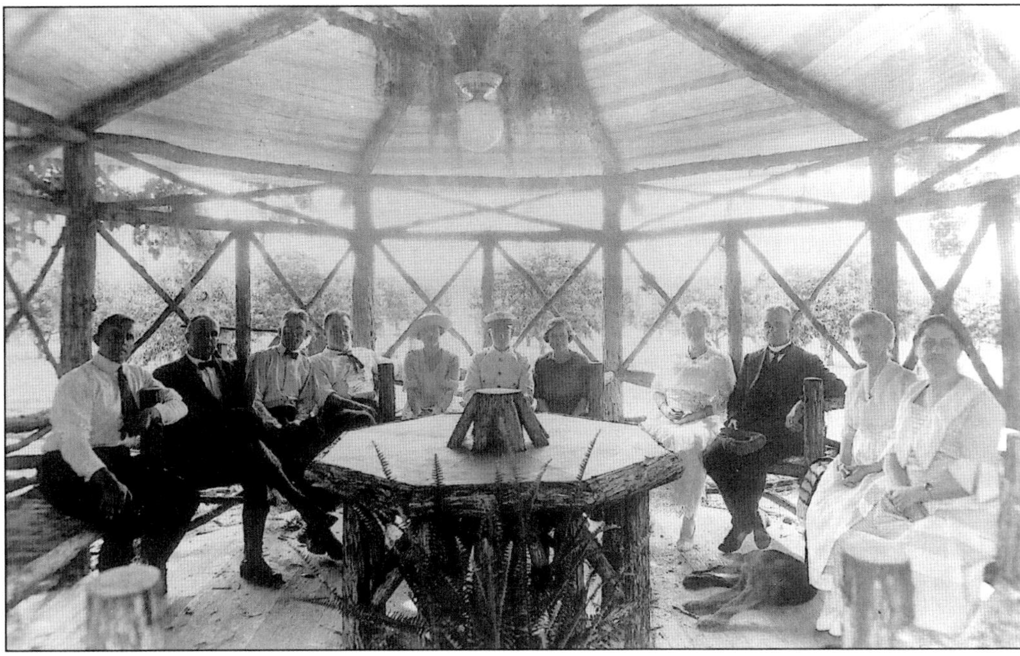

The Haines family and friends assemble inside a gazebo in the Haines groves on Lake Orienta in 1923 when William Jennings Bryan visited. The photo may have been taken before Bryant's arrival or after he left. He is not shown.

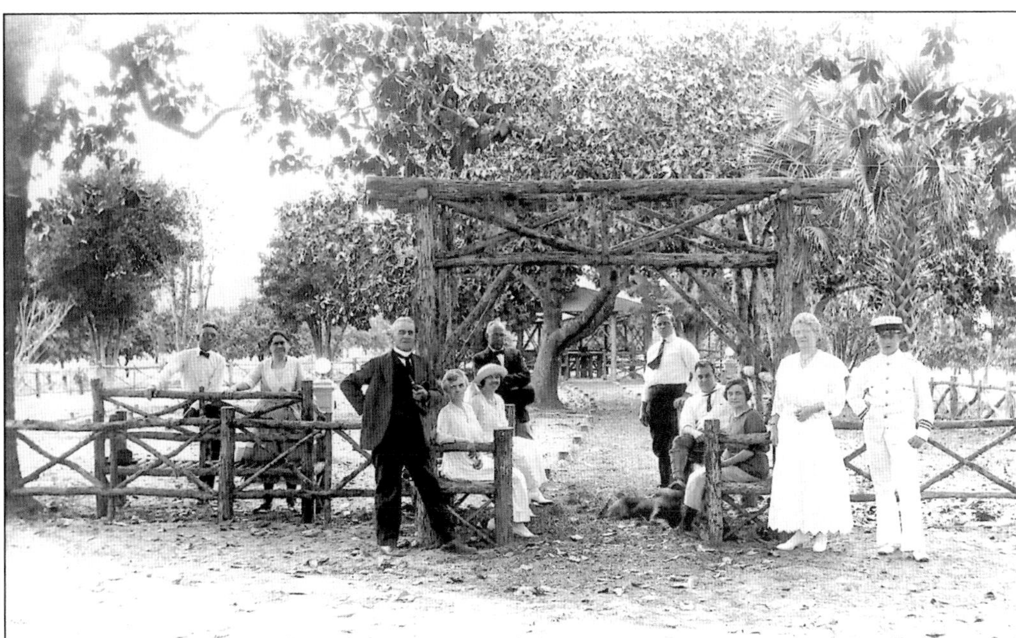

This 1923 photograph shows the Haines family and friends gathered at the entrance to the Lake Orienta grove that included a gazebo for entertainment. C.D. and Katherine Haines stand at the posts of the entrance gate. The man in the sailing uniform is Webber Haines. On the far left behind the fence is Howard Lyman.

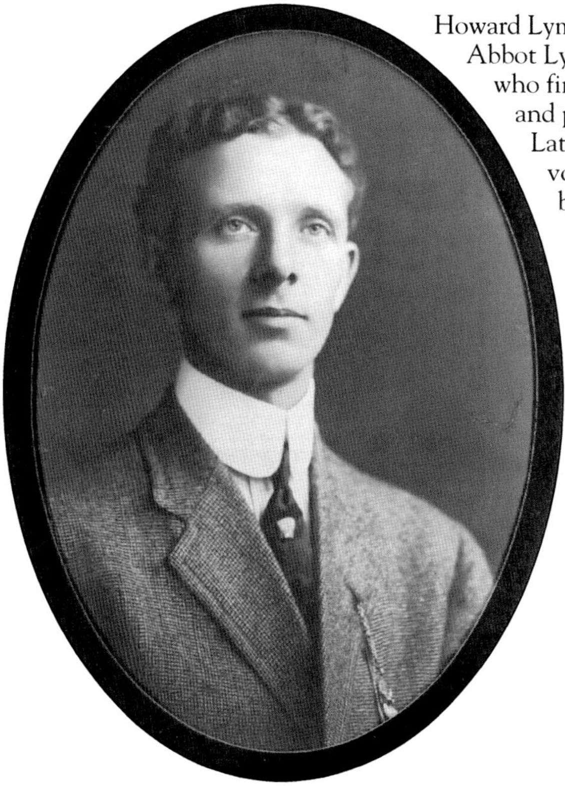

Howard Lyman, shown here, and his wife, Emma Abbot Lyman, were New York entertainers who first came to Altamonte Springs as guests and performers at the Jasmine Theater. Later, they became community leaders, voting to create the town and Howard being elected to serve on the county school board. The Lyman School was named after him and opened in 1924, the same year he died. The original Lyman, now the campus of Milwee Middle School, became a gathering place for various community events.

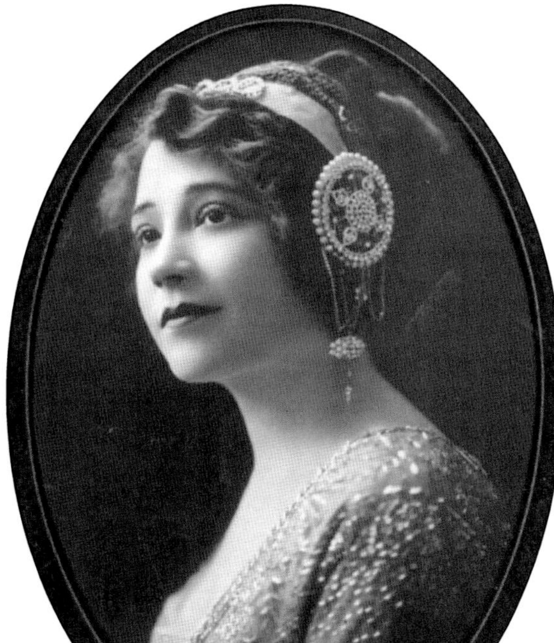

Emma Abbot Lyman, shown here, organized activities at the Community House, which sat on the site that now includes the city library. The Community House later became the city hall and served as a meeting place for the chamber of commerce and civic and religious groups. As chairman of the town's board of aldermen in 1925, Lyman often served as mayor when B.L. Maltbie was away on business. To keep civic organizations active during the Great Depression, she sponsored community picnics and political rallies. Lyman also formed a civic association that took over maintenance of the center when the town was having trouble keeping up with the bills.

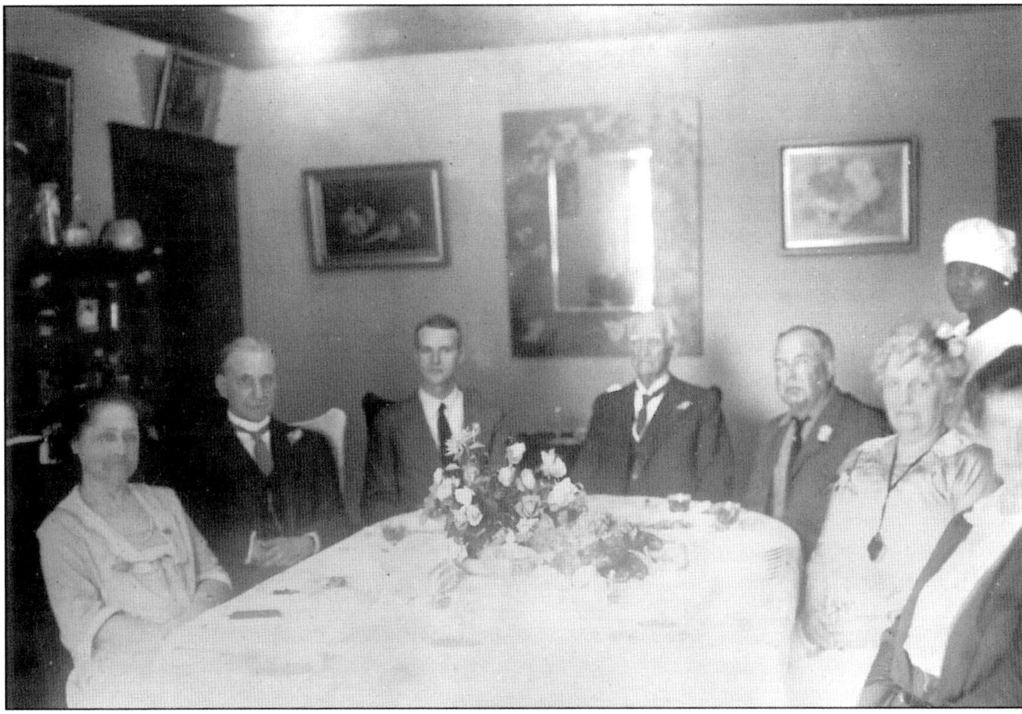

C.D. and Katherine Haines sit opposite each other during a dinner party at the Jasmine. Katherine's brother, Simone Phillips, sits at the head of the table.

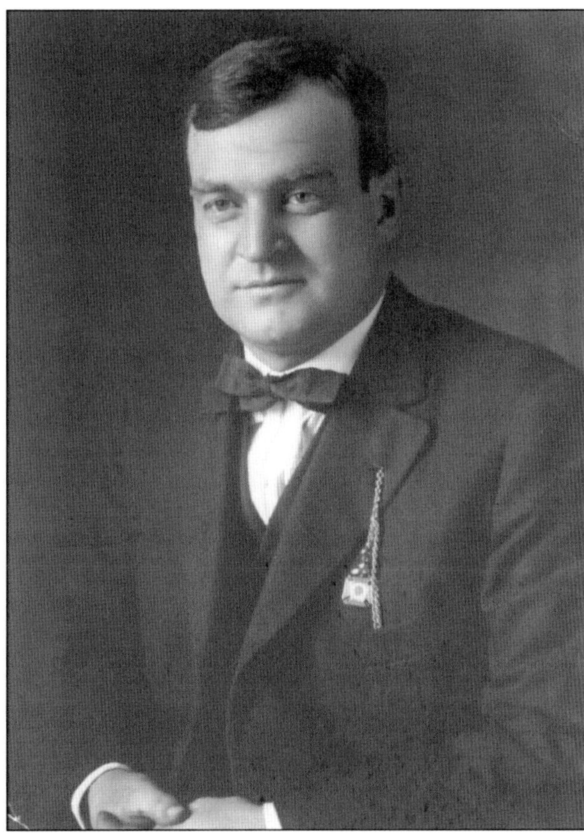

Benjamin F. Haines helped his father, C.D. Haines, establish south Seminole County as the home of the world's largest ferneries.

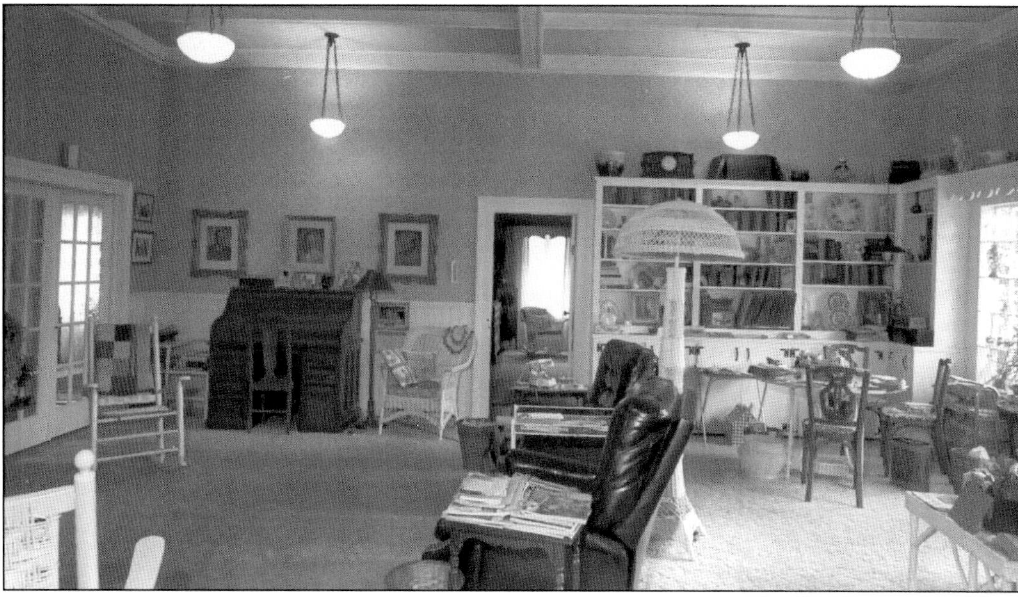

Before the Jasmine Theater was renovated as a house, this area was the theater seating. The wall with the doorway to the bedroom was added. The stage was where the bedroom window can be seen through the doorway.

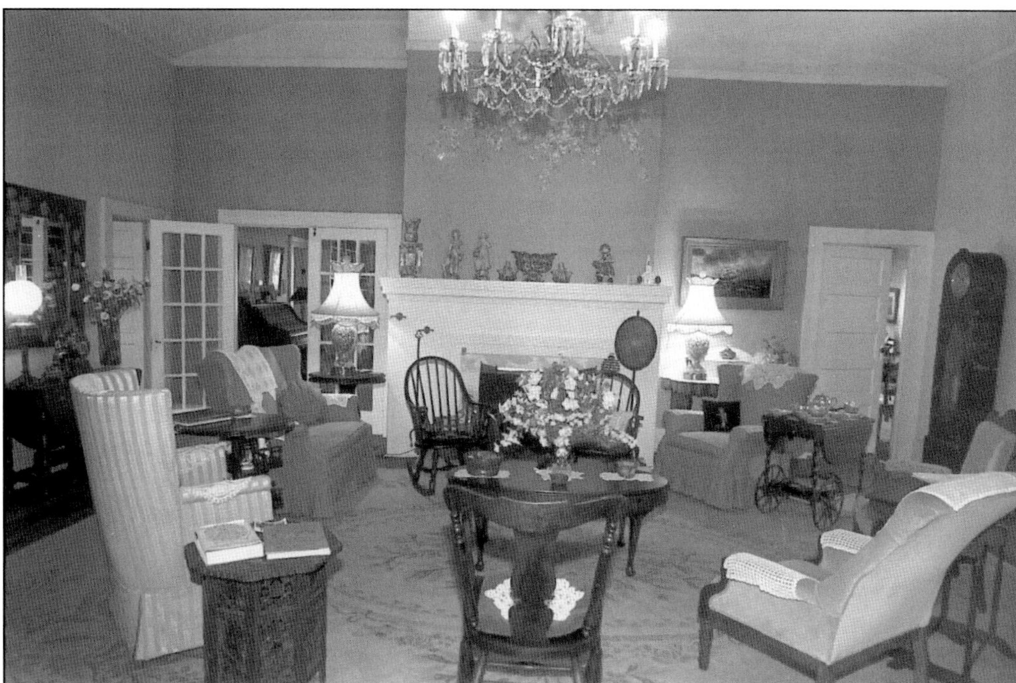

The living room area of the Jasmine Theater was once the lobby. Haines once entertained the idea of turning the theater into a retirement home for journalists, but plans for the National Newspaper Men's Home fell through when the International Press Association wanted more land than Haines could offer. The theater at 447 Orange Drive off Boston Avenue was later remodeled as a residence.

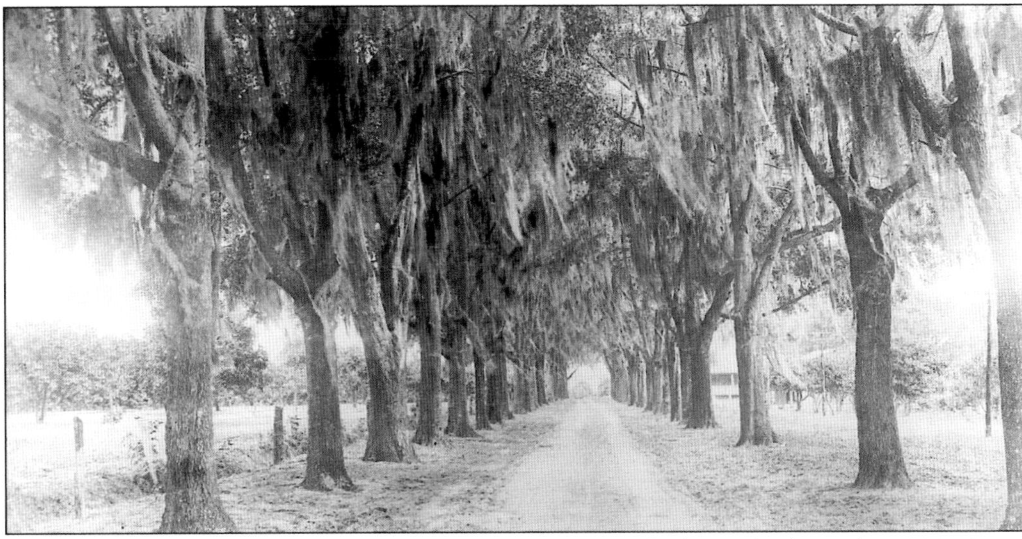

This driveway led to the home of Benjamin F. Haines, which was built in the 1920s during Florida's real estate boom. C.D. Haines, Benjamin's father, died in 1929 as the nation slipped into the Great Depression, and the son became the estate's sole owner. Benjamin Haines would later attempt to dissolve the town his father helped create. Because much of his property was farmland and citrus groves, he did not see the need to pay city taxes.

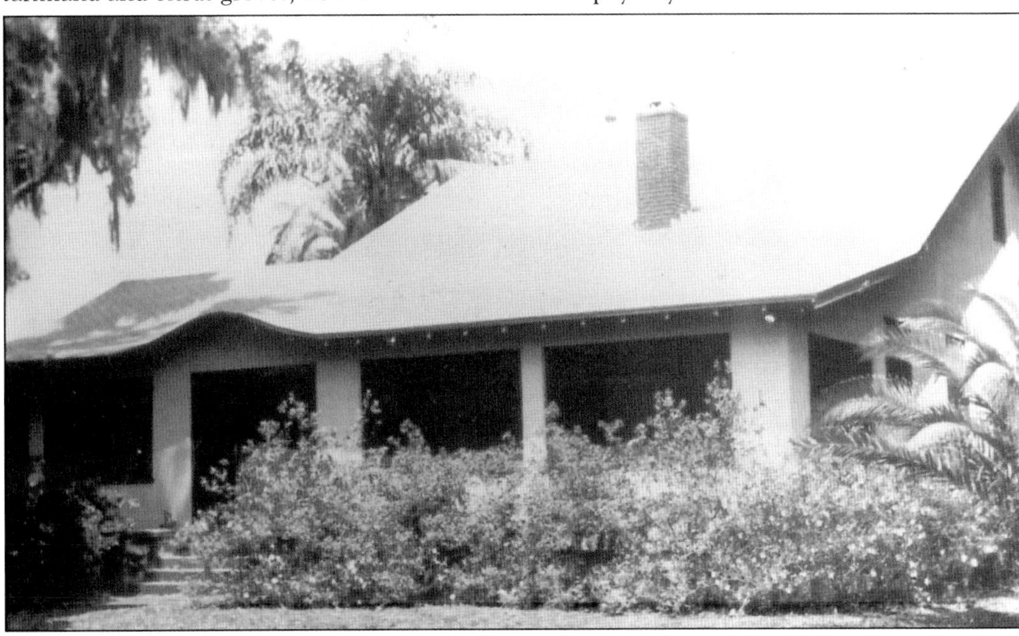

This was the home of Benjamin F. Haines during the boomdays of the 1920s. Once the Great Depression struck, tax money dropped as people stopped buying lots for new houses. Several major development companies had closed down. The railroad even closed the depot. Haines led a tax revolt by farm and grove owners in 1927 to abolish the city. A referendum failed in 1931, but Haines won election as mayor in 1932. Two relatives, E.T. Haines and Webber B. Haines, along with their political allies, won election as aldermen. They cut the budget. Haines filed suits with others to exclude larger amounts of their agricultural land from the city limits. The courts trimmed the town's size in half for the rest of the 1930s.

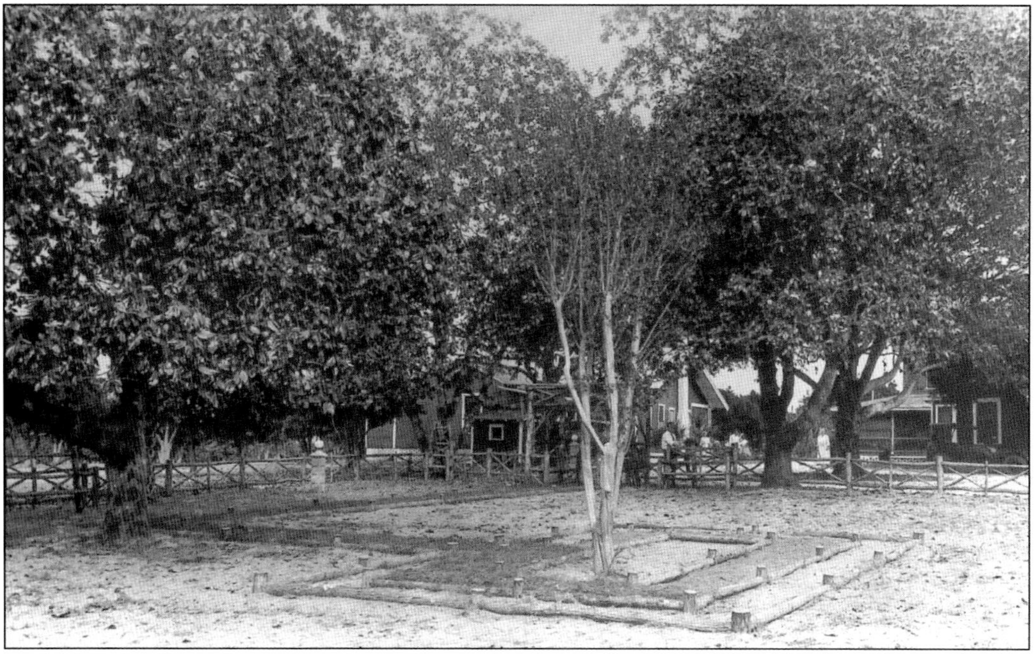

This property was located between the Kingsley house on the right and the Haines house on the left. George Kingsley was one of the Altamonte Springs property owners who opposed creating the new county of Seminole and failed in the efforts to have their land restored to Orange County. He later joined efforts to create the municipal government of Altamonte Springs, serving as one of the first seven aldermen, and was one of the stock investors in the Haines ferneries.

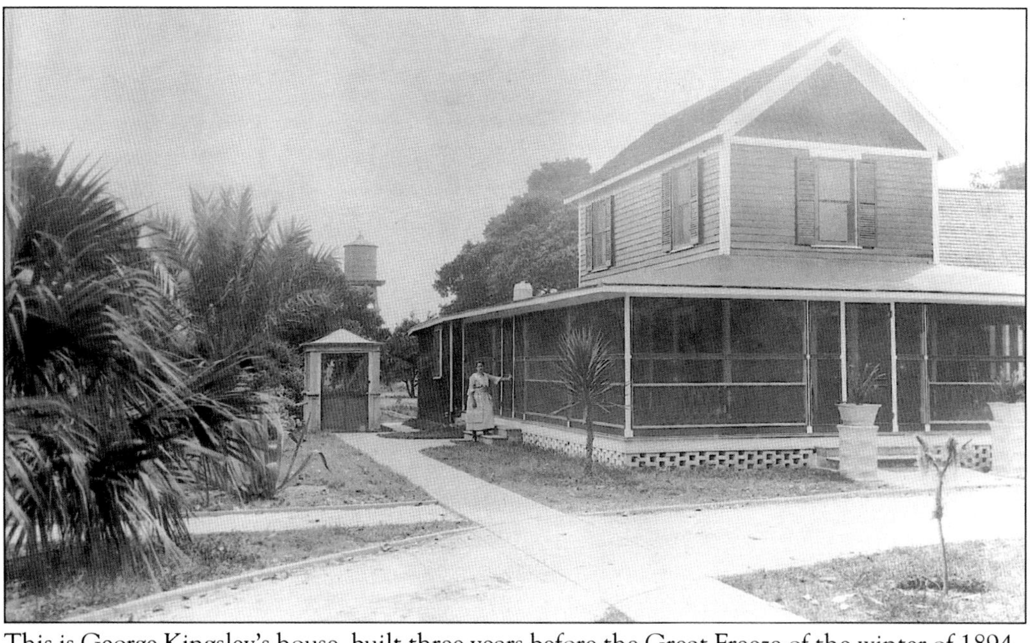

This is George Kingsley's house, built three years before the Great Freeze of the winter of 1894–1895. Lida Kingsley of Round Lake, New York, shown at the steps, was the first wife of C.D. Haines. She died in 1913.

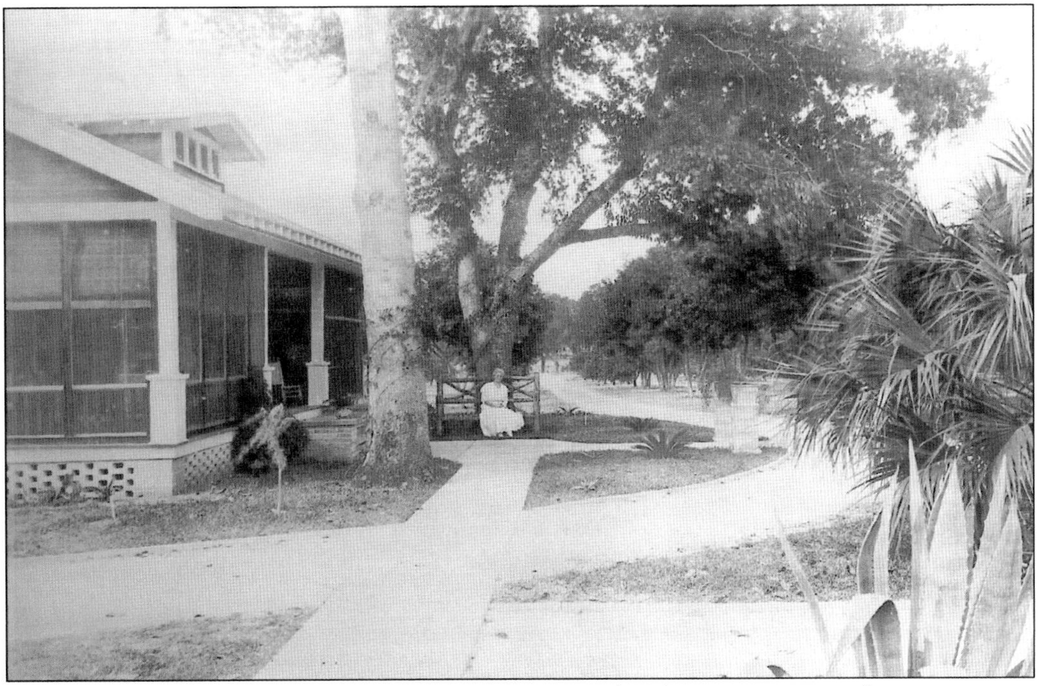

Katherine Haines sits outside her house in 1917. The driveway is now the entrance to Lakepoint Apartments.

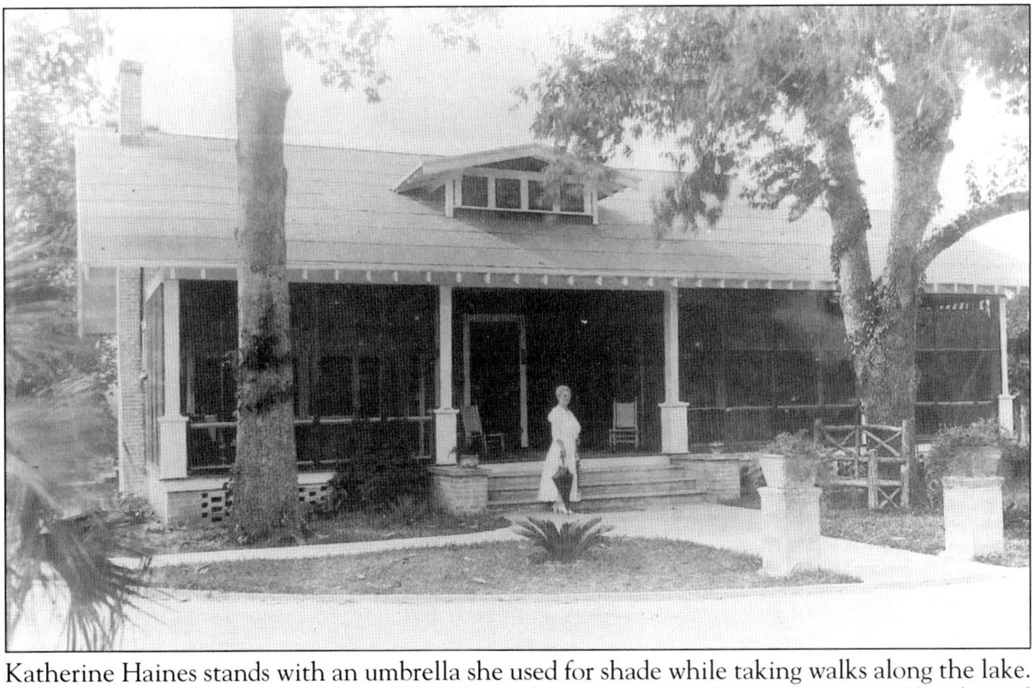

Katherine Haines stands with an umbrella she used for shade while taking walks along the lake. The house was a Sears and Roebuck "kit house," prefabricated, shipped by rail to Florida, and assembled in Altamonte Springs in 1917.

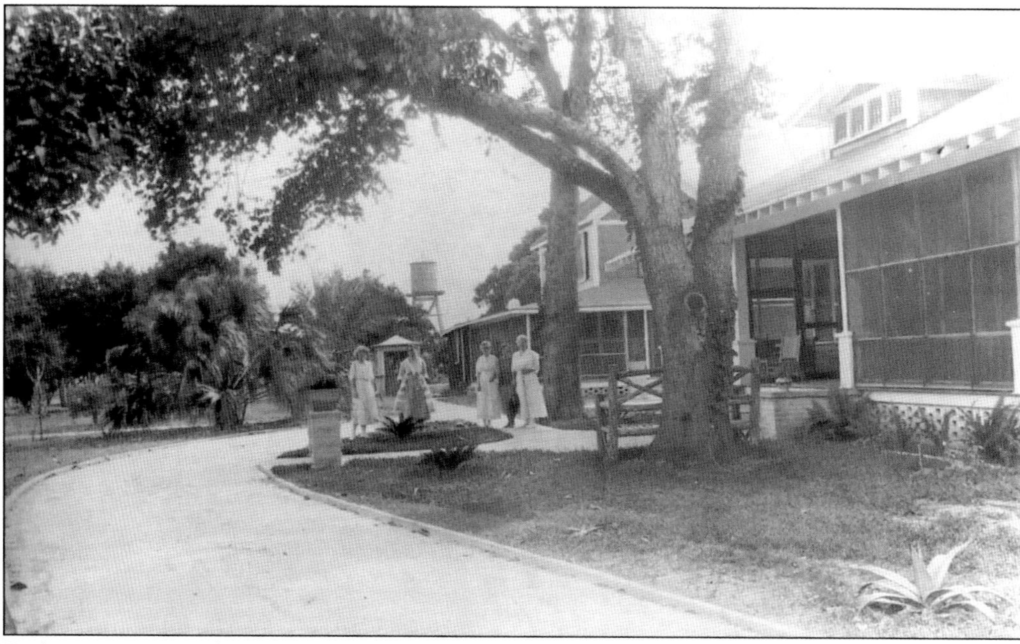

Katherine Haines, shown on the far right, stands with others between the Kingsley and Haines houses. A gasoline engine pumped water from the lake to the tower in the background to provide irrigation for the Haines fernery and groves.

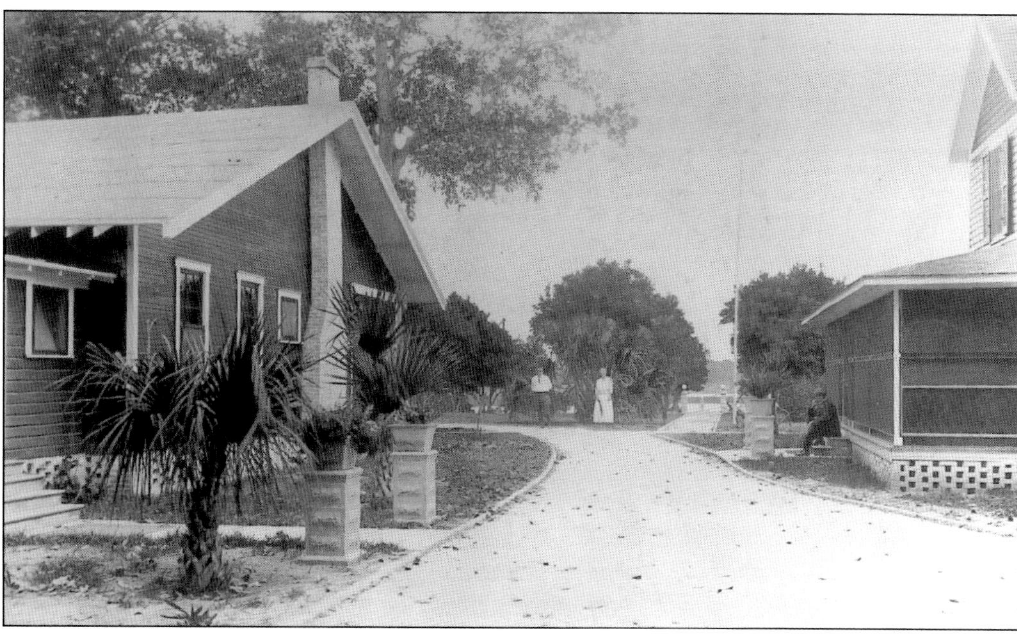

This view of the Kingsley and Haines houses shows the walkway to the lakefront. At night, the generators that Haines had installed provided electric lighting. He also provided lights for the walkways between the houses and along the lakefront.

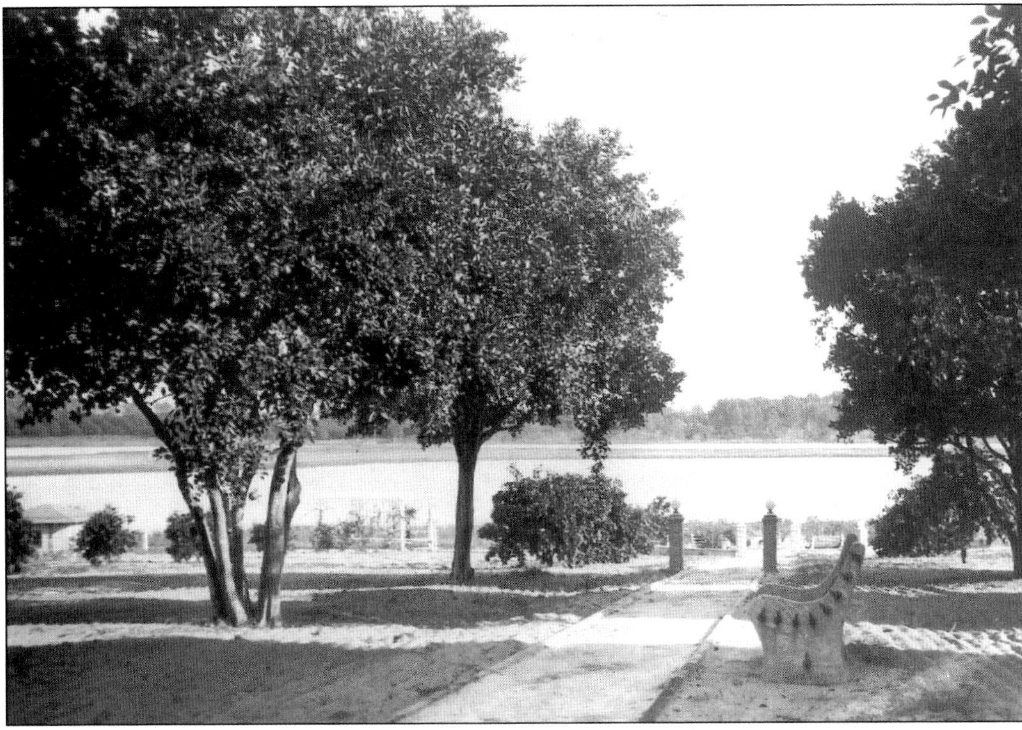

This walkway leads from the Kingsley and Haines houses to Lake Orienta.

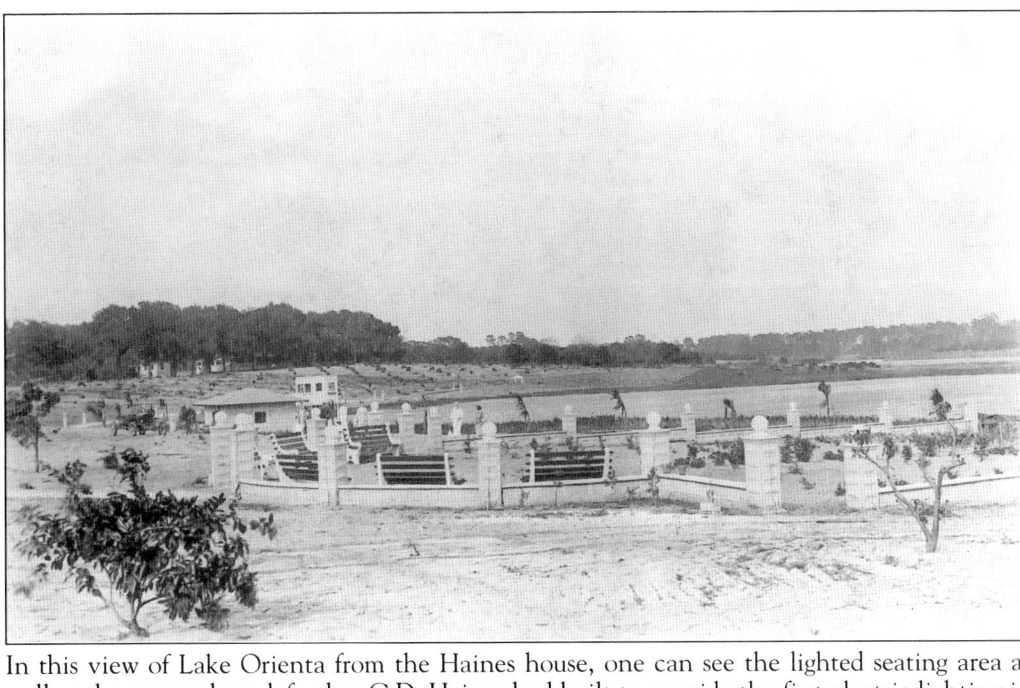

In this view of Lake Orienta from the Haines house, one can see the lighted seating area as well as the powerplant, left, that C.D. Haines had built to provide the first electric lighting in Altamonte Springs.

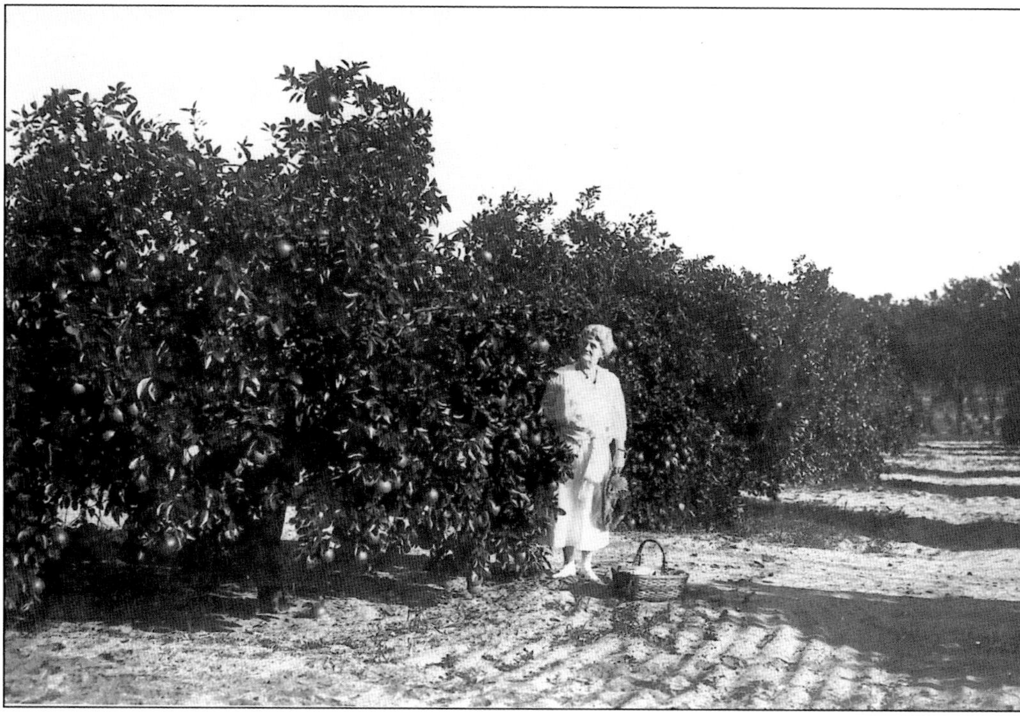

Katherine Haines picks oranges at one of the groves on the Haines property west of Lake Orienta.

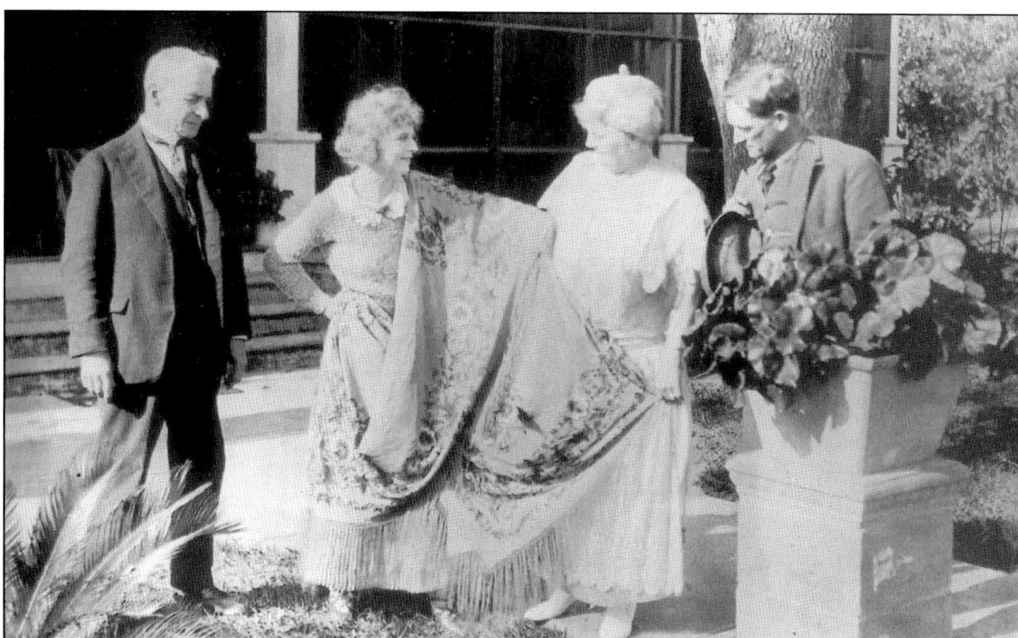

Katherine Haines, shown second from the right, displays a shawl once owned by King Maximilian and Carlotta of Mexico. C.D. Haines, shown on the left, bought the shawl for $20,000 in the 1920s, and it remains in the family. The photo was taken prior to 1929 in front of their house on Lake Orienta.

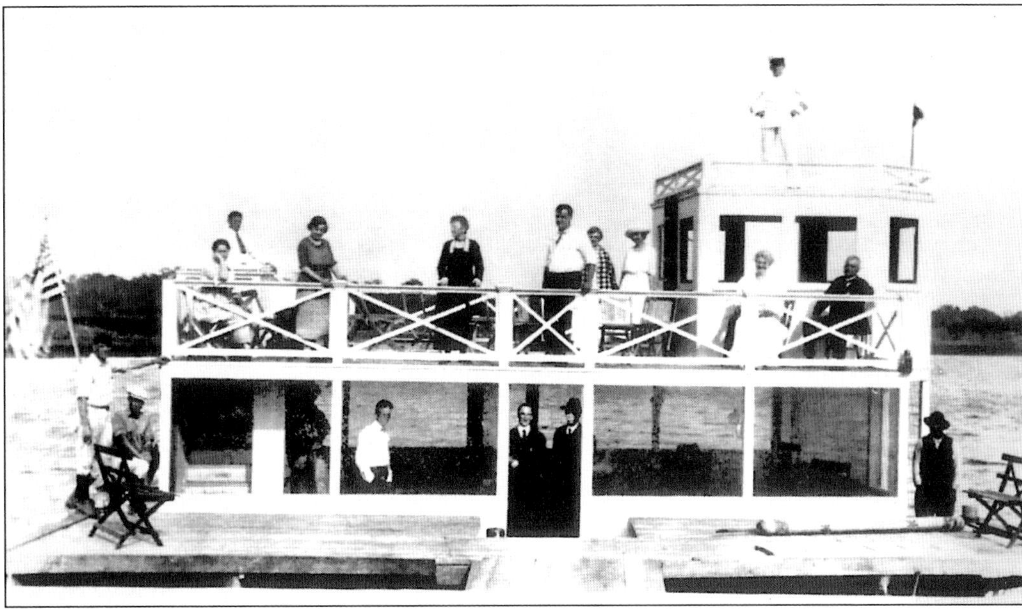

This is the double-decked, 50-passenger party boat that C.D. Haines bought for his wife to entertain guests. The boat was painted with the misspelled name "Kathryn." Katherine and C.D. Haines are seated in front of the wheelhouse. The man standing above in the sailing uniform is Webber Haines. The boat was built in sections at a Jacksonville shipyard in the 1920s and assembled on Lake Orienta. Guests were often treated to a cruise on the lake, a barbecue, and afterwards, shows at the Jasmine. Overloaded with revelers one night in 1925, the boat sank. Many believe its remains are at the bottom of Lake Orienta.

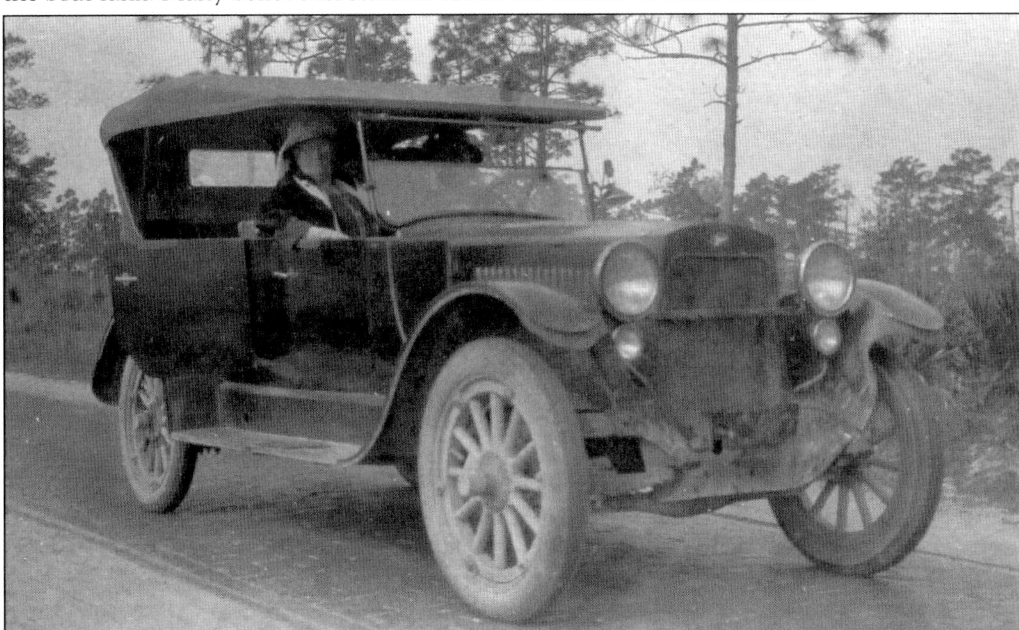

Katherine Haines rides in the passenger seat of a touring car in the 1920s heading south on Maitland Avenue when it was a nine-foot-wide brick road with concrete borders. A short stretch of this brick road survives today around Maitland's Lake Lilly.

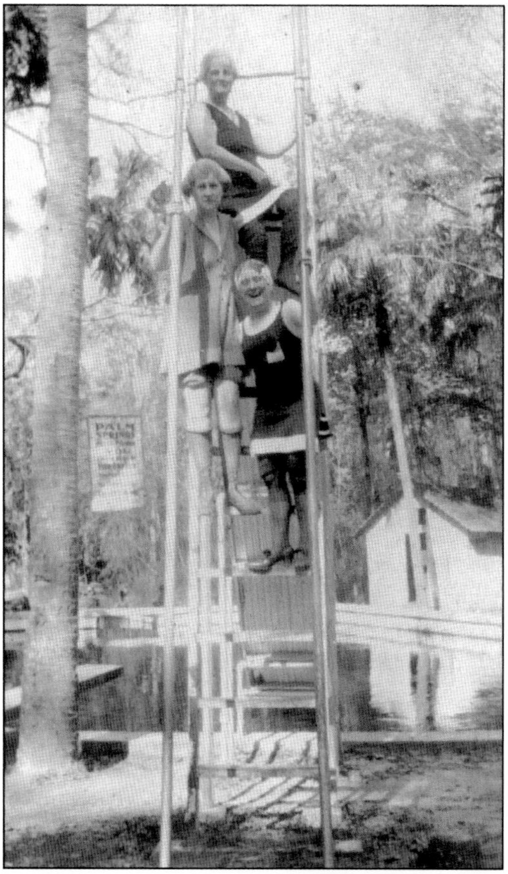

Katherine Haines, shown at the top, poses with friends on the ladder of the slide at the Palm Springs pool in 1918. Newspaper reporters and advertising promoted Altamonte's many springs, suggesting bathing as a cure for many illnesses. The smiles here suggest the cooling "medicinal qualities" of the springs were working.

Katherine Haines, in the center, takes a morning swim with her friends at Palm Springs in 1918.

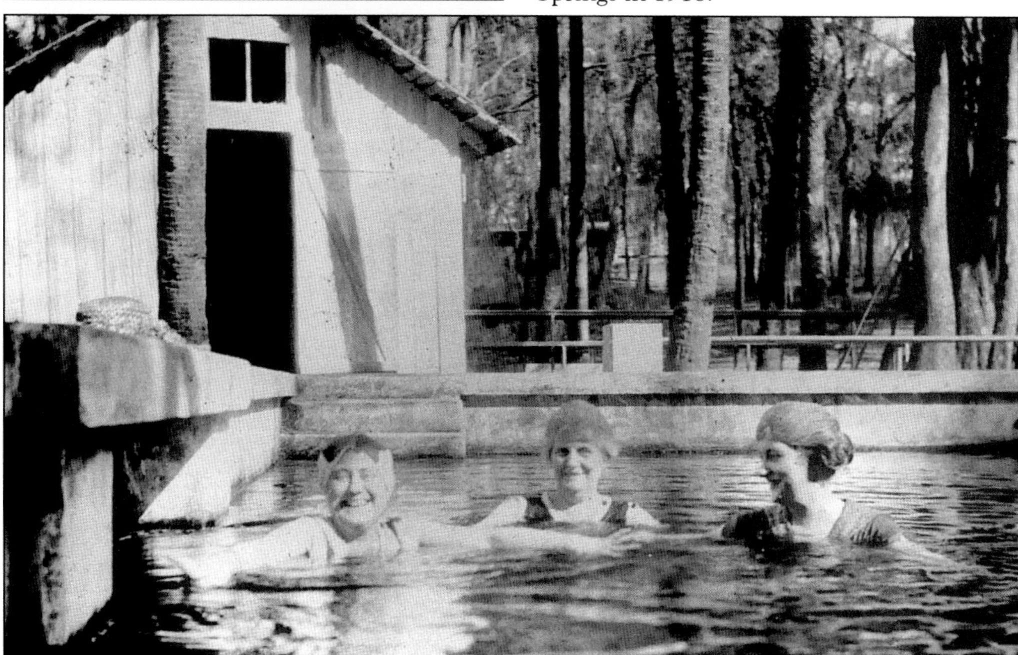

Four

AGRICULTURE BUILDS A COMMUNITY

Altamonte Springs had its ups and downs as a resort town, but agriculture provided year-round employment and its farms and groves fueled the regional economy. Hard freezes in the late 1800s ruined the citrus groves, but timber, sawmill, and turpentine companies thrived well into the 1930s. Commerce near the railroad depot and Fuller's Store peaked in the 1920s because of the world market for the area's ferns. The Lake Orienta ferneries were one of the hobbies entrepreneur C.D. Haines started because he could not just sit around. The hobby he started in Florida to fill up his free time provided jobs and industries for the young town. The Haines ferneries were the world's largest, holding that distinction for nearly three decades before 1940. Ferneries later reached into Casselberry and Fern Park. And, the orange groves returned, once again making a leader in orange packing and juice manufacturing.

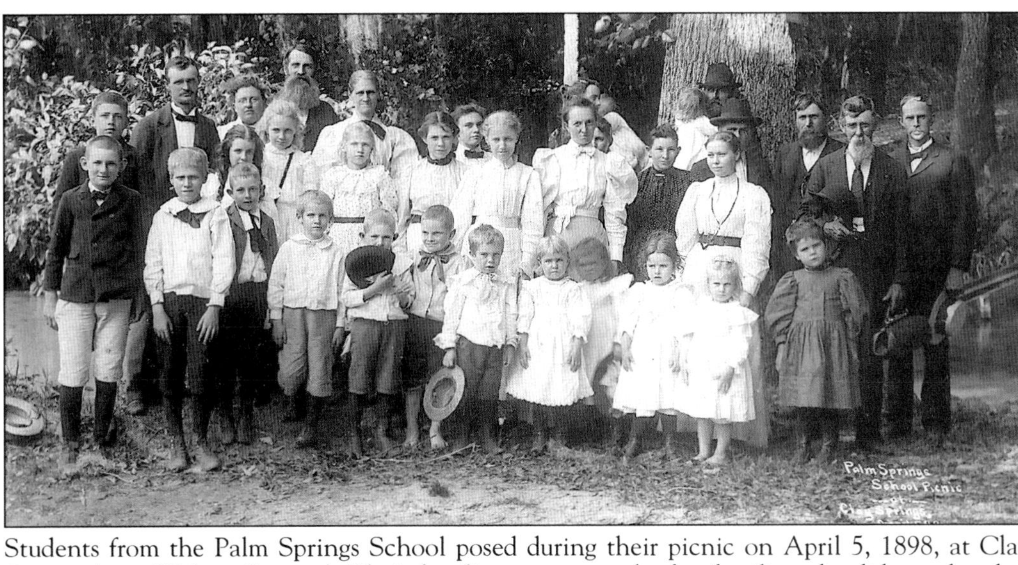

Students from the Palm Springs School posed during their picnic on April 5, 1898, at Clay Springs (now Wekiva Springs). Their families are among the few families who did not abandon their homes and groves after back-to-back hard freezes during the winter of 1894–1895, which killed nearly every citrus grove in Central Florida.

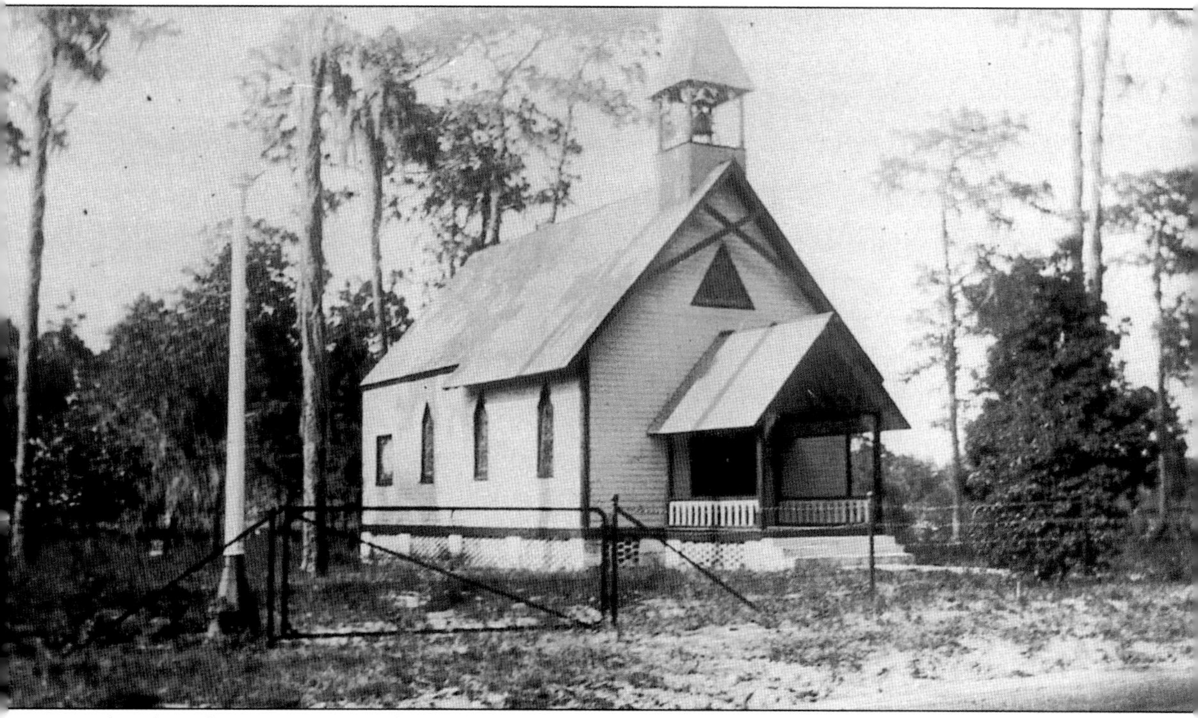

The chapel at Hermits Trail stands as a memorial to the Great Freeze and the early settlers whose economy was destroyed during the bitter winter of 1894–1895. Notice the street light, which was an addition in the 1920s. Most people today call this the Altamonte Chapel, and it sits off State Road 436 just east of Maitland Avenue in Altamonte Springs. It was once the Lake Brantley Union Church. Josiah B. Clouser, the master carpenter recognized by the state through its Great Floridians program, built it between 1882 and 1885 as a gift to the community from Bostonian Carlos Cushing. The site on Lake Brantley was near the Cushing family home, also built by Clouser. Cushing was an investor in Longwood founder E.W. Henck's three-story hotel. The chapel was abandoned after the winter of 1894–1895, which cut that season's fruit harvest to 20 percent of the previous year and killed most of Central Florida's orange trees. Many of the people who relied on citrus in the early communities of Lake Brantley, Altamont, Palm Springs, Forest City, Piedmont, and Glen Ethel packed up and left.

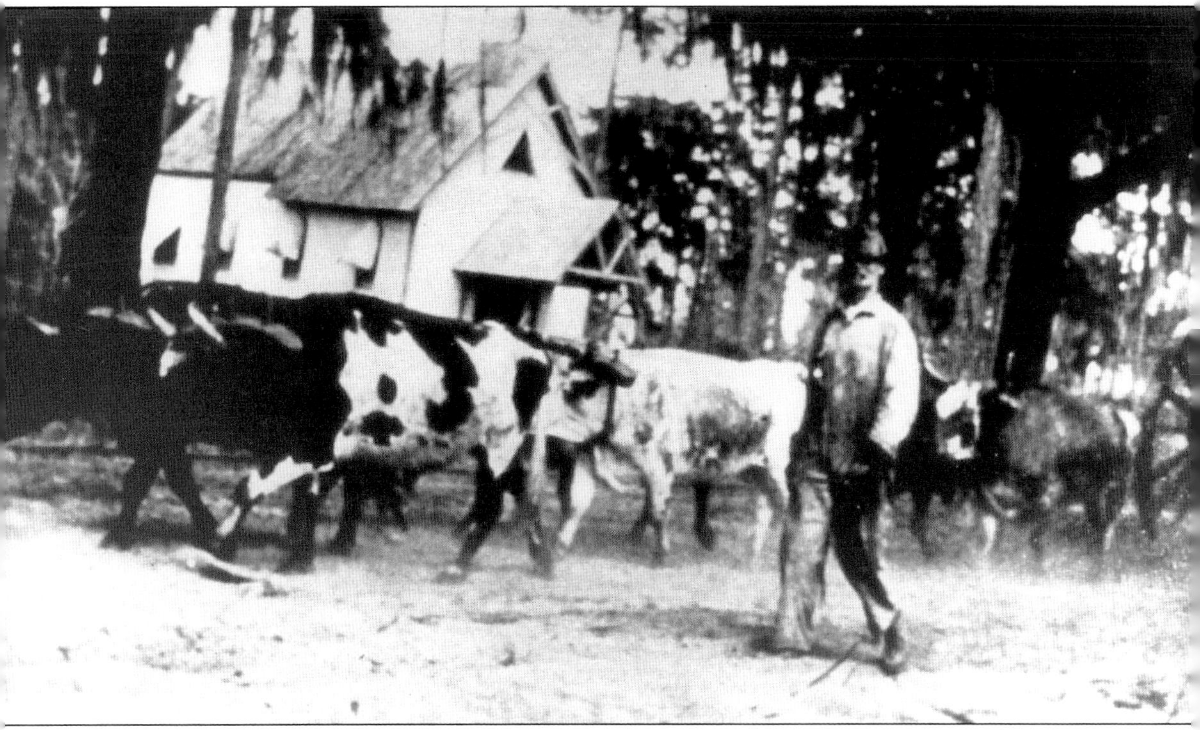

Ollie Braddock, who worked for the Fargo Lumber Co. owned by B.D. McIntosh, drives three teams of oxen pulling a lumber wagon along a dirt trail that later became Altamonte Avenue (State Road 436). The landmark Altamonte Chapel is visible in the background. A decade after the chapel was abandoned at its Lake Brantley site, citrus grower Arthur Fuller and wealthy Bostonian Maxwell McIntyre stumbled on the church in the woods while hunting. After moving the chapel to its current site near Hermits Trail Park, Fuller and building contractor Joseph Lewis renovated it. The chapel served the winter residents of Altamonte Springs and the guests at the Altamonte Hotel. George and Louise Lewton owned the land where the chapel was built. Rollins College accepted the deed as tuition for the Lewtons' daughter. McIntyre, a winter resident from New Hartford, New York, who in 1906 bought the Altamonte Hotel and much of the surrounding land, paid Rollins College $600 for the sanctuary. McIntyre's nearby 15-room winter home is known today as the Bradlee-McIntyre house, which was moved in the 1970s to Longwood's historic district.

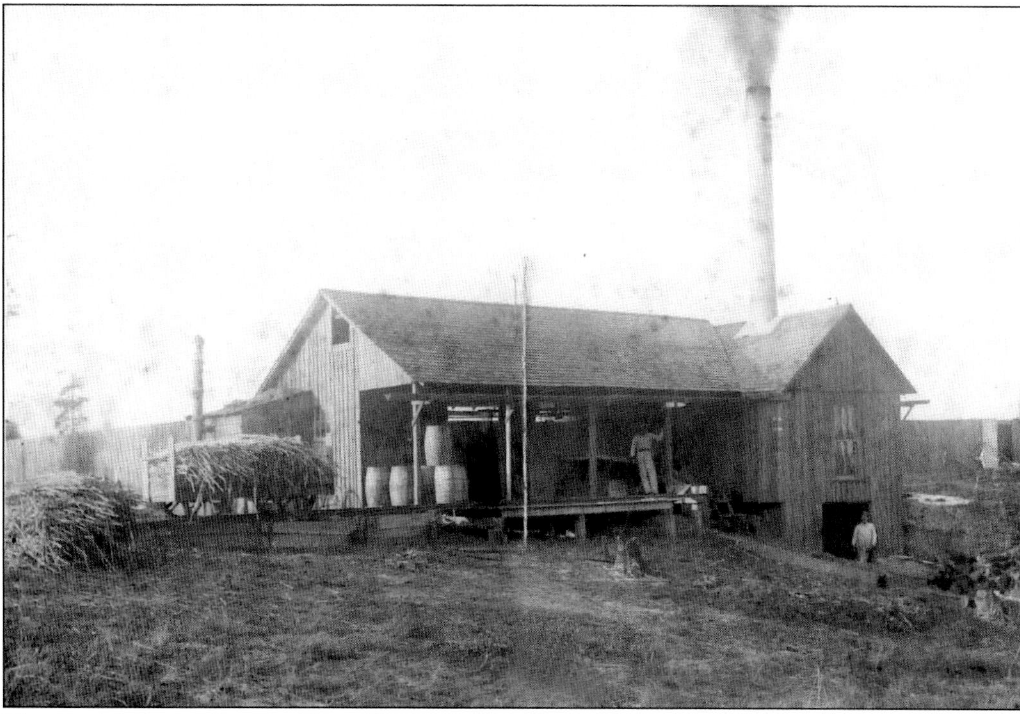

This is the steam-driven sugar cane mill at Spring Lake. Arthur H. Fuller managed Henry Westinghouse's land that included 10 acres of Japanese sugar cane, 2 acres of pineapples, and Westinghouse's Spring Lake Grove.

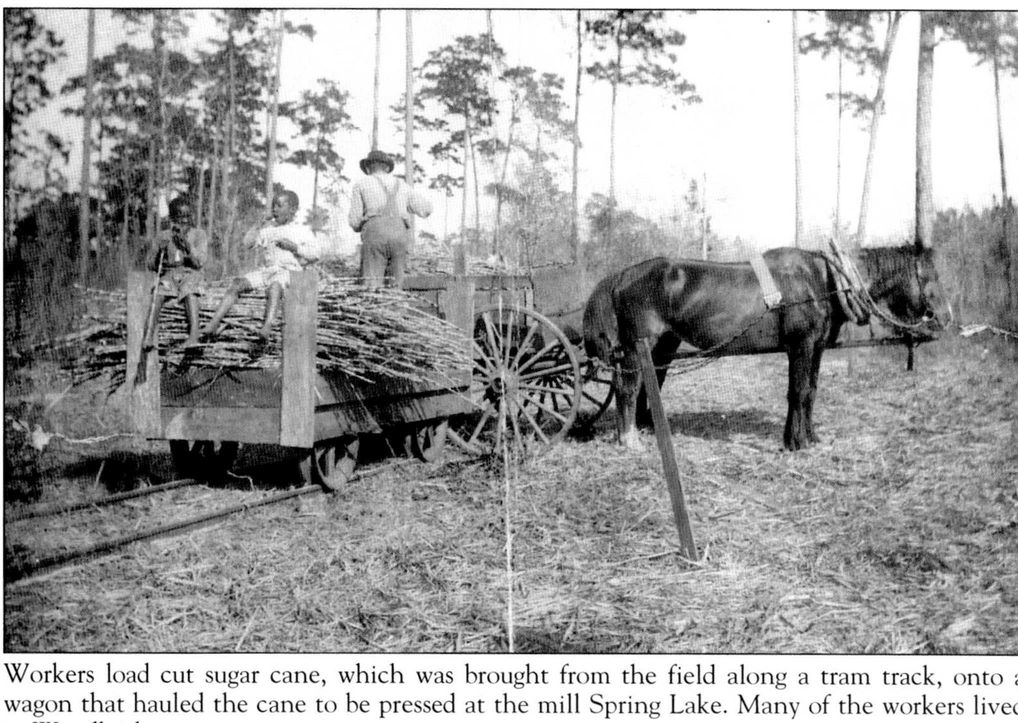

Workers load cut sugar cane, which was brought from the field along a tram track, onto a wagon that hauled the cane to be pressed at the mill Spring Lake. Many of the workers lived in Woodbridge.

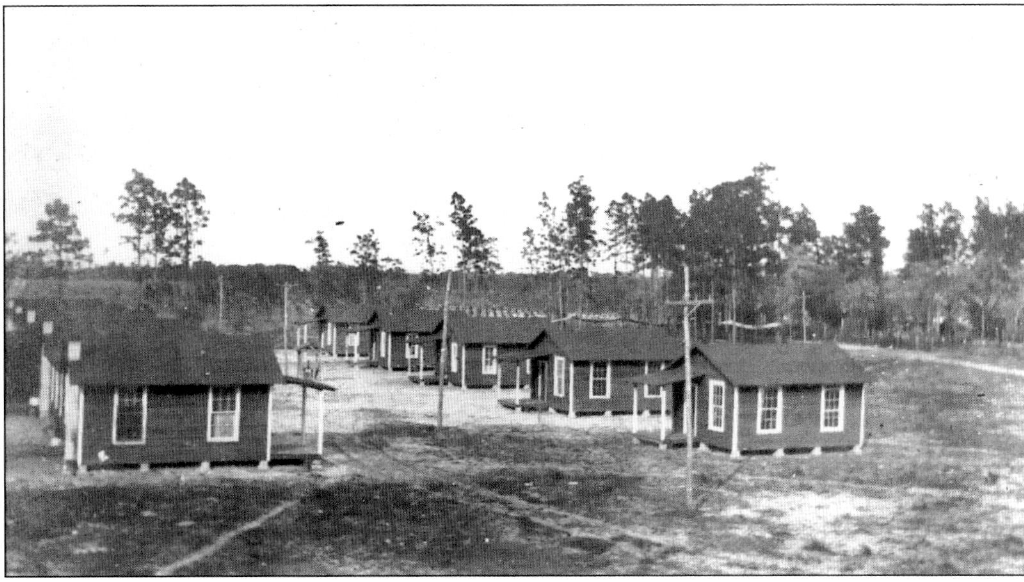

The Royal Fernery provided 40 houses at The Quarters for fern workers. Father and son C.D. and B.F. Haines established the world's largest ferneries in south Seminole County for nearly three decades prior to 1940.The Haines family enterprises employed 200 workers who lived in 30 company houses. The company also built a church, a school, and a store.

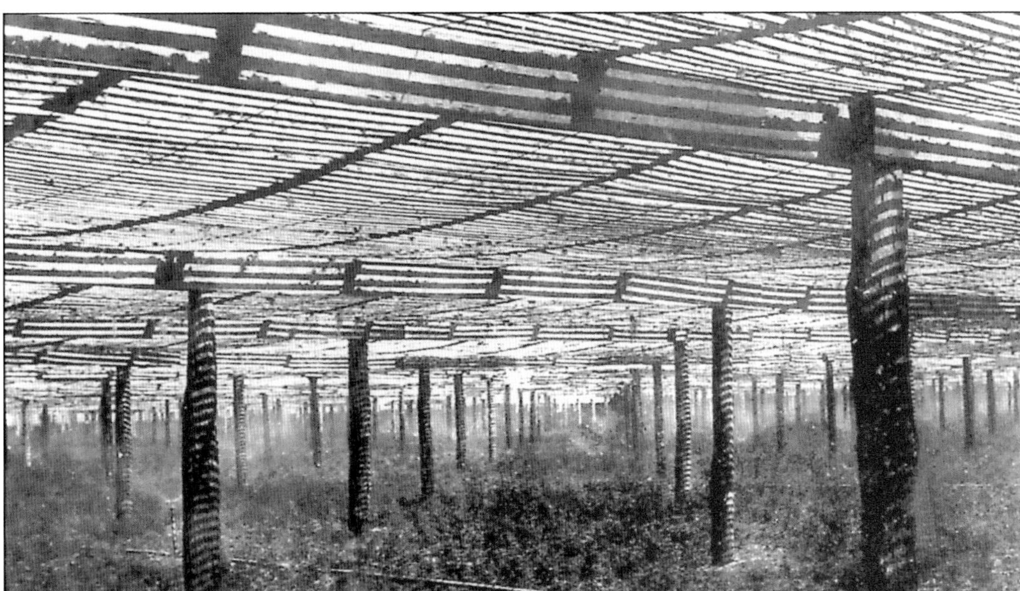

The Royal Fernery kept its tender plants shaded under these slated structures.

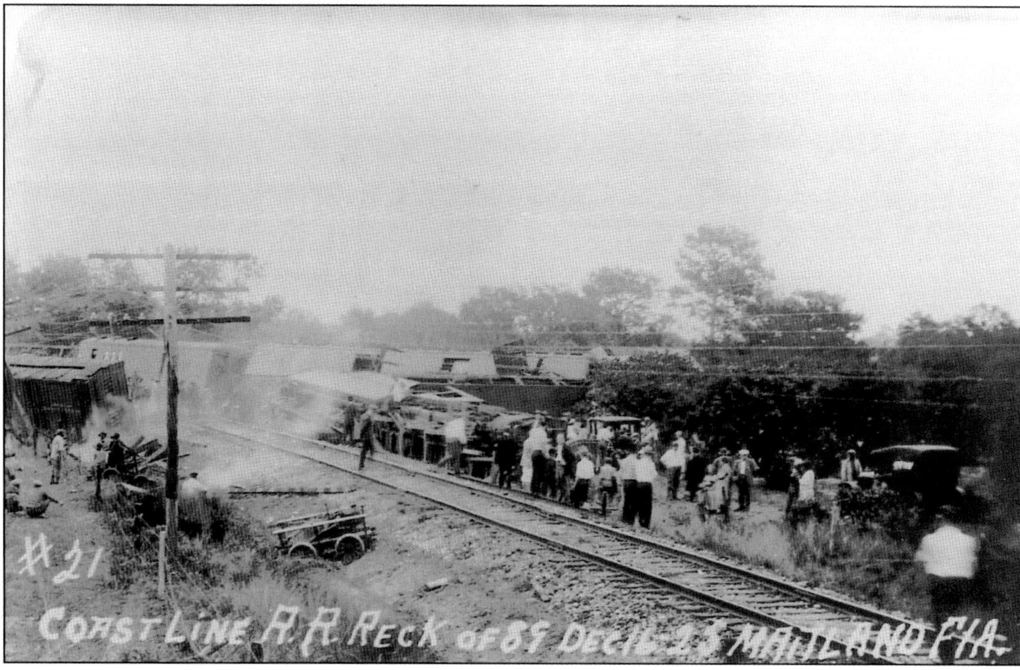

A train wrecked on December 16, 1925, near the area known today as Mayo at the north end of Maitland where Maitland Boulevard meets U.S. Highway 1972. It drew onlookers from many surrounding communities, including the lakefront community of Woodbridge, where black citrus workers lived beginning in the 1880s. Woodbridge was a little more than a mile south of Altamonte Station. The community included the junction of the South Florida Railroad and the Apopka and Atlantic Railroad.

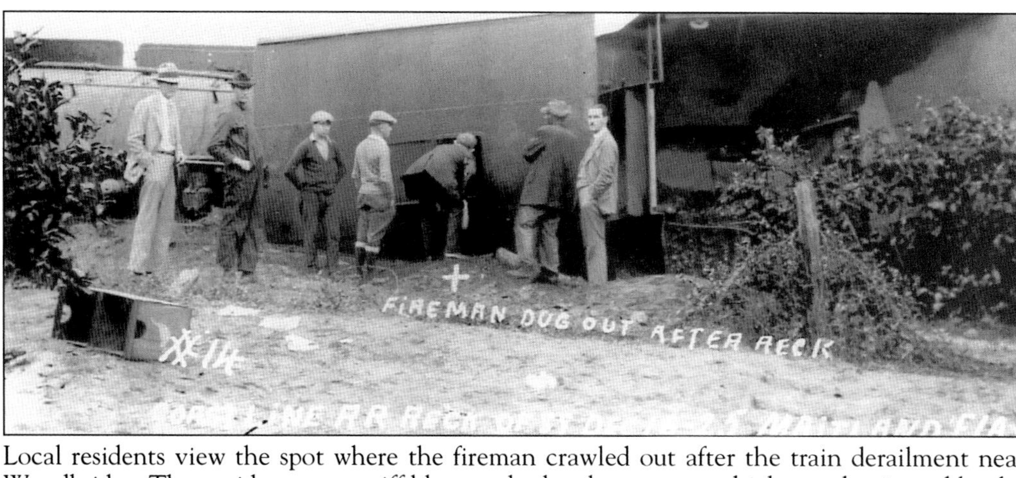

Local residents view the spot where the fireman crawled out after the train derailment near Woodbridge. The accident was a stiff blow to the local economy, which was dominated by the shipment of winter citrus and other crops to Northern markets.

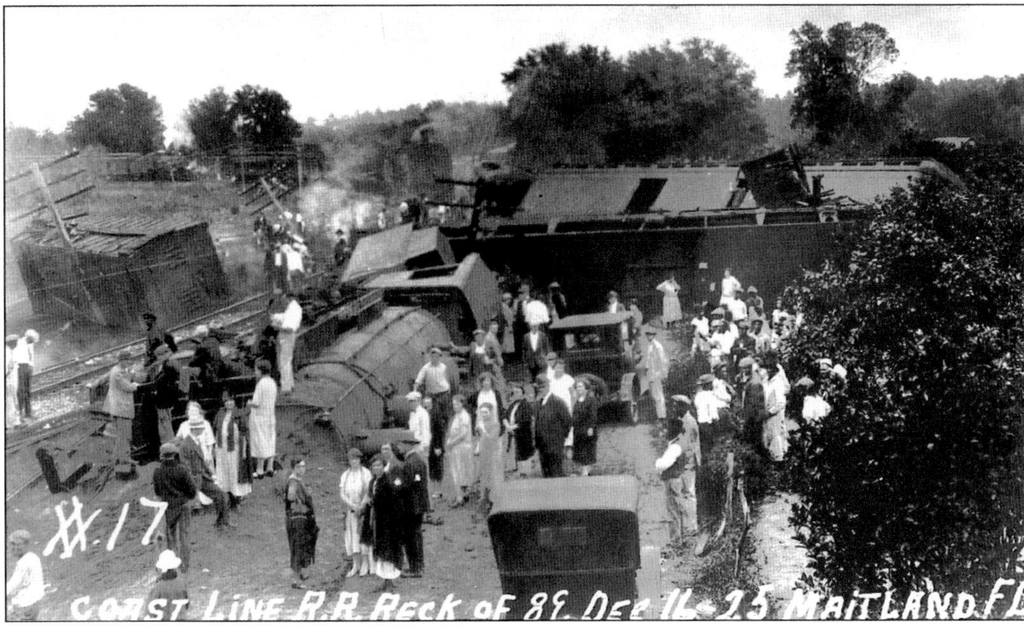

The 1925 derailment of the Atlantic Coast Line train attracted people to watch the clean up. Spoilage of fruit ready for a shipment was a major concern. The railroad carried the iced box cars of citrus to markets in cypress and pine crates made in Woodbridge and Mayo.

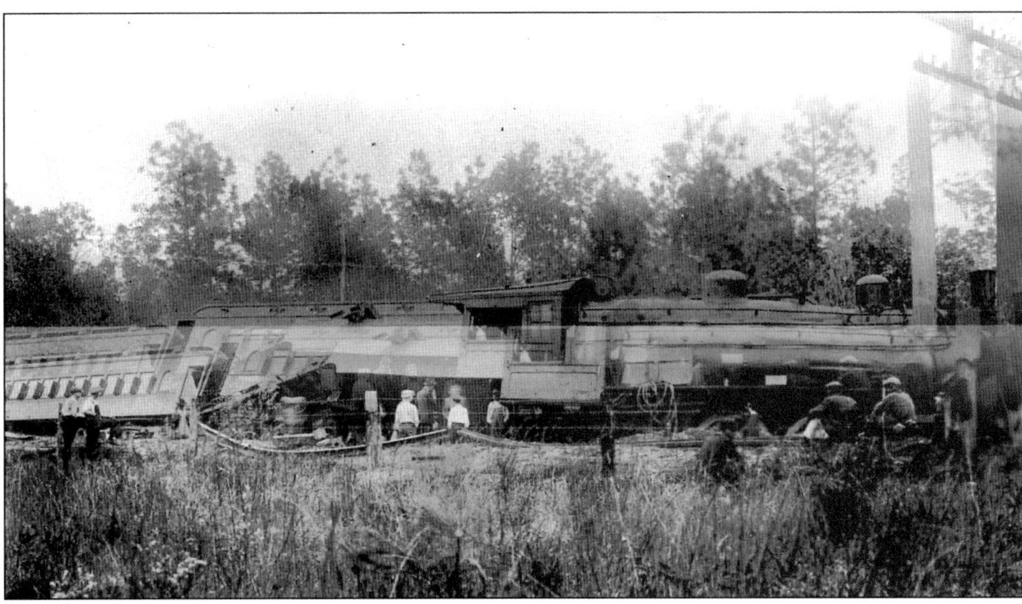

After the 1925 train wreck, this engine was used to clear wreckage from the track.

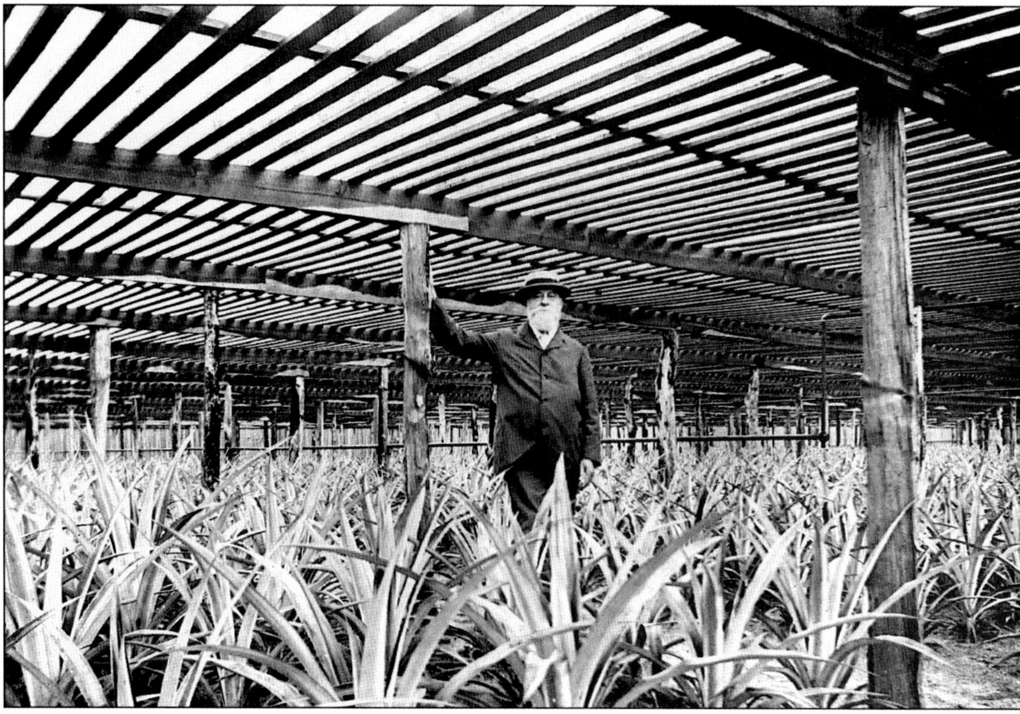

George Frost, one of the Boston investors in the Altamonte Land, Hotel and Navigation Co., poses in the shade under the slants protecting pineapple plants. Pineapples were among the exotic fruits grown in Florida at the turn of the century.

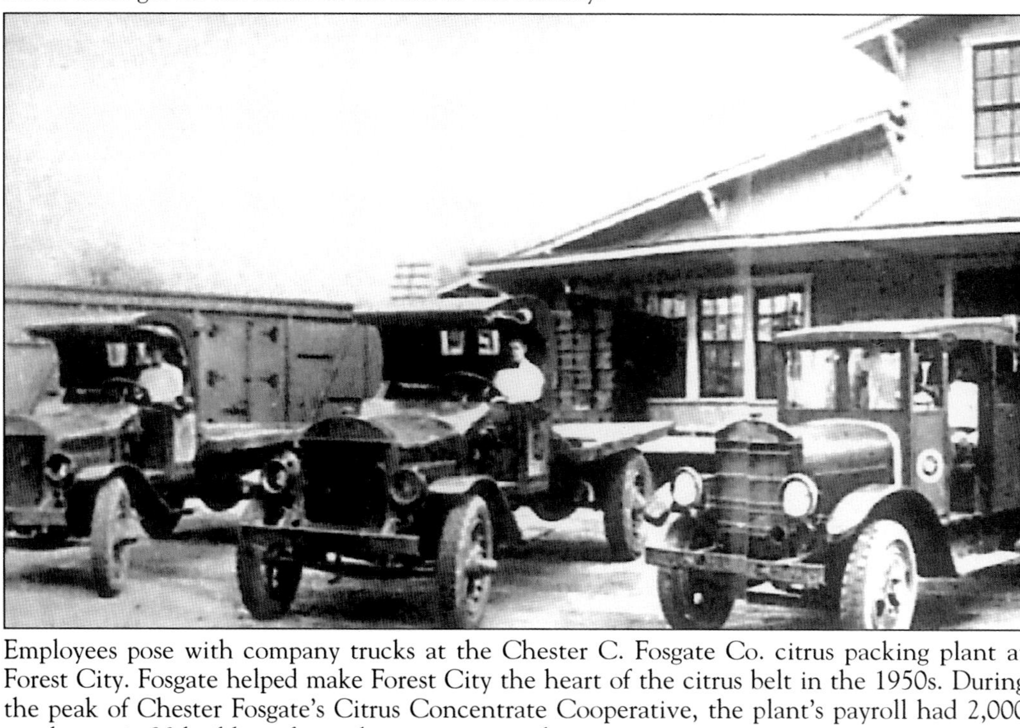

Employees pose with company trucks at the Chester C. Fosgate Co. citrus packing plant at Forest City. Fosgate helped make Forest City the heart of the citrus belt in the 1950s. During the peak of Chester Fosgate's Citrus Concentrate Cooperative, the plant's payroll had 2,000 employees in 20 buildings for packing, storing, and processing concentrate.

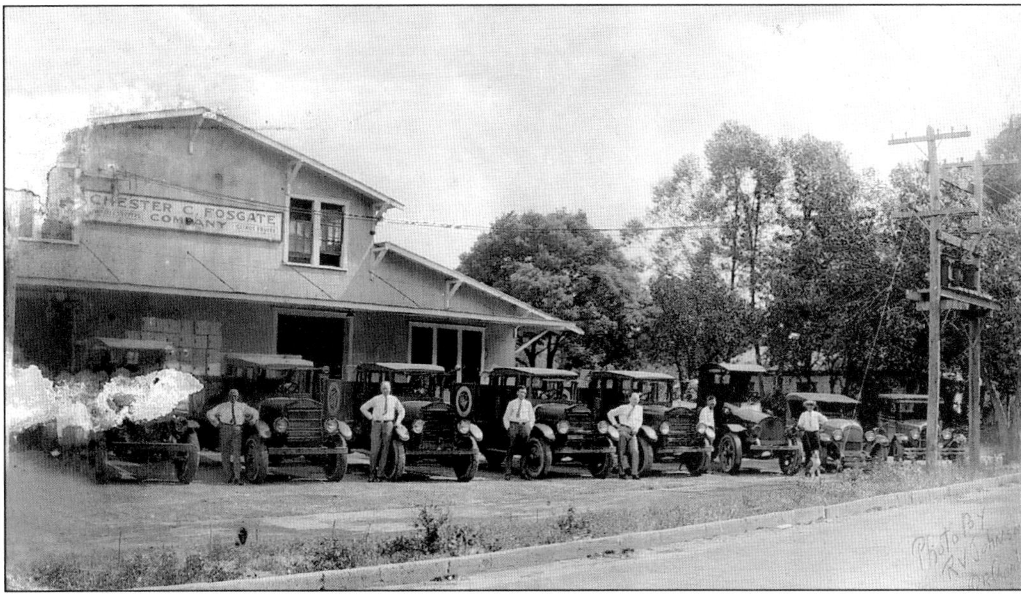

Fosgate trucks and employees line up in front of the packing plant. Chester Fosgate came to Florida from Boston in 1907 when he was just 16 to learn the citrus business. During those early picking seasons, he shuffled between the Florida groves and packinghouses and the Boston markets where he had learned the produce business from his father. In 1928, Highland Stanford Co. of Los Angeles built the first juice canning plant in Florida at the site of the old Forest City sawmill. The stock market crashed in 1929, and Central Florida groves were quarantined after Mediterranean fruit flies were found in Orlando. The company failed after the 1929 season, and Fosgate bought the plant.

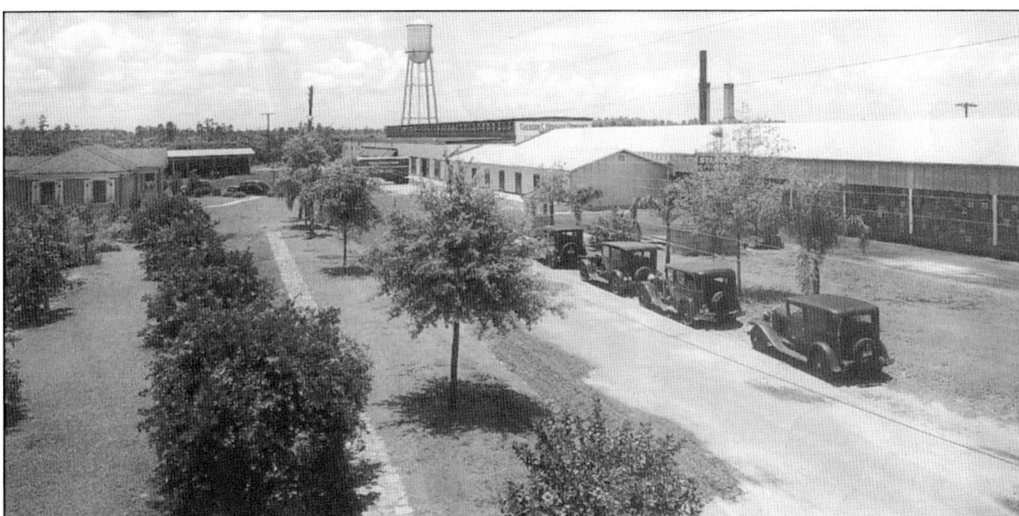

The Fosgate groves are in the foreground of this view of the Chester C. Fosgate Co. packing plant. The double-barreled freezes of the winter of 1894–1895 brought disaster for almost all of Central Florida's citrus families. In the decades to follow growers replanted, and Fosgate founded his Forest City packinghouse. He built his business into one of the largest in the South. His plant was the first in the state to pack and ship a million boxes of fruit in one season.

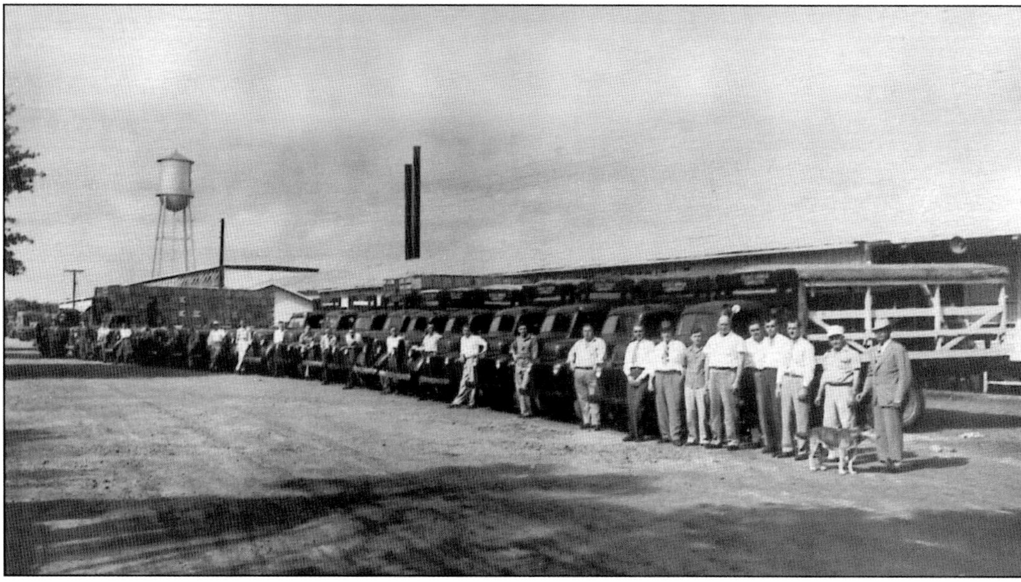

Fosgate employees pose with a new fleet of trucks in the late 1940s. Citrus had been a major influence around Forest City since Swedes planted orange trees in the 1800s. Three families, believed to have migrated from the Swedish colony in Sanford, planted groves and shipped fruit from the Forest City area for more than 20 years. Others planted groves in the same area where Fosgate would later build his packinghouse and concentrate plant. Most of the packing plant's employees were seasonal workers.

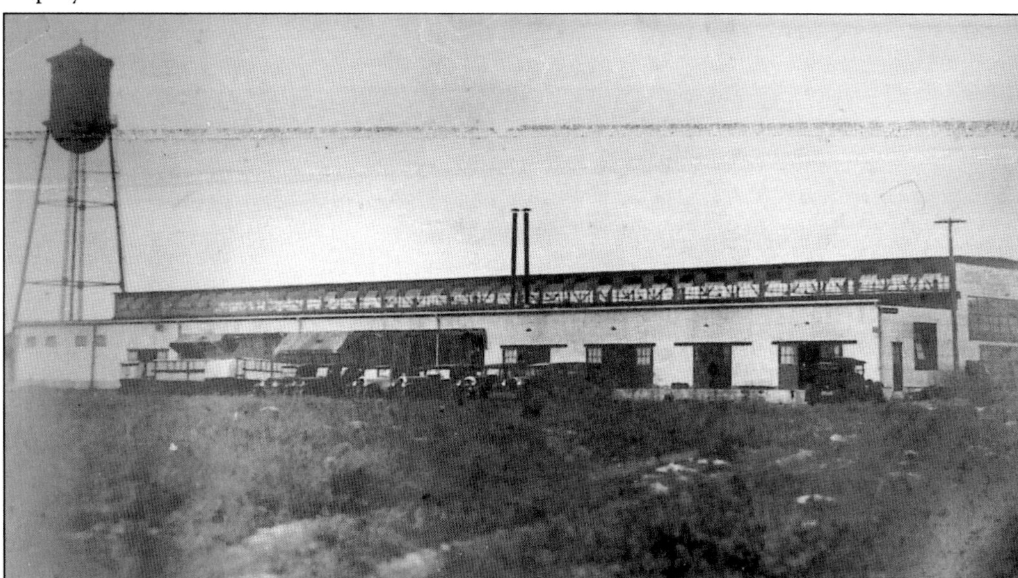

The 1930s view shows the east side of the Fosgate packing plant. Forest City's junction on the railroads connected Sanford with Jacksonville, Tampa, and Orlando and would become a major factor in fostering the small settlement and the citrus boom. An 1886 timetable lists Forest City as one of the stops on the Midland Railroad. Just south of what today is the intersection of state roads 436 and 434 was the heart of Forest City, including a schoolhouse, a railroad depot, a general store, and a two-story boardinghouse. Lots were platted in 1883.

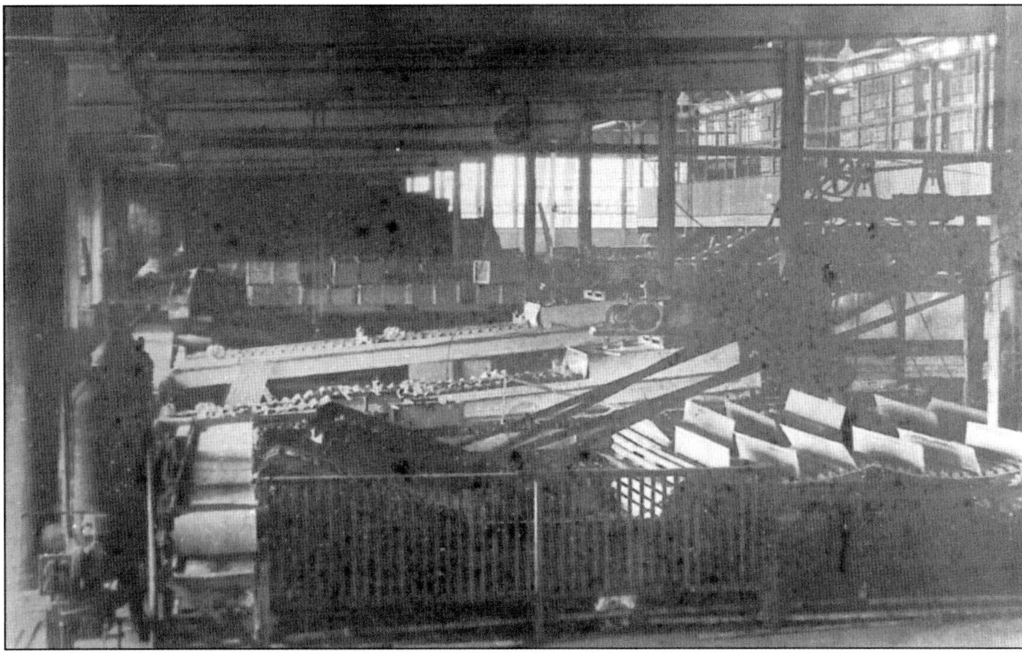

These are the machines used to sort and pack citrus at the Fosgate plant. The Forest City was a rural settlement when Fosgate sold his produce store in Orlando to devote all of his efforts to his citrus enterprises. Fosgate in the late 1920s started one of the first juice canning plants in the state. He would later market orange and grapefruit juices and a citrus blend under the trade name Ace High. He also was the exclusive packer for Duncan Hines concentrate.

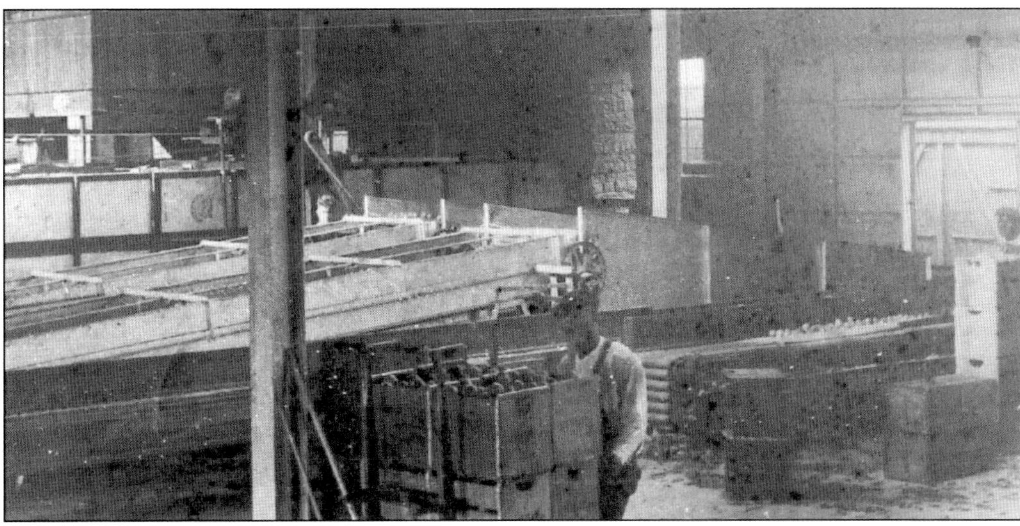

This view shows the crates of citrus brought to the Fosgate plant for sorting and packing. Fosgate sold the packing plant operation, which became Hi Acres. He sold a marmalade-making business to Deep South, a Winn-Dixie subsidiary. Coca-Cola later bought the concentrate plant from Hi Acres. Fosgate was 74 when he died in 1965. His landmark citrus plant closed after the 1983 freeze. That same year, his heirs decided not to replant freeze-burned groves. Instead, they sold off his land holdings to developers. Fosgate was inducted posthumously into the Florida Citrus Hall of Fame.

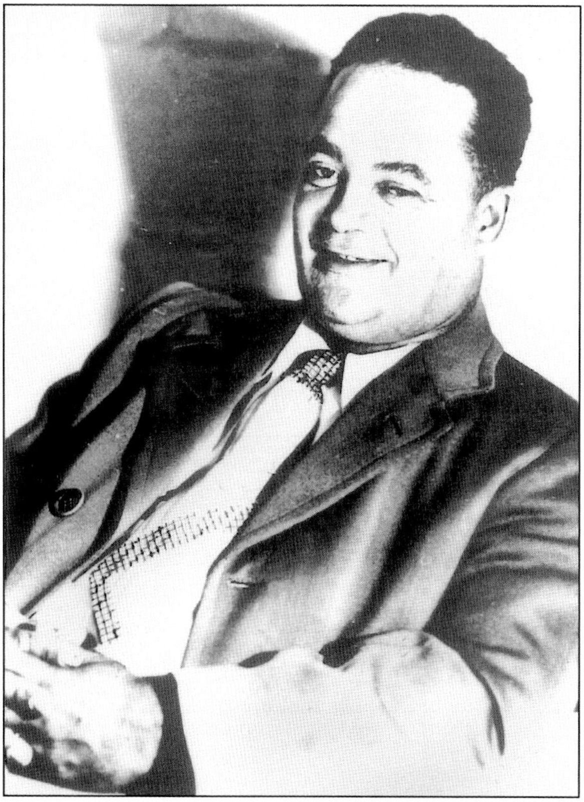

Condor Merritt was one of Central Florida's most powerful African Americans. Merritt developed the Winwood community of Altamonte Springs after World War II with money he made as a fruit picker.

Club owner Condor Merritt, shown here in the center behind the bar at the Club Eaton in Eatonville, opened nightclubs and country stores and invested in real estate. His jazz clubs, both in Winwood and Eatonville, were among the most popular in Central Florida.

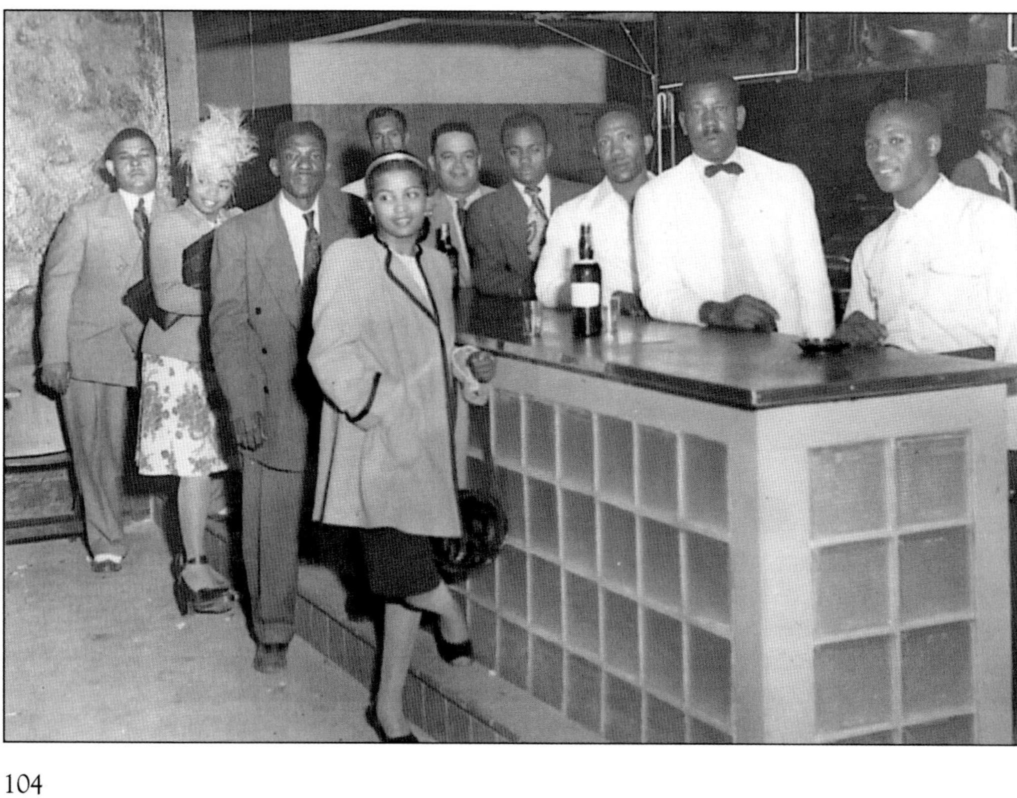

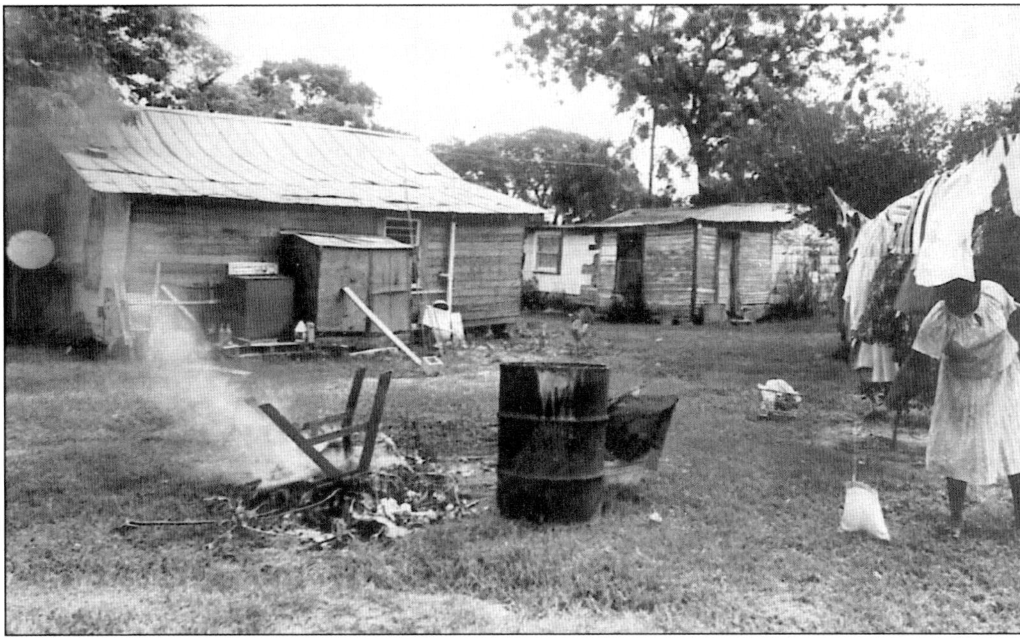

This 1980s photo shows the housing in the Winwood community east of Altamonte Springs. The community was part of the city until Condor Merritt and other community leaders won the right to withdraw from the city because the property taxes they paid were used to provide services elsewhere in the city.

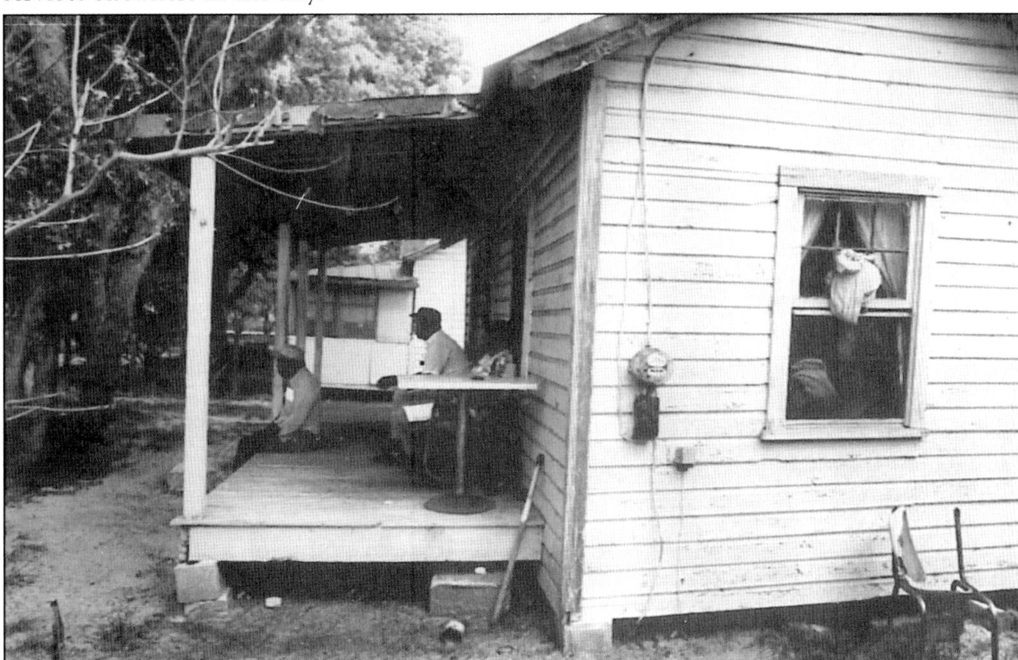

Many of the older houses in Winwood were built when the community provided workers for the area's fern growers. Condor Merritt's family still lives in Winwood and his estate still owns other rental property in the neighborhood.

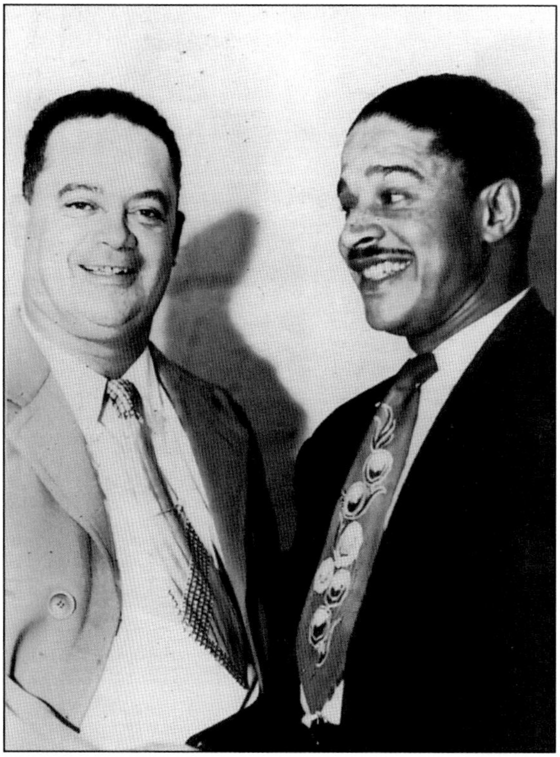

Condor Merritt shakes hands with Dr. Boykin of Orlando. Merritt, who owned many of the businesses in Winwood's commercial area at Merritt Street and Longwood Avenue, helped end the whites-only Democratic primary that dominated Florida politics in the 1940s.

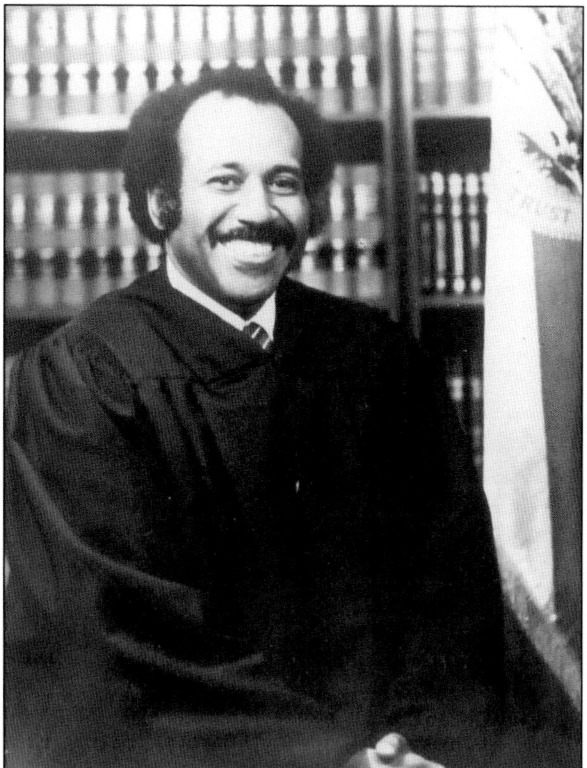

Alcee Hastings, a U.S. Congressman now representing South Florida and Florida's first African American to be named a federal judge, was born in Winwood. Recalling the racism of his youth, he told a reporter a few years ago: "A cross was burned in front of a black-owned drugstore, and some people came and extinguished it and moved it to a white-owned store and relit it. That was the end of cross-burning in Altamonte Springs." One of his uncles was Condor Merritt, who paid for the education that allowed him to excel.

Five

Sanlando and the Springs

James Franklin Haithcox bought Sanlando Springs back when it was called Hoosier Springs. Haithcox renamed the springs, marketing it as an amusement park near his new residential developments. The route of a 1926 dirt road to the springs from Haithcox's Sanlando Golf and Country Club followed roughly the same path as State Road 434. In the mid-1920s, he developed Wilmott Pines on the 2,000 acres surrounding Palm Springs and Sanlando Springs. He and investors put up $2 million in their Sanlando Springs Corporation, founded in May 1925. An estimated 3,000 lots were sold in its first five months. Much of the land was part of the Altamonte Land, Hotel and Navigation Co. It would become known as "Sanlando, the Suburb Beautiful." Haithcox told an Orlando Reporter-Star *writer in 1925, "I won't sell a piece of real estate that I would not buy."*

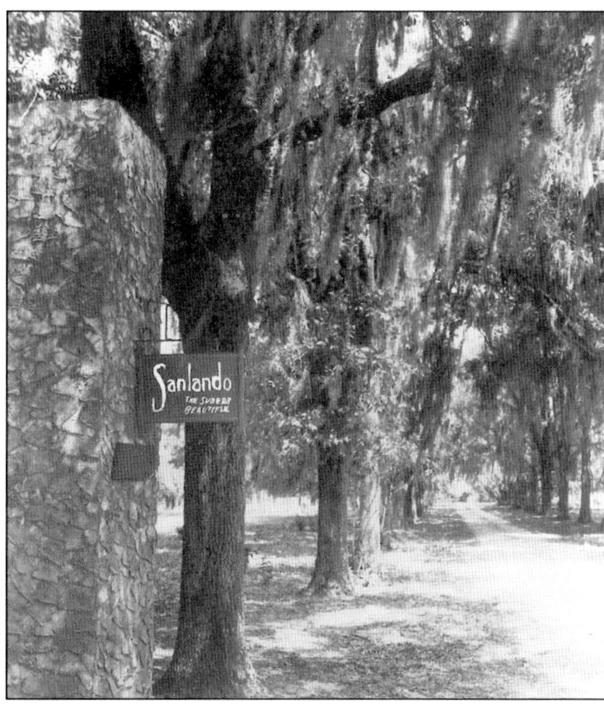

This is the entrance to Sanlando, "The Suburb Beautiful," at Hermit's Trail and Altamonte Avenue in 1925. During the boom times, Haithcox bought more tracts from the springs southeast to his Altamonte development. Much of the land came from the Overstreet Investment Co., which mortgaged it to him in April 1925 for $120,000, then considered a pricey sum.

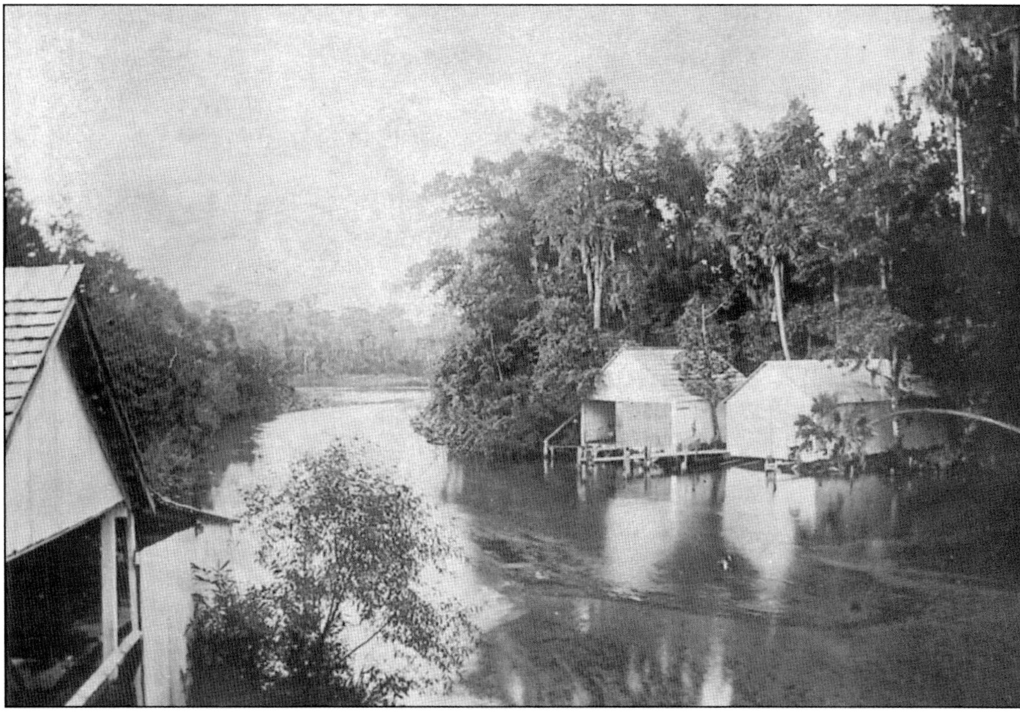

This is the Wekiva River-front community of Clay Springs, which is now known as Wekiva Springs. It was one of the first of many springs to attract bathers.

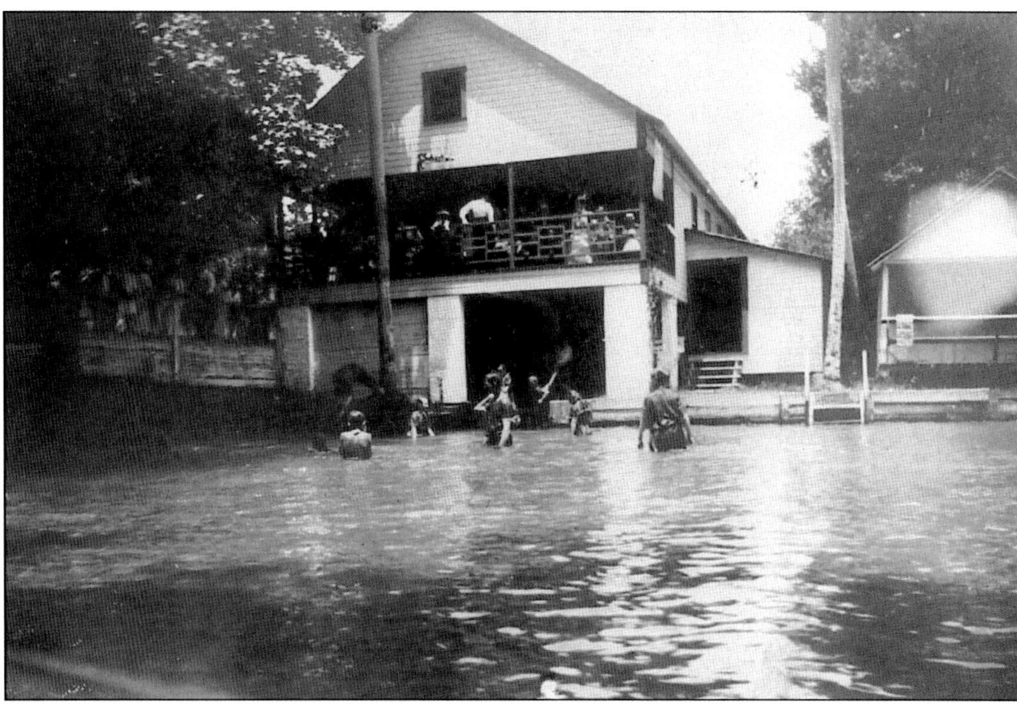

The clubhouse at Clay Springs (now Wekiva Springs) was a popular gathering spot in the early 1900s.

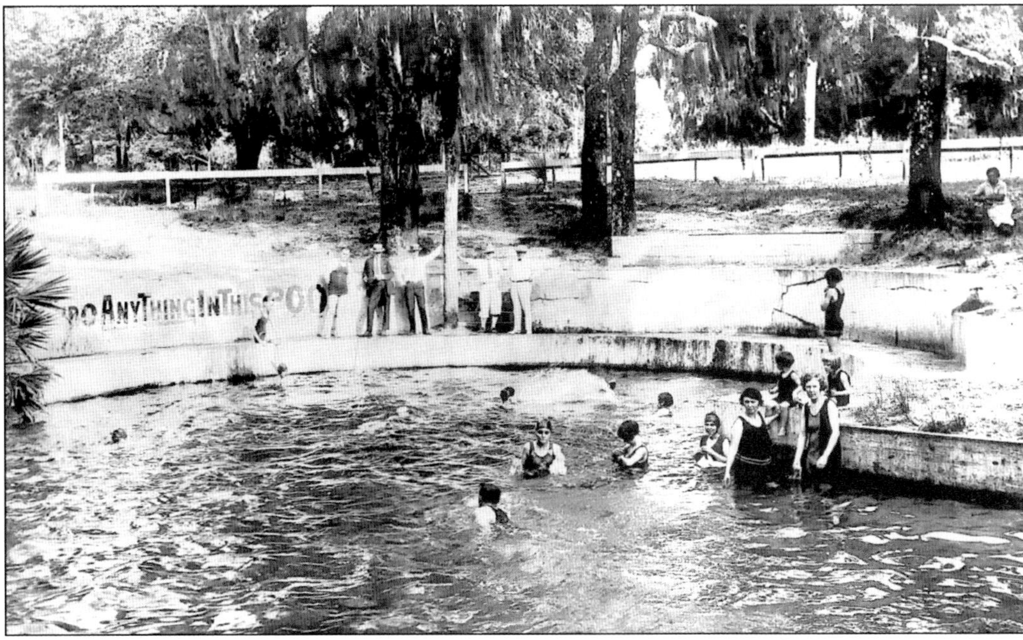

This image shows Sanlando Springs bathers in 1920 at what now is The Springs community. James Haithcox made Sanlando Springs the leading attraction for some of the best communities in Central Florida. Haithcox soon became a major stockholder and officer in five furniture and real estate companies. He also served as mayor of Altamonte Springs for one term.

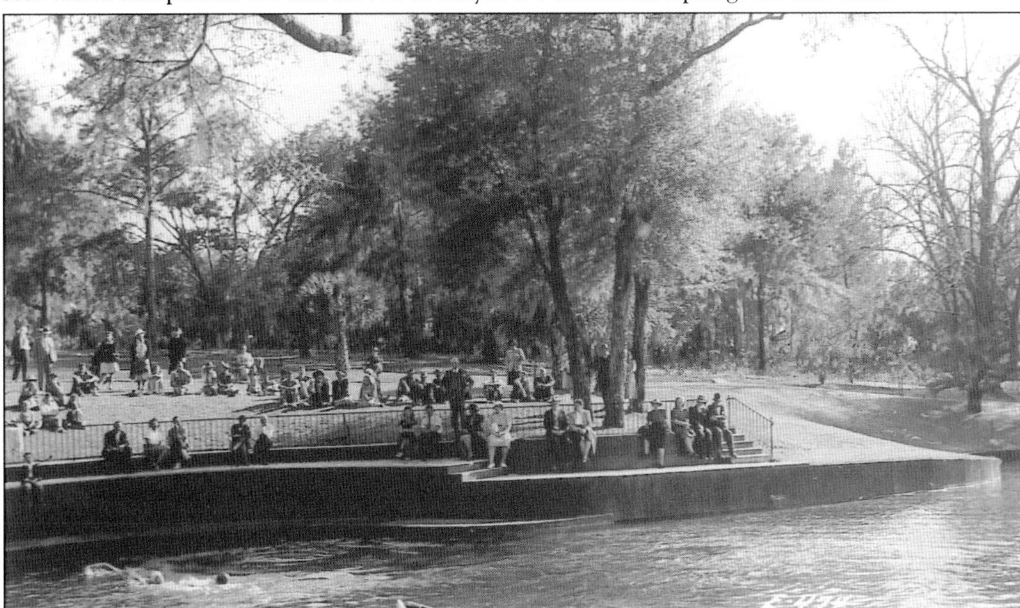

Parents gather on a Sunday afternoon at Sanlando Springs, still dressed up from church services. For at least three generations, young people and families enjoyed Sanlando Springs and its slide into cool, clear water. In the 1930s, when Sanlando Springs drew large crowds on the weekends as families searched for relief closer than Daytona Beach's shores, a newspaper advertised, "It's fun to be cooled swimming in fresh, clear spring water."

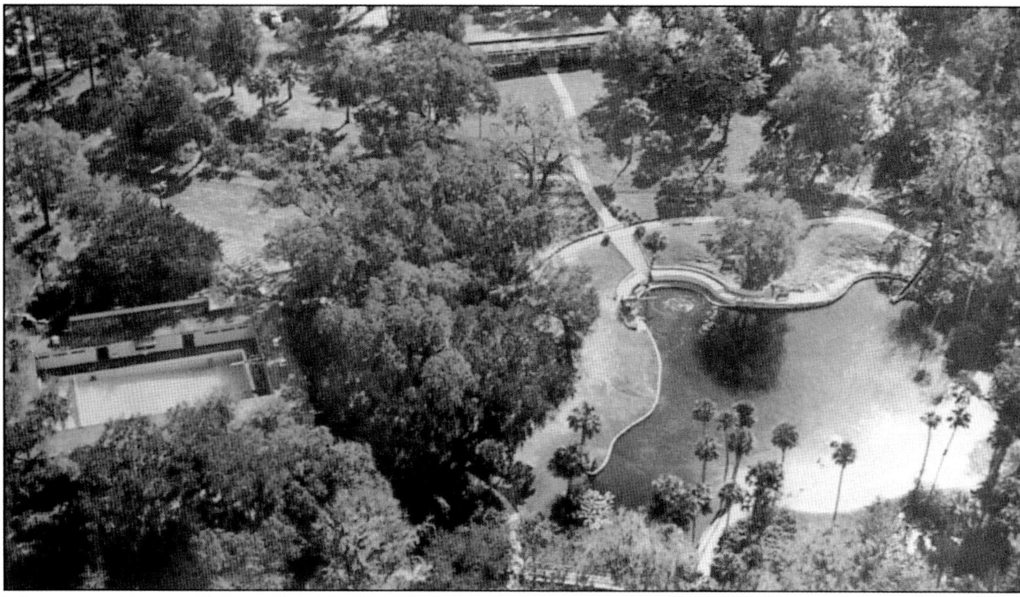

This aerial view shows the pool at Sanlando Springs, the spring's boil, the slide, and the clubhouse. James Haithcox built a dam to raise the water level, landscaped the shoreline with tropical plants, and added a swimming pool and bathhouse. It would become Sanlando Springs Tropical Park. The Sanlando swimming pool, the first in-ground pool in the area, opened in April 1926.

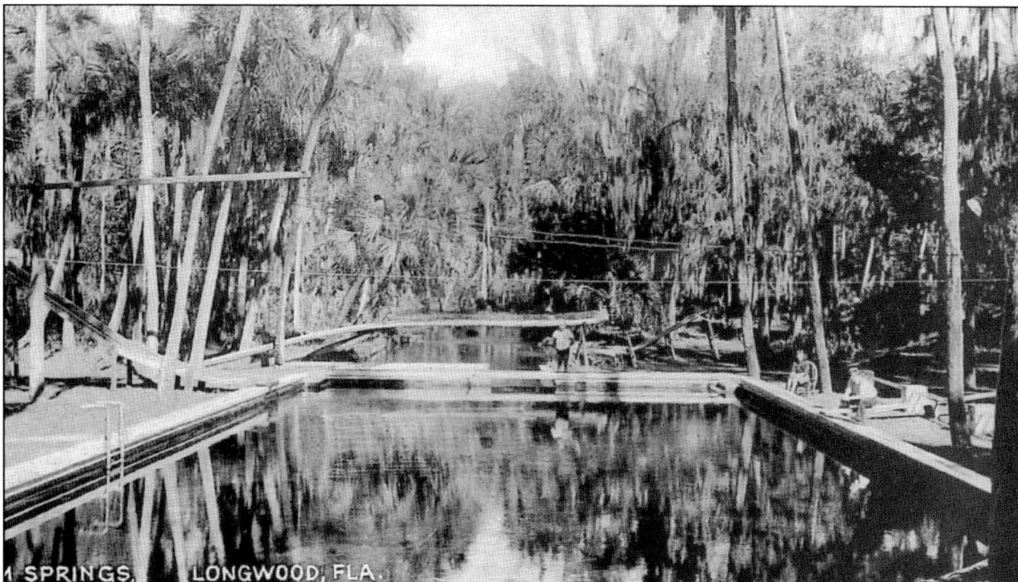

Sanlando Springs was called Palm Springs, which also was the name of one of the early communities that became Altamonte Springs. The pool and slide were built at the springs just after a road was opened between the community of Palm Springs and the spring near the Little Wekiva River. Sanlando Springs had the best waterslide in Central Florida. Hour after hour, kids could climb the steps of a giant slide and scream their heads off before splashing into the cool spring waters.

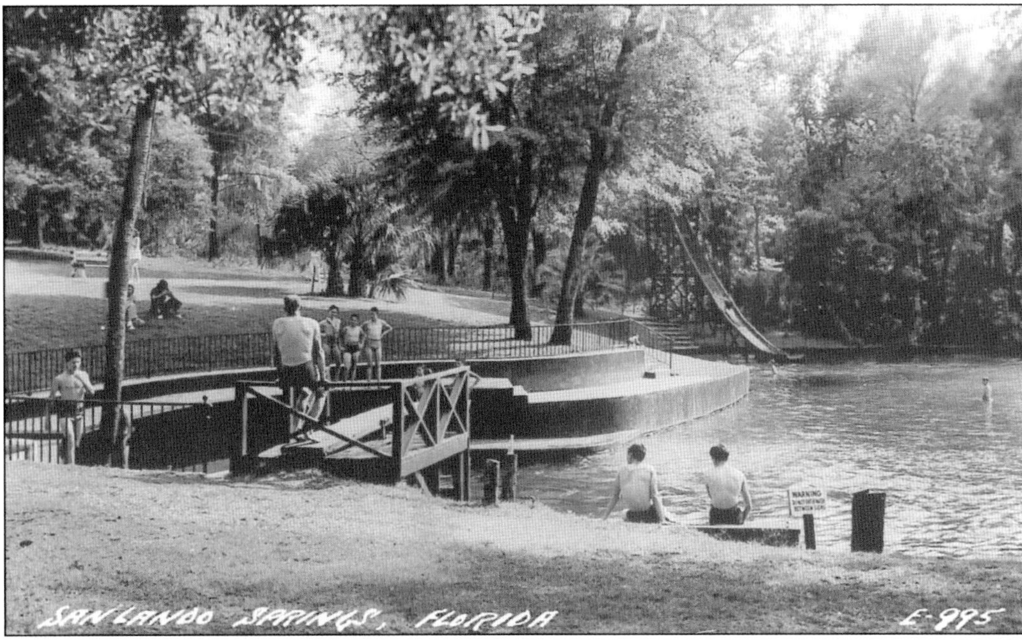

A platform and springboard were built over the boil of Sanlando Springs. The slide in the background stretched over shallow water.

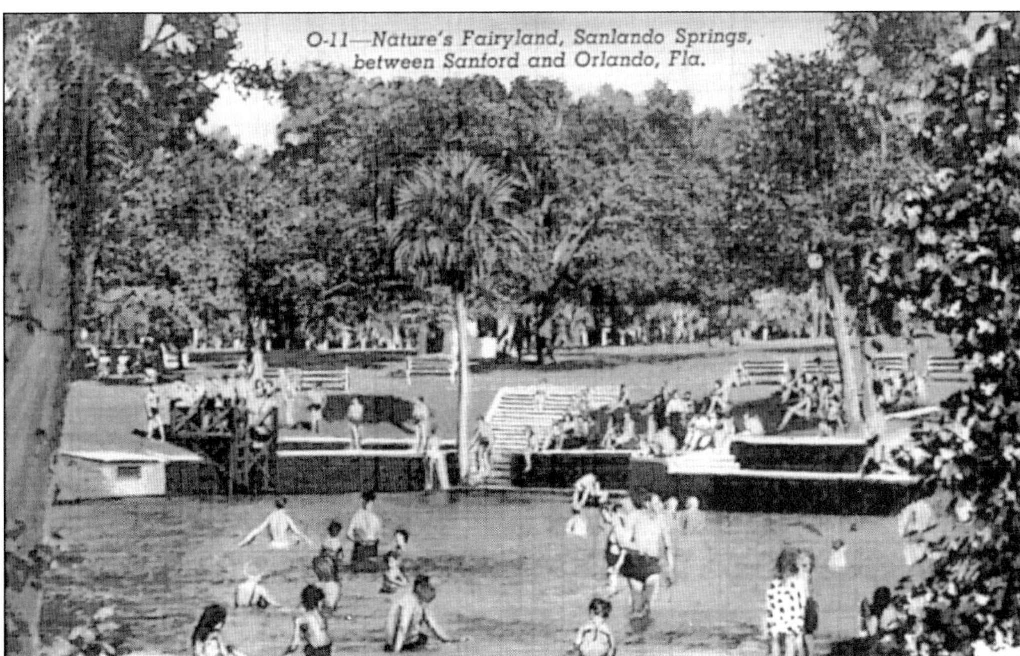

Sanlando Springs, shown in this 1960s postcard, was one of the most popular spots in Central Florida during the summer.

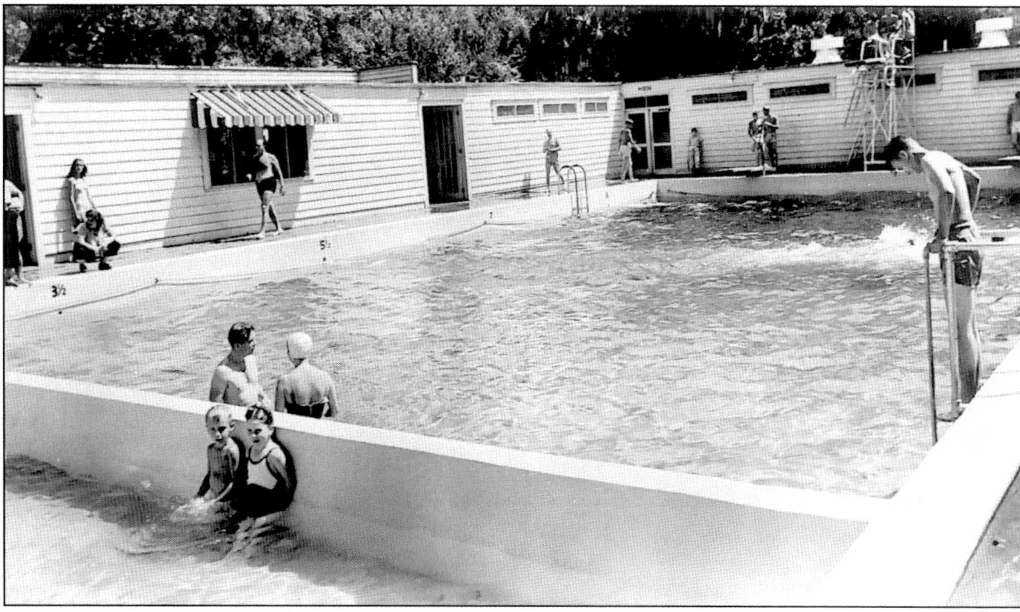

This 1960s scene shows the pool at Sanlando Springs. "Summers" at the springs lasted until Halloween and often well after Thanksgiving. Generation after generation enjoyed activities at Sanlando Springs.

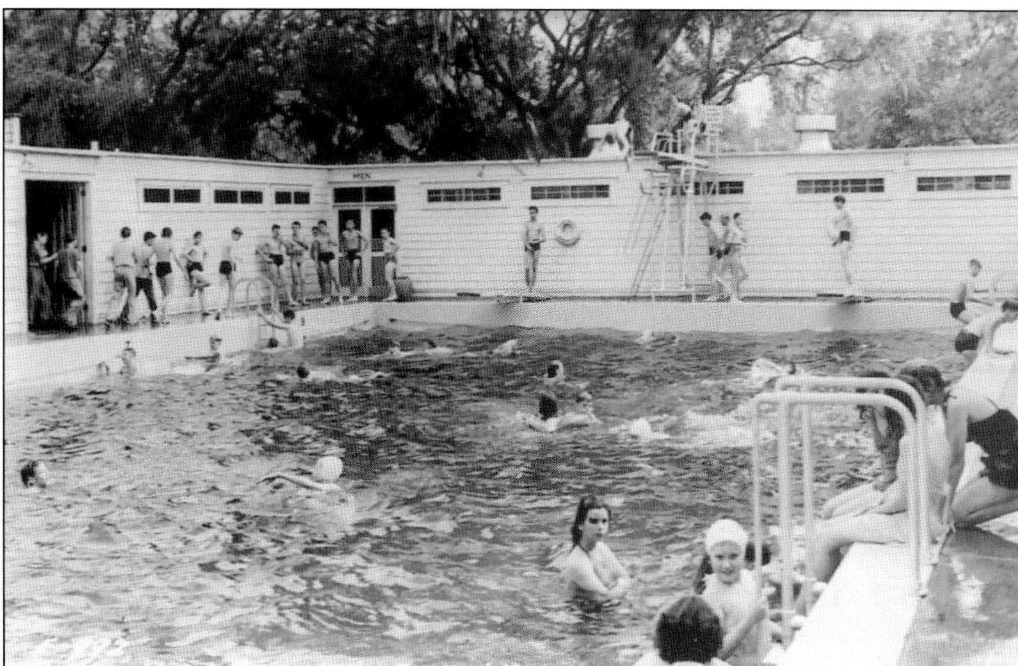

Shown here is the new pool built at Sanlando Springs after Frank Haithcox bought the springs and much of the surrounding land.

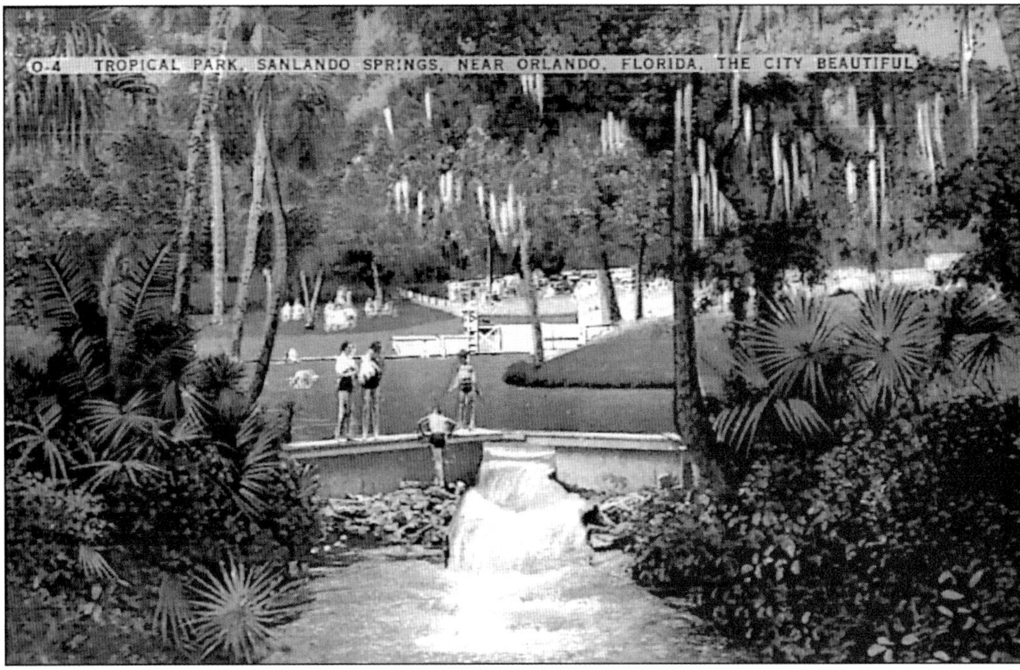

Water from Sanlando Springs in the 1960s flowed over this waterfall into a creek leading to the Little Wekiva River.

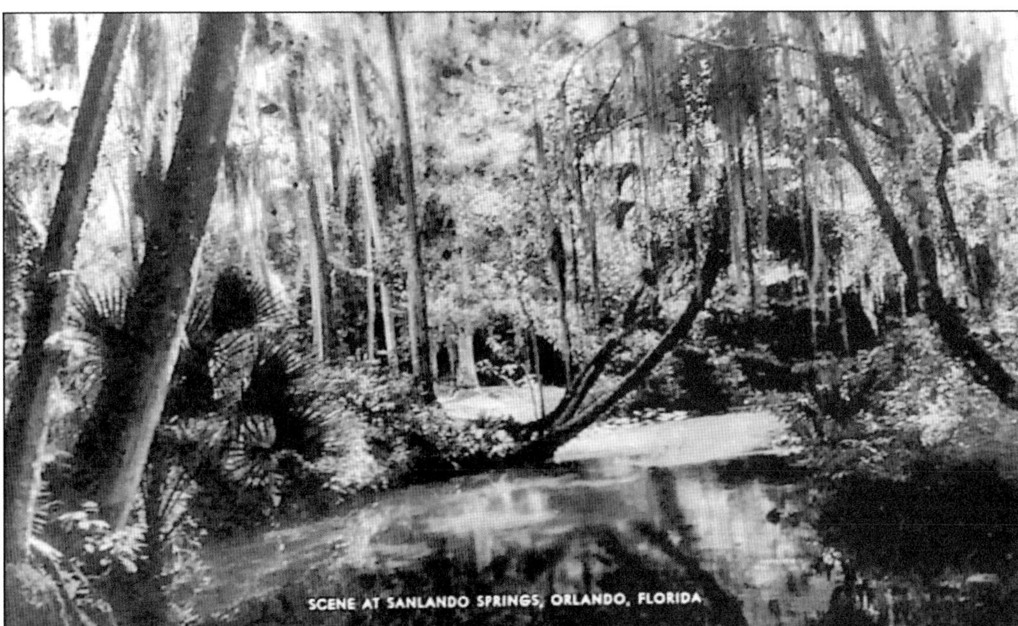

Palms bend over the Little Wekiva River near Sanlando Springs. Moses Overstreet, the Florida senator for whom the more than 3,000-year-old bald cypress "The Senator" is named, owned timber and turpentine companies that controlled thousands of acres along the Wekiva and Little Wekiva Rivers. He was forced to repossess Sanlando Springs Tropical Park after the 1920s boom busted and James Haithcox lost interest in his developments.

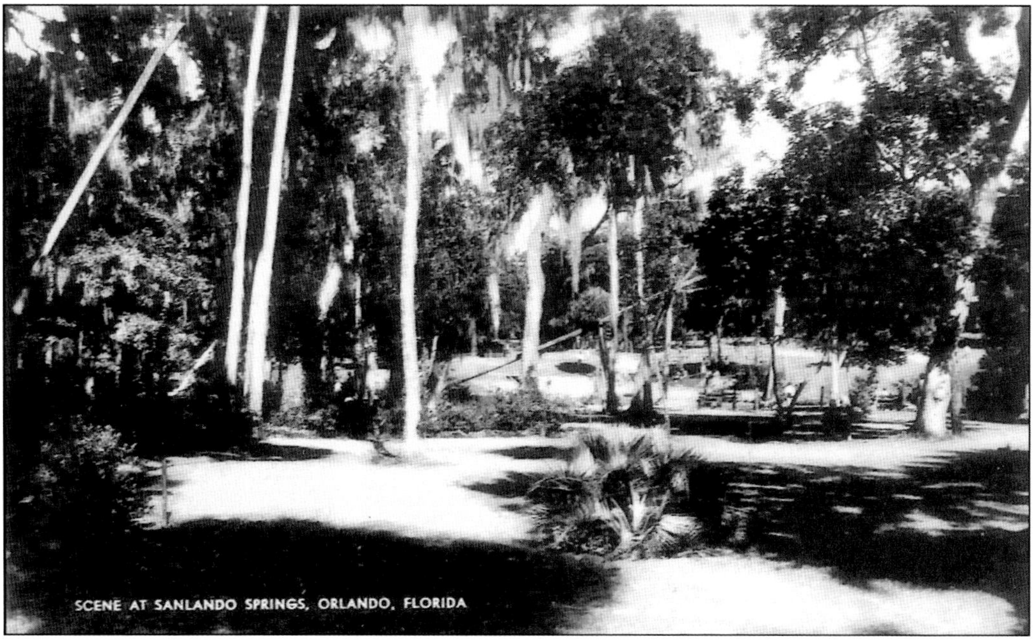

Benches along the garden walkways through the grounds of Sanlando Springs provide quiet spots to rest. The foreclosed parkland reopened in 1935, and visitors came to see the park's addition of more than 10,000 azalea plants. The park also offered swimming lessons and weekly aquatic shows. The Marchand family put on professional log rolling contests and demonstrations in 1941. After dark, the pavilion at Sanlando Springs opened for dances that drew many young people in the 1940s.

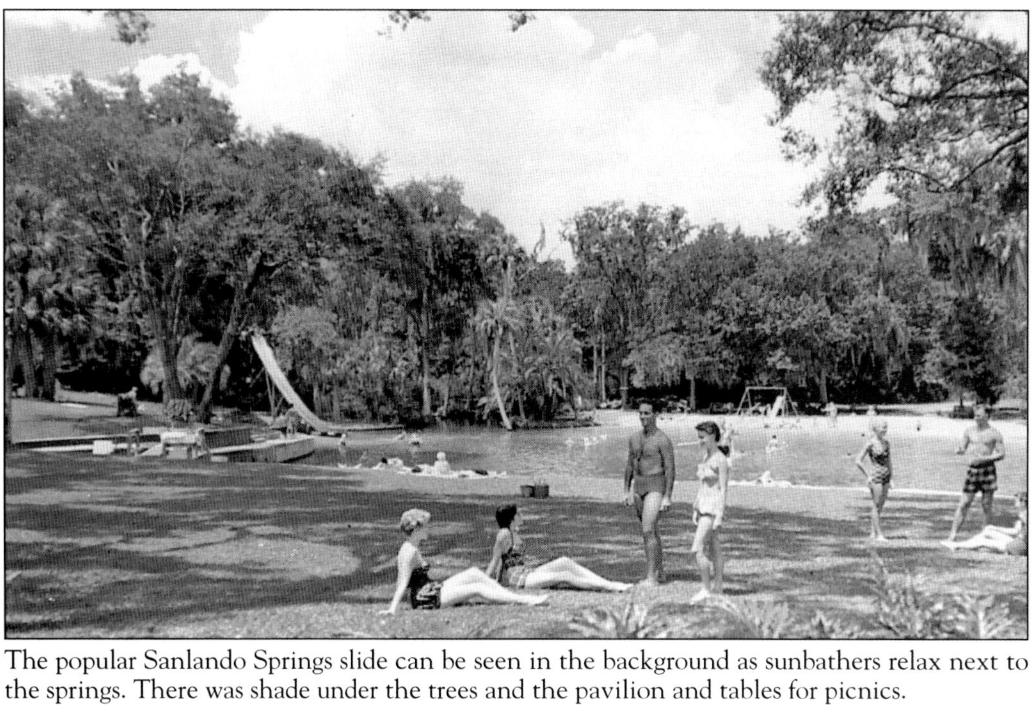

The popular Sanlando Springs slide can be seen in the background as sunbathers relax next to the springs. There was shade under the trees and the pavilion and tables for picnics.

A couple shares a pleasant moment on the footbridge at Sanlando Springs. Teenagers and families gathered by day at the springs and young adults showed up for dances at the pavilion at night.

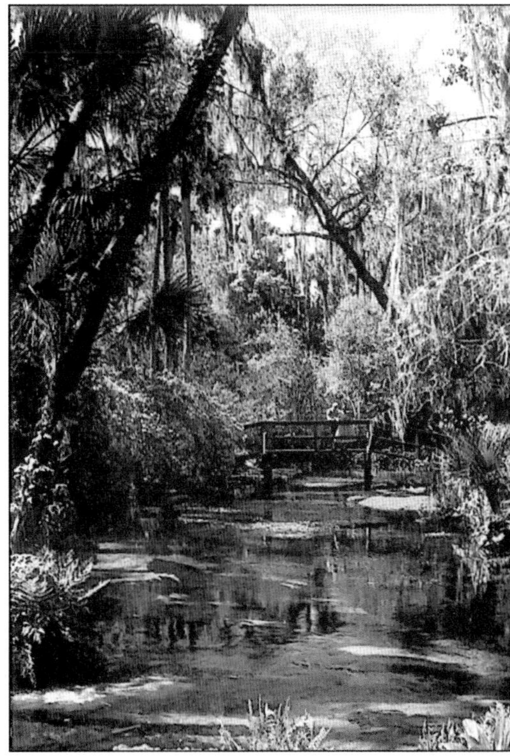

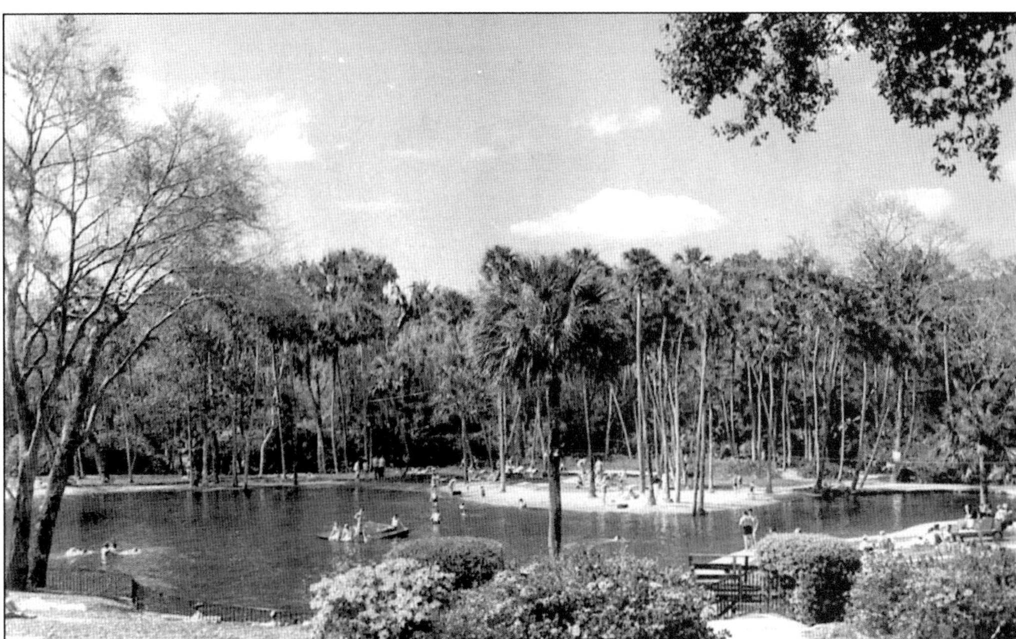

This scene from 1954 shows the beach across Sanlando Springs from the clubhouse. One dollar was all it cost to get into Sanlando Springs on a hot Saturday in the 1960s. A youngster with a few extra coins could eat at the snack bar or play the pinball games in the clubhouse. A large pool had three diving boards.

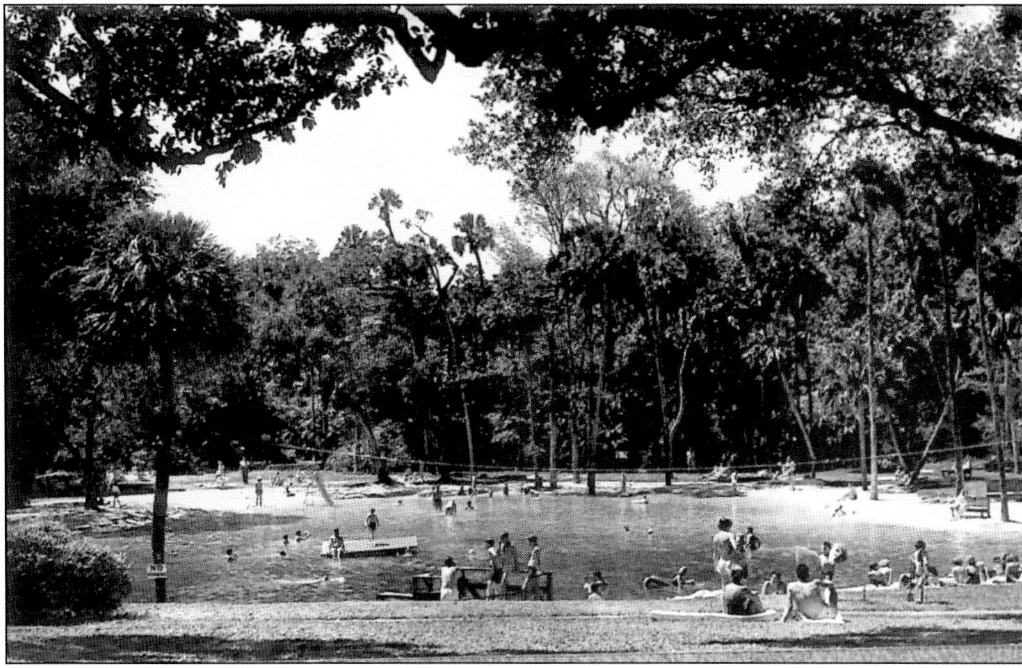

Sunbathers watch from the grounds surrounding Sanlando Springs in the 1960s.

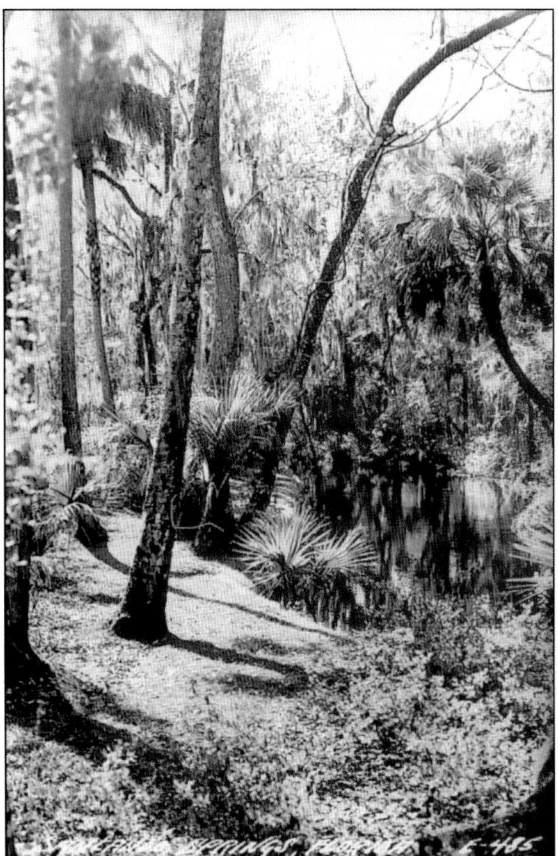

The banks of the Little Wekiva River near Sanlando Springs are shown in this 1950s view.

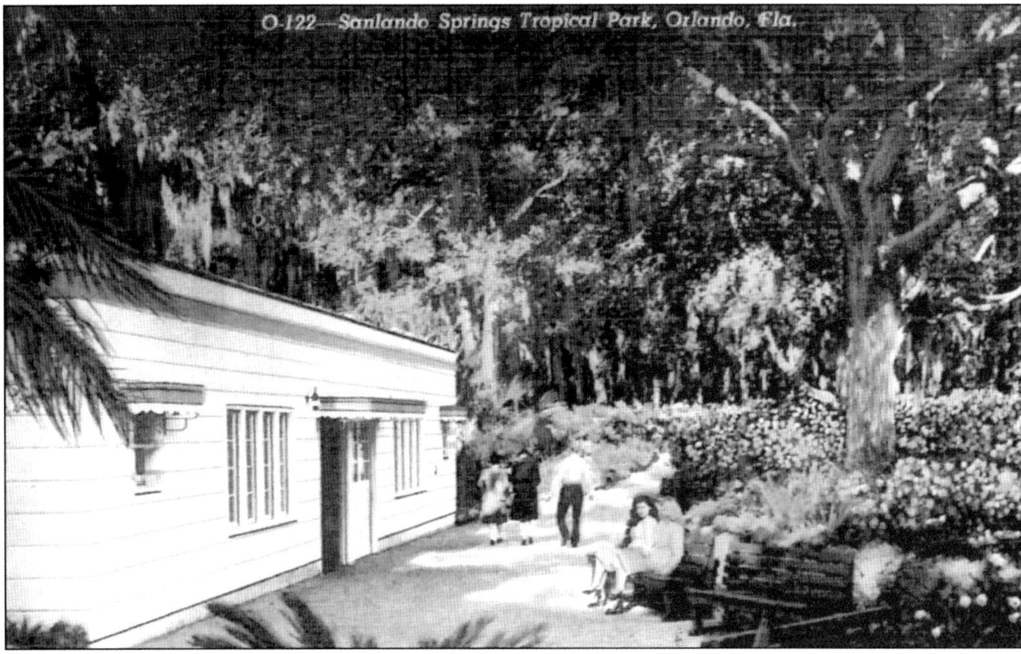

The clubhouse at Sanlando Springs and the walkways through the surrounding gardens were popular gathering places for youth during the 1960s.

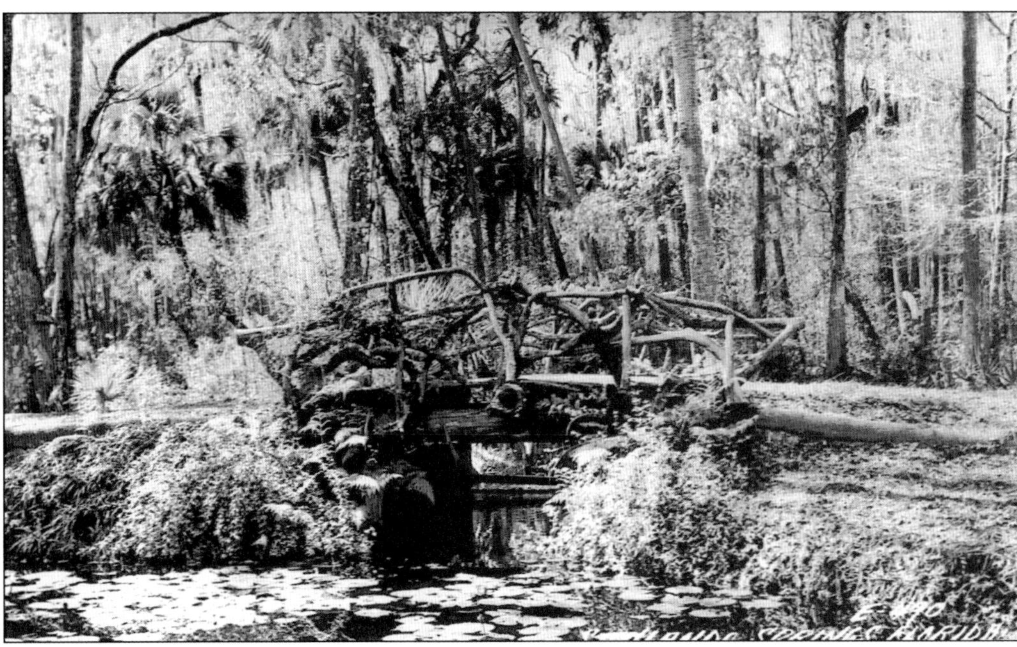

The grounds at Sanlando Springs included this footbridge over one of the spring-fed creeks that flowed into the Wekiva River.

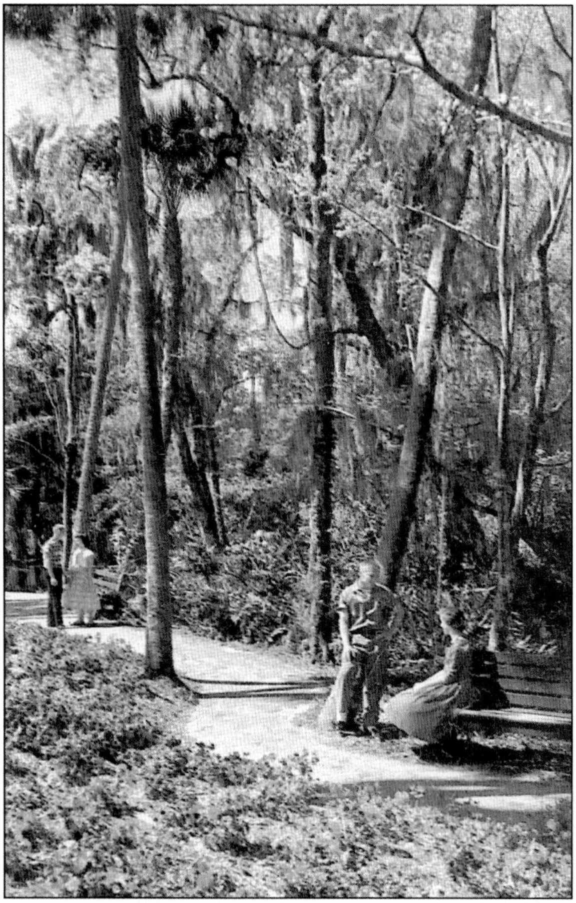

Two young couples chat on the winding walkway through the gardens at Sanlando Springs.

Two women stand on the shoreline of the springs, across from the beach at Sanlando Springs.

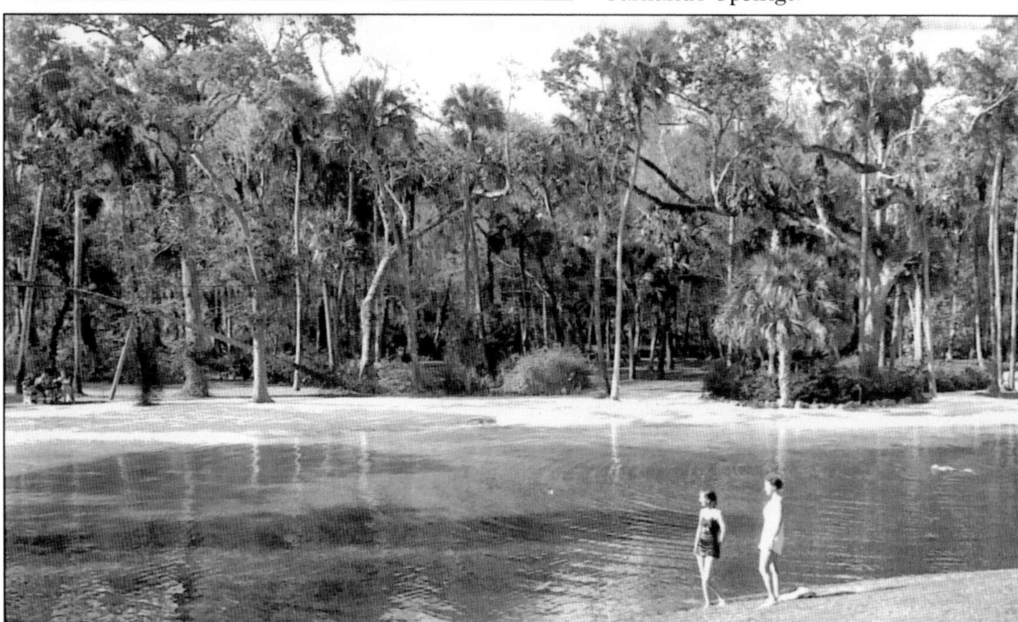

Two women pose on one of the footbridges leading from the springs to the beach at Sanlando Springs in the early 1950s. The springs drew gatherings of friends and families as well as school and church picnics. One farm family treated everyone to ice cream, bringing its hand-cranked freezer to the shoreline.

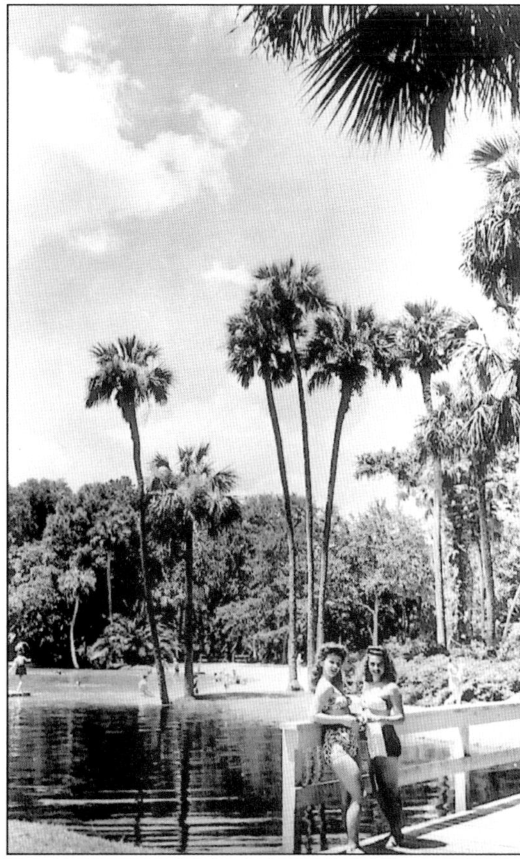

Bathers at Sanlando Springs in 1946 play on an elephant barrel.

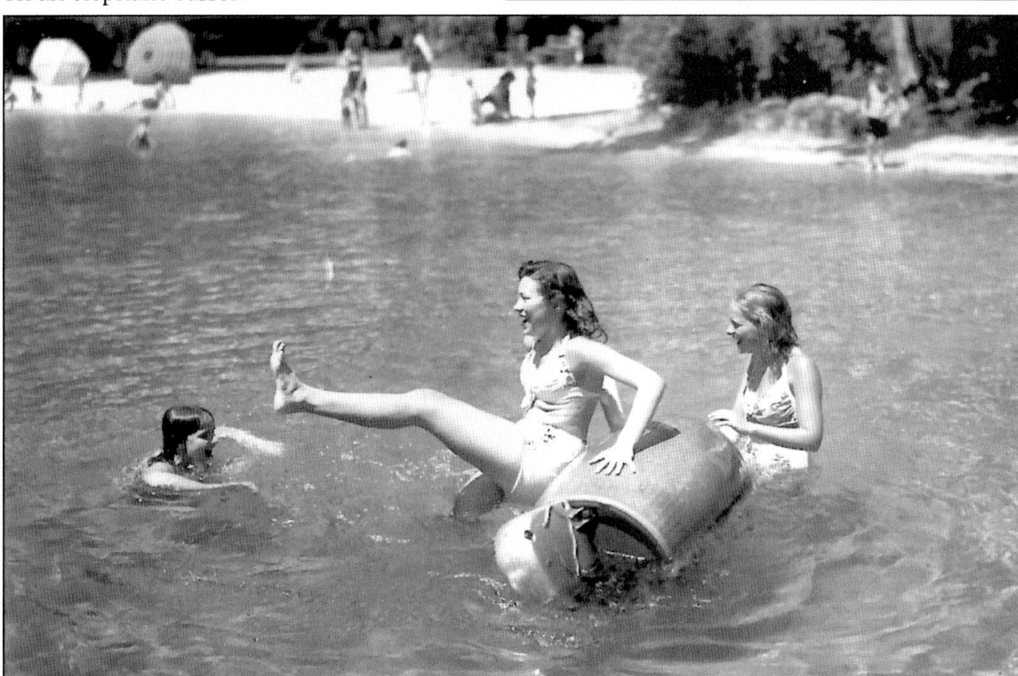

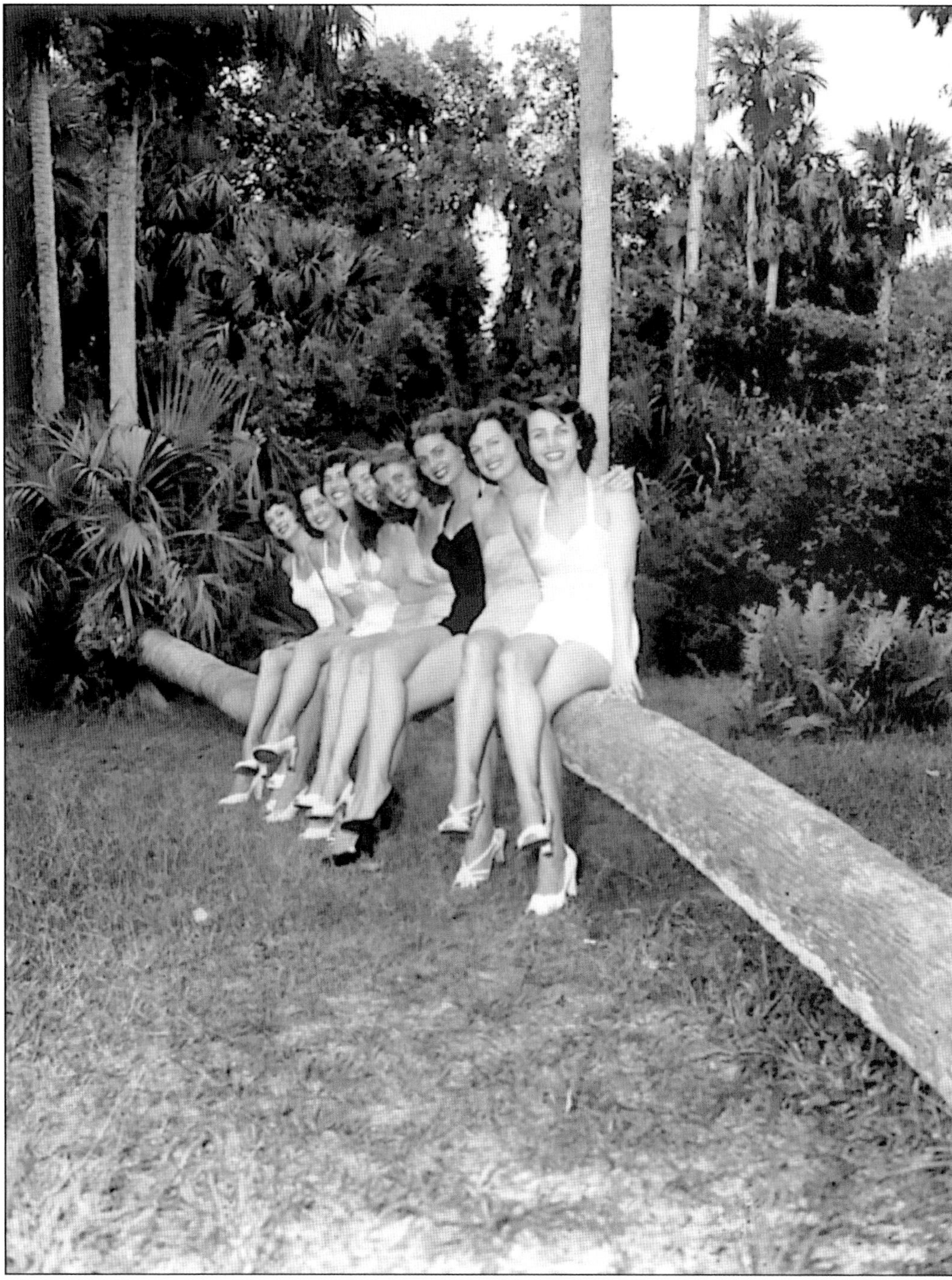

These are the 1951 contestants for Mrs. Sanlando Springs. The winner, Peggy Creel, is third from the front in the dark bathing suit. J.E. Robinson owned and ran the park from about 1950 until 1970 when it remained one of Central Florida's most popular water parks. Sanlando Springs and its 350 acres of rolling forest and crystal-clear waters that feed into the Little Wekiva River closed to the public in 1970 when the property became the gated community The Springs.

Six

TODAY'S ALTAMONTE SPRINGS

The symbol of Altamonte Springs as a winter resort burned to the ground in July 1953. As in previous years dating back to the late 1800s, the Altamonte had opened for the winter season in December and closed in April. The fire alarm sounded early on the morning of July 1. Volunteer firefighters pumped water from Lake Orienta, but witnesses reported seeing towering flames from miles away. Other firefighters from Orlando, Winter Park, Pine Castle, Casselberry, Maitland, Longwood, and Sanford joined in the failed effort to fight the blaze. The last flames were put out early the following day. The Bates family decided not to rebuild. For the balance of the 1950s and the early 1960s, Altamonte remained what some have called a quiet sedentary town. It would emerge in the 1970s as the first Seminole County city to take advantage of the retail and residential growth opportunities made possible by Interstate 4 and the widening metro-Orlando economy.

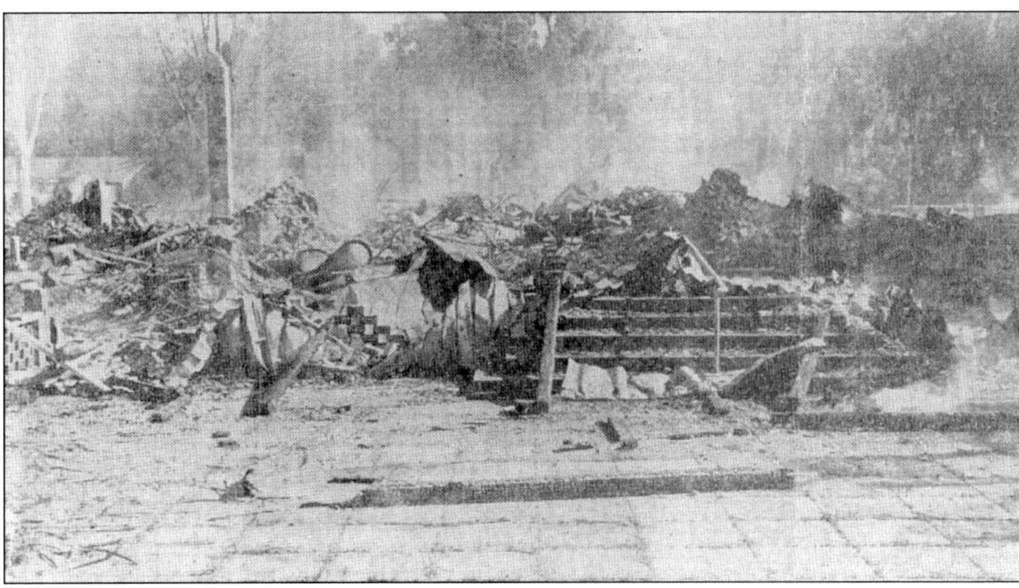

This is the *Sentinel-Star* (now *Orlando Sentinel*) photograph showing the charred remains of the Altamonte Hotel after the July 1953 fire. The three-story hotel was 70 years old when it burned to the ground.

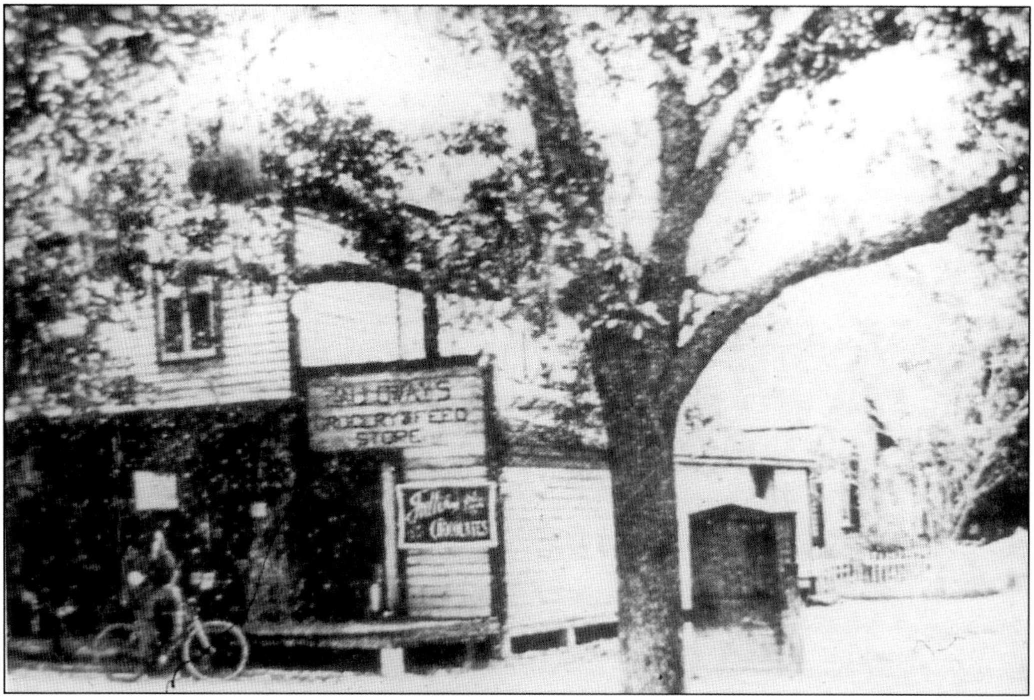

The Winter Park Telephone Co. began in 1910 in the back of the B.A. Galloway and Son Grocery Store on Maitland Avenue in downtown Maitland. Galloway's company reached 10 phone subscribers in Altamonte Springs a few years later.

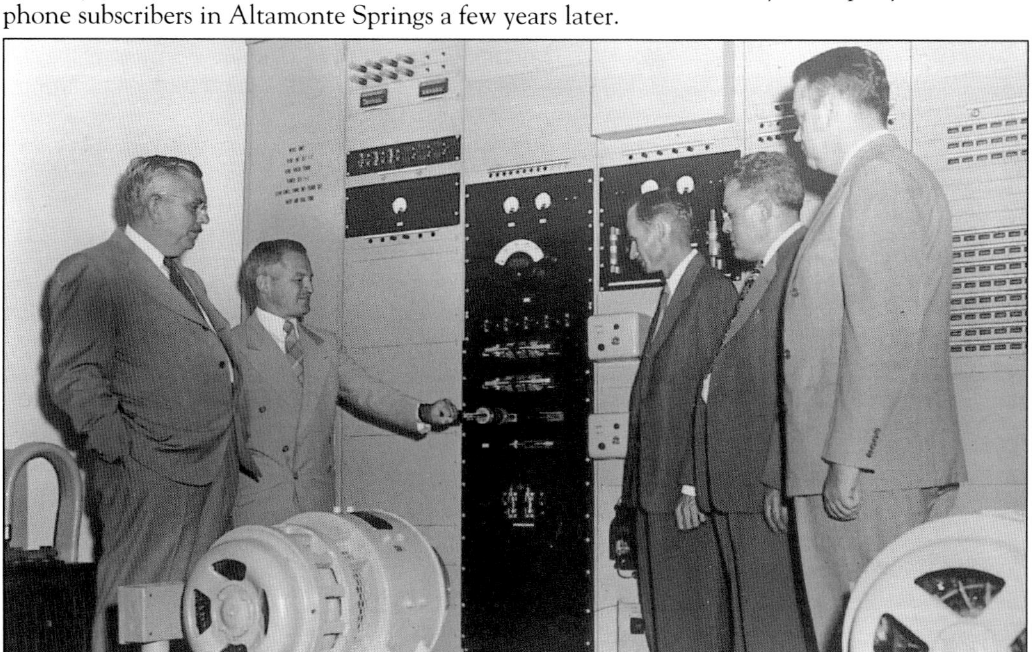

Winter Park Telephone and local government delegates in 1949 watch as the switch is thrown for automatic dialing equipment. The Altamonte office served the city as well as Casselberry, Fern Park, Longwood. and Forest City. Winter Park Telephone was later absorbed into United Telephone of Florida, which is now owned by Sprint.

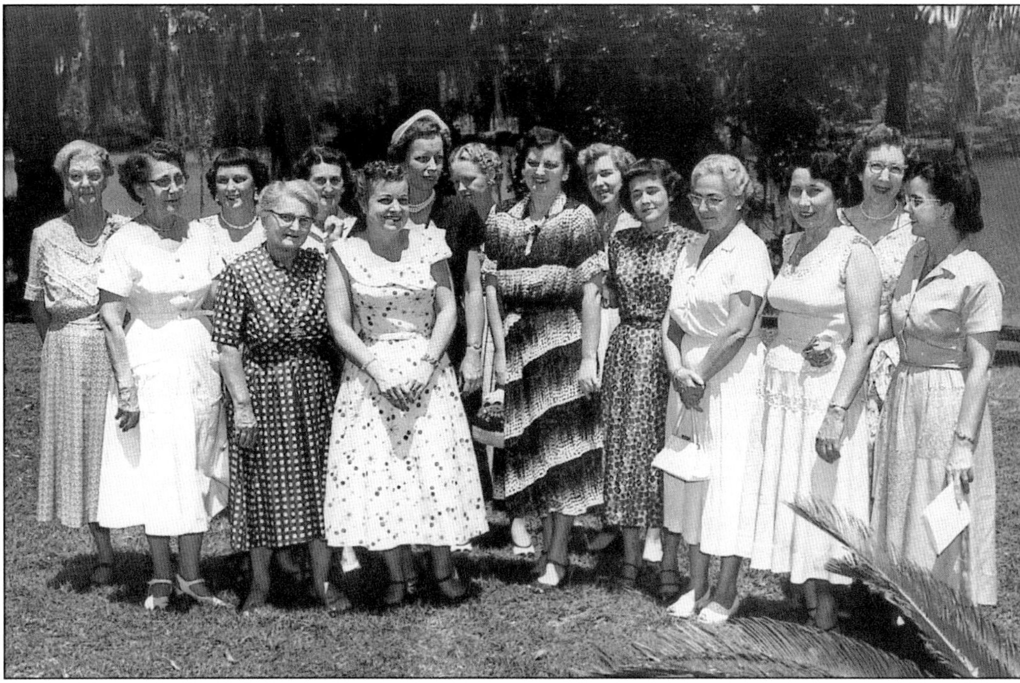

The members of the Altamonte Springs Women's Club gathered in the late 1950s. These ladies, through the Women's Club and other civic groups, had sponsored care of city properties since the 1920s.

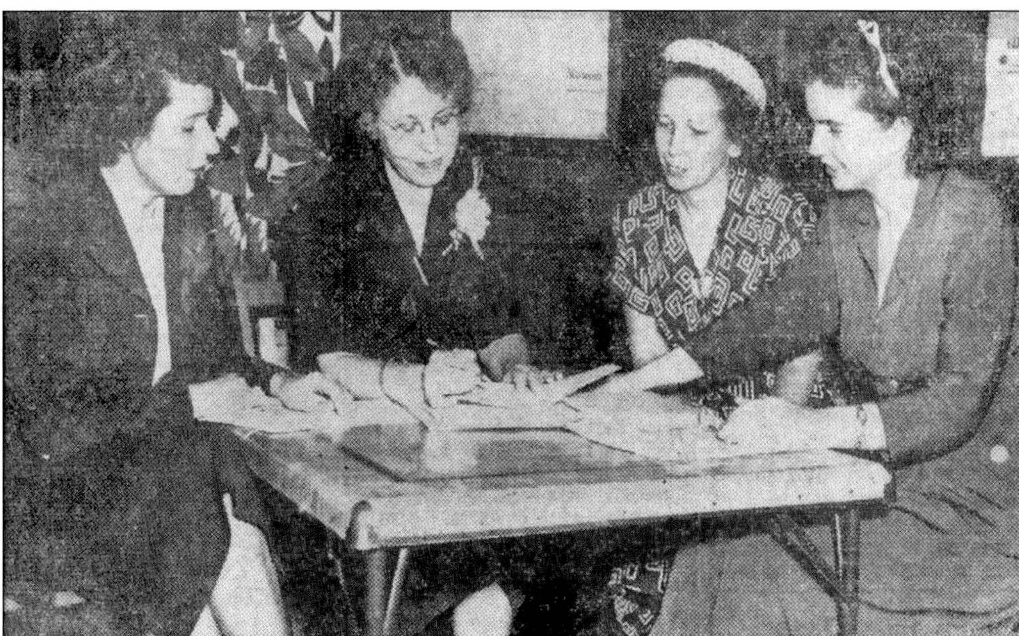

This photograph was taken during one of the Women's Club's blood drives. The group later merged with the Garden Club to become Altamonte Springs Civic Club in the mid-1940s. Members were active in helping care for the city's Community House, parks, tennis courts, streets, and the chapel.

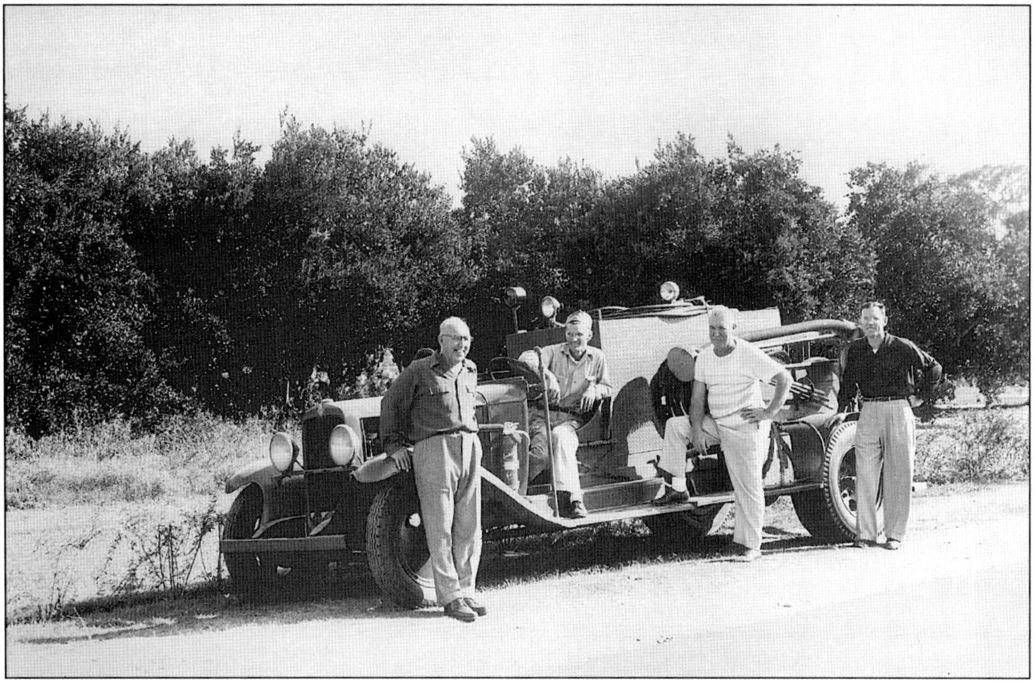

From left to right are Earle W. Riley, B.D. McIntosh Jr., Clifford Sands, and J.E. Martin with the Altamonte Springs fire truck in 1952.

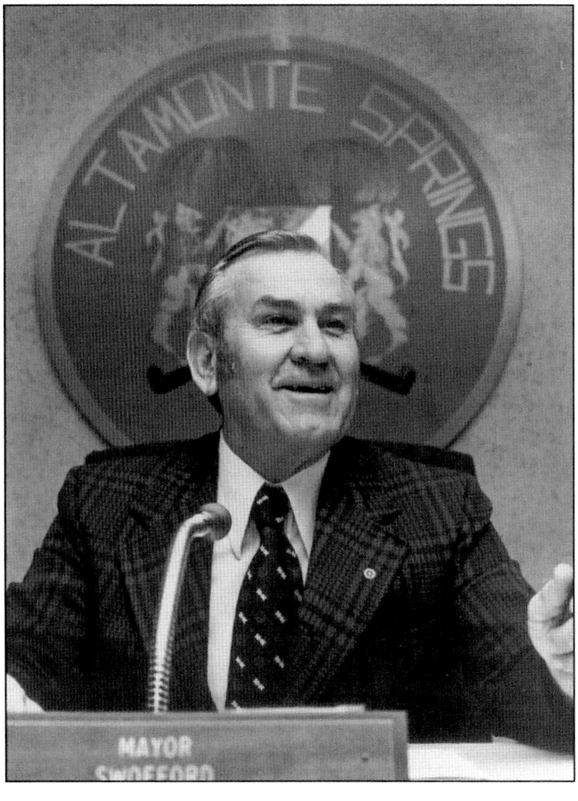

Lawrence Swofford, mayor of Altamonte Springs from 1961 to 1973, led the city during the era that included the blossoming of what had been little more than a village into Seminole County's leading retail center. Altamonte and other areas of south Seminole County became Central Florida's bedroom community as Martin-Marietta and other space and missile companies brought good jobs to the region. Construction of Interstate 4 and State Road 436 opened up new land for development. The opening of Walt Disney World prompted the construction of the Altamonte Mall, making the city the regional retail center of the late 1960s and early 1970s. Altamonte's many quiet neighborhoods provide homes for the region's growing employment base.

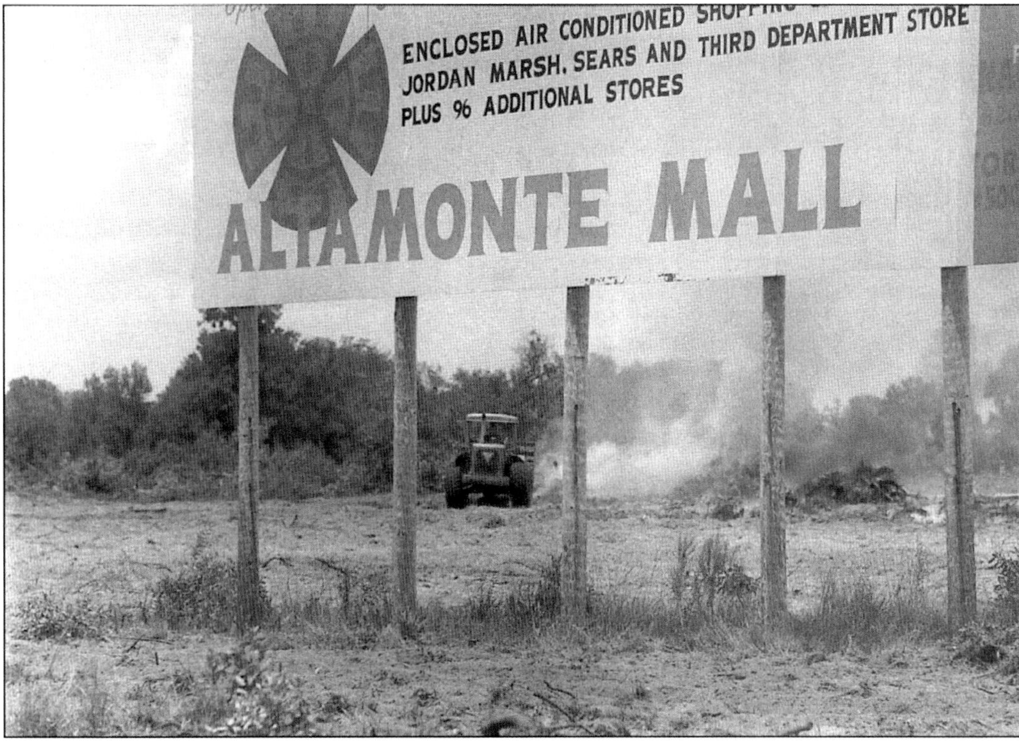

This photo was taken July 26, 1972, during site clearing for the Altamonte Mall. The site had been citrus groves and cattle pastureland for decades.

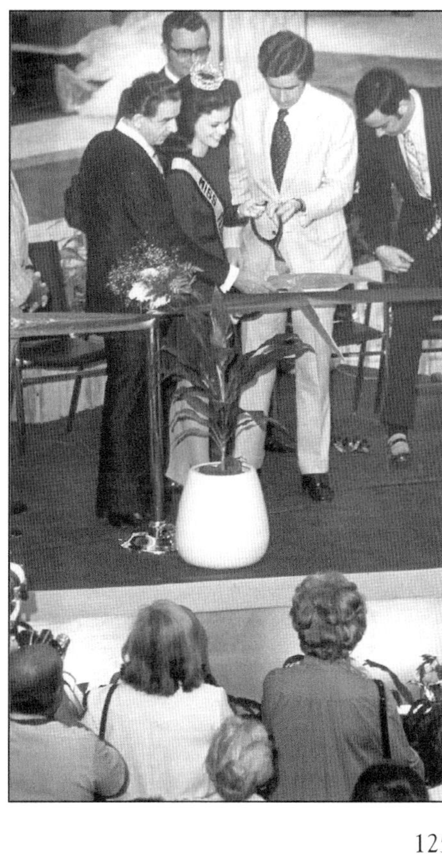

Snipping the ribbon in August 1974? at the opening of the Altamonte Mall, clockwise from the top, are Norman Floyd, mayor of Altamonte Springs; Michael O'Brian, vice president of Homart Development Co., a Sears Roebuck Company; Delta Burke, Miss Florida; and Edward DeBartolo.

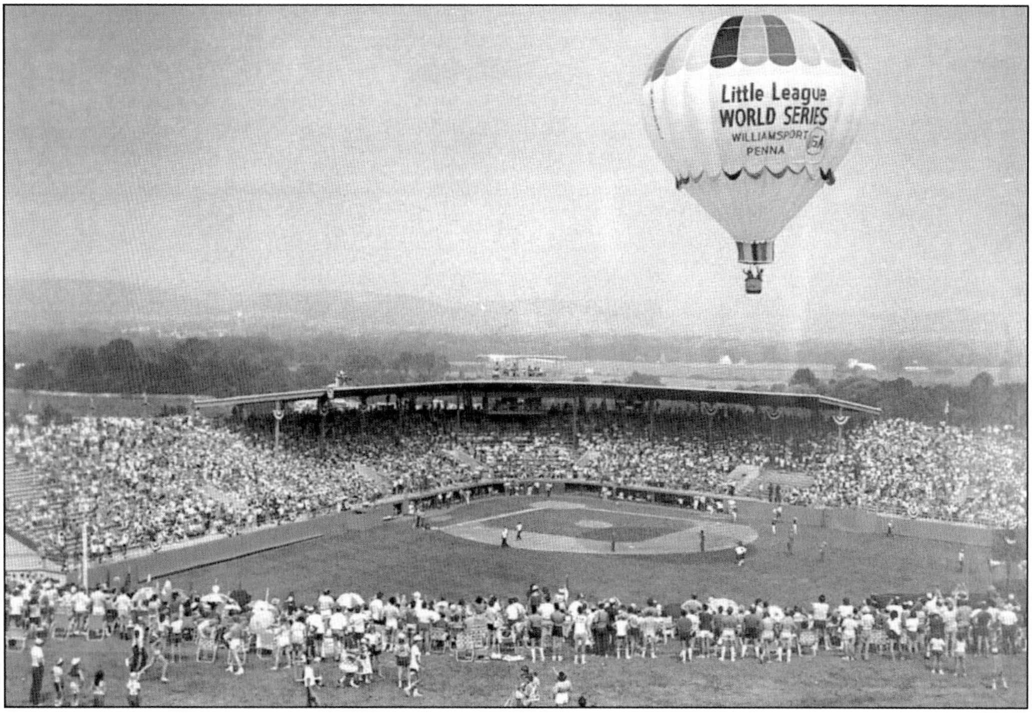

In 1984, the Altamonte Springs Little League 12-year-old All-Stars won the United States championship and the right to compete for the World Series title at Williamsport, Pennsylvania. The Altamonte team lost that year to Korea.

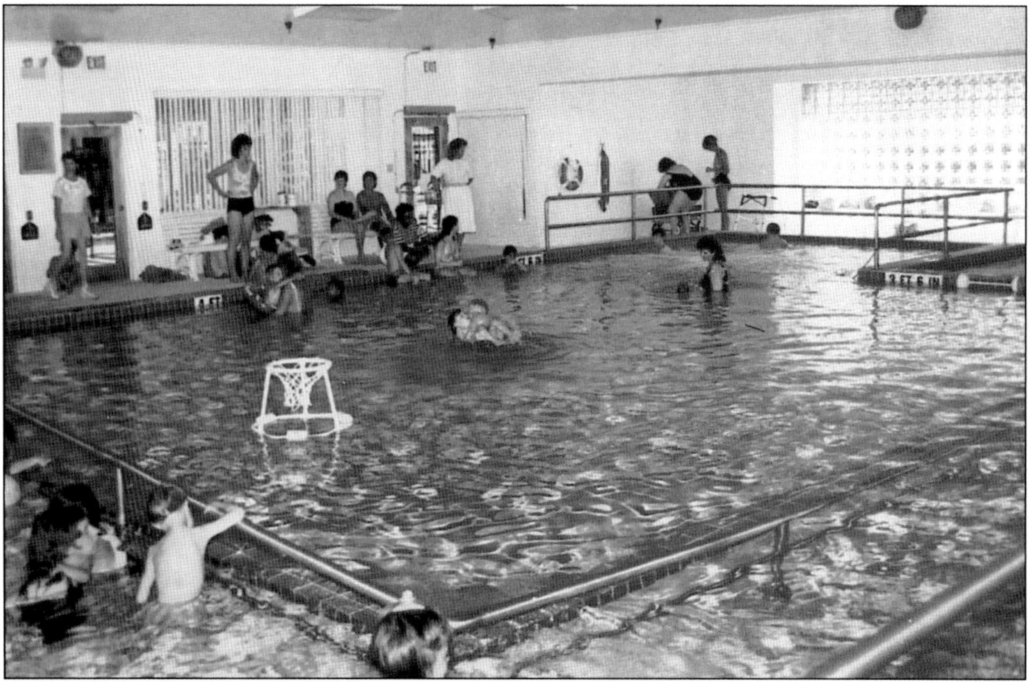

This is the Westmonte pool, Central Florida's first enclosed therapeutic exercise pool. It draws seniors and others with health problems from throughout Central Florida.

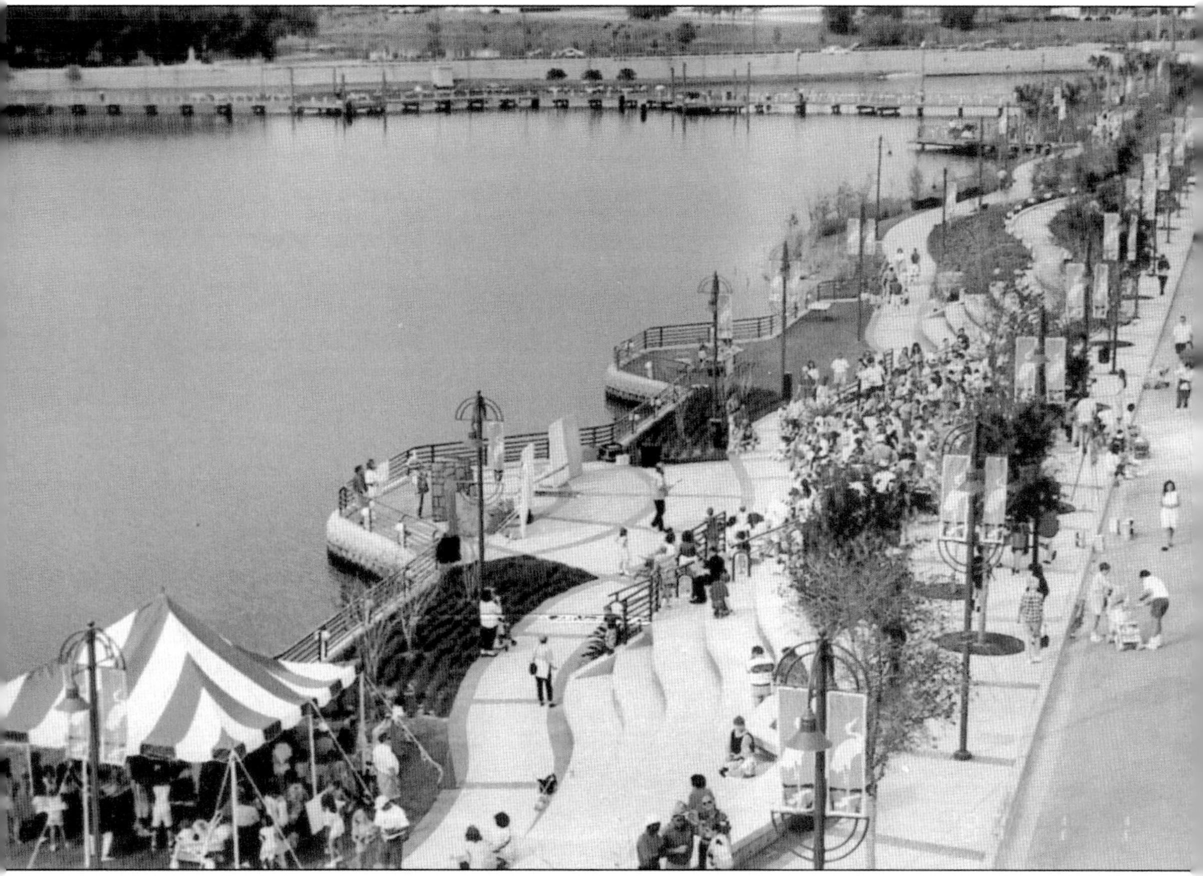

Cranes Roost Park, south of the Altamonte Mall, holds an April 1994 art festival. Altamonte celebrated its 75th anniversary in 1995 after redefining its "downtown" as an office park around the centerpiece lakefront at Cranes Roost Park. The park and its floating stage have become the site of many community events.

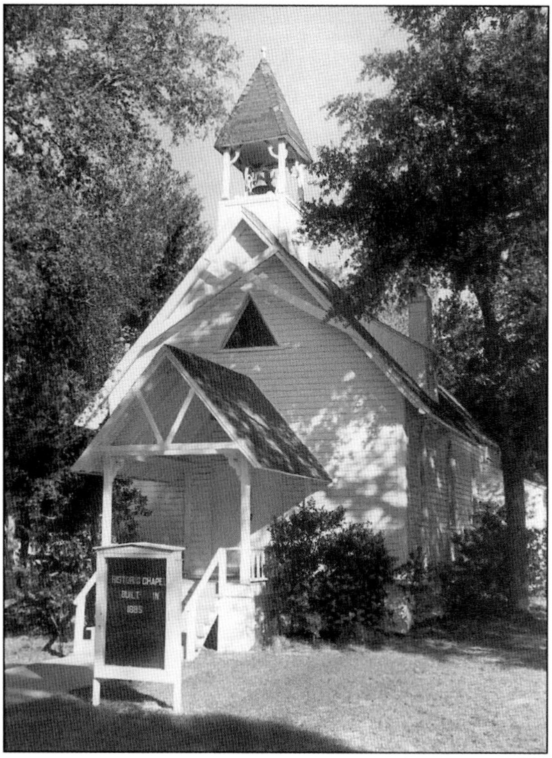

EPILOGUE

The Altamonte Chapel and its bell tower stand today near Hermit's Trail along State Road 436 as the city's most visible landmark of its early years. Rescued from the Lake Brantley area after it was abandoned when hard freezes in the late 1800s killed orange groves, the restored chapel was used for winter services in Altamonte Springs when Northern visitors filled the town for the season. Retired ministers who spent their winters in Central Florida provided a pool of visiting preachers in the early 1900s. A century later, the chapel remains the focal point of community pride. Central Florida's first tourism boom turned the flagstop village of Snowville/Snow Station into the winter resort town of Altamonte Springs in the late 1800s. The Altamonte Hotel and a winter community-economy thrived because of the wealthy Northerners, many from Boston, who built fine homes. Altamonte remains a shoppers' and diners' destination in Central Florida. The Altamonte Mall—the first in Seminole County, built at the time of the opening of Walt Disney World—is surrounded by other stores and restaurants that draw patrons from throughout the region. Altamonte and Seminole County's agricultural and winter tourism economy of the late 1800s and early 1900s disappeared by the mid-1900s as families made much of the former farm and grove lands into new bedroom communities of Orange County and its major city of Orlando. Although many residents still make their livings in the Orlando area and return to homes in Seminole County, Altamonte has established its own strong neighborhoods while providing its residents with employment in the Interstate 4-corridor's growing high-tech market and the retail and restaurant row along State Road 436. The city draws private high-rise office investment into its downtown corridor behind the mall and its lakefront centerpiece Cranes Roost Park.

Altamonte enters the new millennium having preserved the best of its heritage for future generations to enjoy and treasure.

